George Barrell Cheever

God's Timepiece for Man's Eternity

Its Purpose of Love and Mercy

George Barrell Cheever

God's Timepiece for Man's Eternity
Its Purpose of Love and Mercy

ISBN/EAN: 9783337183516

Printed in Europe, USA, Canada, Australia, Japan

Cover: Foto ©Lupo / pixelio.de

More available books at **www.hansebooks.com**

GOD'S TIMEPIECE

FOR

MAN'S ETERNITY.

ITS PURPOSE OF LOVE AND MERCY; ITS PLENARY
INFALLIBLE INSPIRATION; AND ITS PERSONAL
EXPERIMENT OF FORGIVENESS AND
ETERNAL LIFE IN CHRIST.

BY

REV. GEORGE B. CHEEVER, D.D.,

AUTHOR OF "LECTURES ON THE PILGRIM'S PROGRESS"; "THE RIVER OF THE
WATER OF LIFE"; "A PILGRIM IN THE SHADOW OF MONT BLANC";
"VOICES OF NATURE TO THE SOUL"; "VOYAGE TO THE CELESTIAL
COUNTRY"; "LECTURES ON COWPER"; "POWERS OF THE
WORLD TO COME"; "FAITH, DOUBT AND EVIDENCE," ETC.

NEW YORK:
A. C. ARMSTRONG & SON,
714 BROADWAY.
1883.

PRESS OF J. J. LITTLE & CO.,
NOS. 10 TO 20 ASTOR PLACE, NEW YORK.

PREFACE.

From Alpha to Omega, THE VOLUME OF THE BOOK WRITTEN OF ME, is One and Eternal; perfect, infallible, indivisible, even as Christ is one and the same, yesterday, to-day, and forever. In its purpose of Love and Mercy, its absolute plenary inspiration, its all-sufficiency in Time, its ceaseless accumulation and progress of spiritual Light and Life through Eternity, it is "*the Law of the Spirit of Life in Christ Jesus.*" As God's infallible Word in Christ, it is man's only possible LAW OF LIBERTY; THE SPIRIT AND THE WORD; WHATSOEVER THE SPIRIT SAITH UNTO THE CHURCHES. Being God's Law in Christ, it is our Life and blessedness; the Book of God's ABSOLUTE PREPOSSESSION IN US FROM THE CRADLE TO THE GRAVE. In itself are our appointed tests of its infallible unalterable inspiration and certainty, incapable of diminution or addition; the inspiration and its tests wholly at our own pleasure and power, by our daily experimental use of it, watching not only at the posts of its doors, but within its Holy of Holies; and *praying in the Holy Ghost* for its demonstration in our own soul's experience, and for its fruit in our daily life, by the faith it inspires and produces, working by love, purifying the heart, overcoming the world.

All this, God's Timepiece, OUR BIBLE; with its place and guidance in the soul of Man; God's indwelling telephone of word, thought and impulse; every ray of light, God's voice, God's electric touch, quickening every instant for Eternity; as a perfect watch in the bosom directs a man by its ticking, through the minutes and hours of each single day. He minds his watch every day, and winds it up, and cannot carry on his business without it. Let him keep God's Timepiece in his heart, as he does his watch in his pocket, and it will carry him and his business for eternity, without need of any other guidance. God in Christ lives and breathes in it, and in the soul that hides it. It is perpetual motion and Eternal Life. "Thy Word have I hid in mine heart, that I might not sin against Thee." It is, within and without, a union of Chronometer and Compass; and the MICROMETER-SCREW besides, measuring the vastest and compressing into action the minutest spaces and motions of time, thought, and character.

Take care of the minutes, and the hours will take care of themselves. Words are to Scripture and its texts, what moments are to Time and its seasons. If a single second were wanting, or too much, in the mechanism and motions of the Universe, it would, ere long, become a chaos. And so with the language of a Divine Inspiration. The seconds govern the minutes, the minutes the hours, the hours the days; and so on, through the whole round of weeks, months, seasons, years; and so, with the same accuracy, must the words and sentences of God's Timepiece for Man's Eternity be constructed for the expression and interpretation of God's will, God's thoughts.

It cannot be supposed that God would leave His attributes at the mercy of human beings, to be described in language or style of their own choice or invention. What *are* His thoughts, and what revelations of them men need, God must teach His servants a language to express, without mistake, with the right words in their right places. Therefore παδα γραφη θεοπνευδτος, ALL SCRIPTURE is inspired of God, is GOD-BREATHED, for Man's Eternal Salvation, and is infallible through Jesus Christ. This is the argument and intent of the present volume, for which we earnestly desire a patient consideration, and upon which we humbly implore the divine blessing.

CONTENTS.

INTRODUCTION. The Divine Revelation is of Certainties, not Obscurities—The Unknown must be studied by the Known—The Uncertainties of any Law-book, its condemnation—An uncertain Law, a Trap for Ruin—All the Laws of God the Result of Infinite Love—Only one Code of Laws ever revealed by the Almighty..........................xvii

I,—II.

CHRIST'S DIVINE PERSONALITY THE LIGHT AND LIFE OF THE WHOLE BIBLE.

Christ the central Light, Life, and Proof of the whole Bible, dependent throughout on His divine Personality—The whole written of Him, and for Him, that in Him we may have Eternal Life—The Scriptures therefore of God manifest in the Flesh, the great Mystery of Godliness.............. 1

The Things REVEALED are OURS FOREVER—Everything dependent on the disclosure of God's Attributes, and of our own Character and Responsibility before Him—All Things concerning God, Christ, and the Soul's Eternal Life or Death foreshown in the Writings of Moses, and gradually demonstrated through the whole Scriptures of God by the Witness of the Spirit—The Bible our infallible Chronometer and Compass, for Time and Eternity, that we may keep all the Words of this Law—The Key-words for the Boxing of this Compass........ 7

III,—IV.

INFALLIBLE AUTHORITY OF THE PENTATEUCH: ITS LANGUAGE AND BOOKS A FIVE-FOLD KEY TO THE SUCCESSIVE SCRIPTURES.

The Pentateuch our only Divine infallible Authority, for all our Knowledge of Creation and Redemption—The seeming Contradictions, and the Means of understanding them, from Eternity to Eternity, in God's Light................... 15

The gradual self-interpreting and accumulating Power of Revelation, from the Old Testament to the New—The Eternal Spiritual Meanings and Teachings of the Words for Life, Death, Hell, and the Grave, Expiation, Atonement, Sin, Sacrifice, Holiness, Redemption, and the eternal Judgment of Men according to their Character in this World...... 20

V,—VI.

THE WHOLE OLD TESTAMENT AND ITS TEACHINGS DRAMATIZED BY CHRIST, AND INTERPRETED.

Stalactites of Homer's Genius in the Caves of Pluto—The Power of a classical Paganism—The Light of David's Psalms—Power of internal Evidence—The great shining Passages of the Old Testament dramatized by Christ........................ 36

Truths for Eternity as well known by Inference as by Miracles—Christ's own Method of Reasoning good enough for us—The necessary absolute Certainty of God's Words for an abiding Faith in Him... 41

VII,—VIII.

THE SILENCE OF GOD, ITSELF A DIVINE REVELATION.

Teachings by the Silence of God—A dividing firmament in the Scriptures between half-truths and whole, and between Falsehood and divine Truth—Immortality of the Soul, and a Belief in the future Life and Retribution, known in ancient Egypt amidst Darkness, but revealed to the Hebrews, in a pure and holy Light—Reasons for the Reserve of divine Revelation—God would not sanction the Traditions of Men, nor of a darkened or defiled Conscience.................. 44

The assured gracious Presence of the Holy Spirit with the Word—Demonstrations in the Fifth Chapter of John's Gospel—Object and Evidence of Miracles—Personal Experiments requisite for all spiritual Proof............................. 51

IX,—X.

DEMONSTRATIONS IN THE MACHINERY AND REASON OF A WATCH.

Consequent Infallibility and Independence of the Word above all human Testimony—Illustrations from the Machinery of the Watch—The Argument from Chance and Atheism; the Argument from God to Man; the Answer from Man to God. 60

Christ's testimony covers all the Scriptures—Man's infallible personal Experiment is in Prayer—Consequences of Protesting God's Drafts from Time to Eternity............. 77

XI,—XII.

NAPOLEON'S THOUGHTS ABOUT CHRIST AND HIS EMPIRE OF INFINITE LOVE.

Thoughts of Napoleon and Rousseau concerning Christ—Christ the God-Man, and His spiritual Kingdom an Empire of Love in the Soul and for Eternity—Forgiveness of Sins and the Power of Miracles in Christ, the Demonstration of God manifest in the Flesh 84

This Manifestation progressive, both in the Human and Divine; in the Claim and Demonstration of Divine Attributes; in the equal Demonstration of human Guilt, sinful Habit, and Despair, unless forgiven and regenerated—Blasphemy of the Man of Sin and Son of Perdition, assuming the holy Infallibility, Omniscience, and forgiving Power of the Son of God... 89

XIII,—XIV.

CHRIST OUR LIFE. DEATH SWALLOWED UP IN VICTORY BY HIS DEATH FOR US.

Christ alone our Eternal Life, dwelling in our Hearts by Faith—Our Lawgiver and King, Creator, Judge, Advocate, and forgiving Saviour, all in One—The successive Terraces of these demonstrated Glories in the Prophecies of Isaiah....... 97

Intuitions of the People and Teachings of the Law of God combining with the Light of divine Prophecy—Death swallowed up in Victory by our forgiving Lord and God—Forgiveness the most absolute Proof of Deity, and the greatest Obligation of Gratitude from Man to his Redeemer—If Mankind were not lost, no need of ever being found—But no Fear of God, if no Hope of Salvation...... 102

XV,—XVI.

CHRIST'S ARMY OF THE WITNESSES AND TEACHERS FROM PROPHECY TO ITS FULFILMENT.

Foreshadowing of the Appearance of Christ in the World—These Realities of Experience and Warning, the Grounds of His

Appeal to Mankind—The great disciplinary Instruction and Experience, arising from the Knowledge of an Existence and Responsibility beyond the Grave—Presumption and Despair the two Extremes of Temptation and Guilt, to be provided against—Who shall lead Christ's Army of Witnesses? David and Paul... 113

Treatment of the Claims of Christ by the Jews—Their Possession already of the Power and the Rules of correct Reasoning from their own Scriptures, acknowledged as God's Word—Forgiveness of Sin impossible but by God only—The Assumption of its Power by Man a Blasphemy against God and the divine Spirit—Any Experiment beyond this Life impossible, and this Men know beforehand................. 122

XVII,—XVIII.

FORGIVENESS BY CHRIST THE ALL-CONTROLLING EVIDENCE.

Character of Christ, and Experience of spiritual Healing and Forgiveness by Him, the central, all-controlling Evidence of Christianity—The Combinations of Promises and Warnings; co-extensive with Eternity—God's alarm-bells of Death, and Jubilee Chimes of Salvation........................ 130

A spiritual and Eternal Kingdom of Grace and Glory demonstrated—All Nations are to call Him blessed, and the whole Earth to be filled with His Glory—The demonstration of Infinite Love is that also of Infinite Blessedness and Power in Heaven and on Earth, from Everlasting to Everlasting. 136

XIX,—XX.

CHRIST'S USE OF THE SCRIPTURES THE RULE OF ALL TRUE CRITICISM, AND THEOLOGY.

The Temptation of the Son of God in the Wilderness, the first explanatory Narrative in the Gospels—Its Connection with the Transfiguration and the Walk to Emmaus—The divine Necessity for Christ, IT IS WRITTEN.................. 142

Position of Satan, as the Tempter, Accuser, and Enemy of Mankind—Position of the Son of God, and the Difference between the Methods of Satan and those of Modern Infidelity—The Power of a "Thus saith the Lord.".................... 152

XXI,—XXII.

CHARACTERISTICS OF DIVINE INSPIRATION SETTLED BY CHRIST.

Characteristics and Limitations of Divine Inspiration, settled by Christ—Its Definitions and Possessions from Genesis to the Apocalypse—Amount of Christ's Testimony on the lowest Computation—Steps in the History of the Temptation—Final Demonstration wrought out by that....... 161
Demonstration from the Temptation completed by Gethsemane and the Death of the Cross—The Limitations of Christ's Omnipotence by the Absoluteness of His whole divine and human Nature—His own Work, as appointed by God's Word—The Blessedness of the Apostolic Participation in His Sufferings—Suffering with Him, to be also glorified together... 169

XXIII,—XXIV.

THE RESURRECTION AND WALK TO EMMAUS.

Argument of the Narrative of the Resurrection: 1. Of Certainty; 2. Variety; 3. Congruity; 4. Forgiveness and Assured Salvation, as in Paul's Testimony in 1 Cor. xv.—IT IS WRITTEN carries this Triumph through Eternity................ 178
The Walk to Emmaus, and its Key to the whole Body of the Scriptures 184

XXV,—XXVI.

THE DESPAIR AND RESTORATION OF THE DISCIPLES.

Temporary Despair of the Disciples an inevitable first Result of our Lord's Death upon the Cross—The divine Presence and Prayer alone prevented its Continuance—The Intercessions and the Spirit of Christ enlightened and preserved their Souls... 197
The whole divine Preparation completed for the Apostles' Preaching and Teaching concerning Christ out of the Scriptures—Then the Propylæum built by Christ for the Acts of the Apostles, and the Epistles Accompanying and Following—The absorbing and triumphant Power of Faith and Love and Apostolic Zeal and Faithfulness............. 204

XXVII,—XXVIII.

CHRIST'S MINISTRY OF SUFFERING LOVE.

Power of the great Personal Revelation after this Survey—The divine Preparations for it—The infinite Privilege and Happiness of the Ministry of suffering Love.............. 219
God's Method of Demonstration, personal, experimental, soul-renewing, beatifying, transfiguring, and consonant with our Nature; destined in Christ to be the Witness of His Infinite Love, Power, and Glory—Vastness of our Lord's Exposition of the Scriptures.................................. 225

XXIX,—XXX.

VASTNESS OF CHRIST'S EXPOSITION OF THE SCRIPTURES.
NO ANCHORAGE IN UNCERTAINTIES.

"In all the Scriptures the Things concerning Himself"—The Sweep and Thoroughness of this Proposition—Christ demonstrated it while Himself on Earth—No Attempts at the Breaking of His Will, no Case left for Chancery, or conflicting Canons of Councils—The whole known Volume of the Bible, and its Documents, God's Vouchers, and His alone......... 231
Sufficiency of our Evidence—No Anchorage in Uncertainties, for Eternity—God's Mercy not hidden in Obscurities, but He sets His Bow in the Clouds—The very Proverbs of this World are Prophecies of the next................... 237

XXXI,—XXXII.

LANGUAGE AND LAWS OF FAITH AND EXPERIENCE.

Questions and Conclusions of Experimentalists—"But they don't come back to tell."—John Foster and S. T. Coleridge—No Uncertainties in the Gospel, but only immutable Things, in which it was impossible for God to lie—Testimony of John and Paul....................... 241
Promulgation of Law in Nature—Language and Laws of Faith—The Experiment of Time one and final; the Invitation and Acceptance of Divine Grace; the Death of Death and Hell's Destruction through Christ; and the Beginning of the Life Eternal in Him................................ 246

XXXIII,—XXXIV.

A PLENARY INSPIRATION NECESSARY FOR THE REVELATION
OF SIN AND ITS ETERNAL CONSEQUENCES.

The Revelation of Sin and its consequences, considered as a central Proof of the plenary verbal Inspiration of the Scriptures.. 253
The infallible Inspiration demonstrated by the Nature of the Truths revealed; and by the Saviour's Words; and by the Consequences of idle Words........................ 258

XXXV,—XXXVI.

CHRIST THE LORD OF THE SABBATH. THE NAZARENE
CRITICS OF HIS FIRST SERMON.

The Law of the Sabbath, with our Lord's Dominion over it, Himself its Soul, and the Gospel to the Poor forever in it, demonstrate a verbal Inspiration—Christ's first Sermon in Nazareth.. 266
Qualifications of the Nazarenes as the highest literary Critics... 277

XXXVII,—XXXVIII.

HUMILITY BEFORE GOD, THE PERFECTION OF REASON.

A plenary verbal Inspiration necessary to sustain the Appeals of Christ to the Old Testament and Moses............... 287
References to Reason and Conscience in the Sight of God—Humility before God the only Security of Reason in the Examination of God's Word—God the Teacher, Reason the Learner—The Prayers of Bacon, the Experience of Coleridge—Lightfoot on the Source of Luke's Gospel by direct Inspiration—Men casting Anchor out of the Stern, and wishing for the Day, meanwhile Dragging and Drifting.... 295

XXXIX,—XL.

NOT YE THAT SPEAK, BUT THE SPIRIT OF YOUR
FATHER IN YOU.

Arguments of Ullmann, Tholuck, Luther, and Bengel, on the Use and Province of Reason, and the Necessity of a verbal

Inspiration—In what Sense is the Bible breathed forth from God?—Argument of Alexander on Isaiah.............. 307
Demonstration from the closing Chapters of Luke's Gospel—Certainty of the Old Testament Canon—The Septuagint Translation—Philo and Josephus—Eichhorn's Historic Investigation - Christ's Verification and Use of the Old Testament Scriptures—"Not ye that speak, but the Holy Ghost"—Neither extempore Speaking nor Writing, in Christ's inspired Messengers..................................... 314

XLI,—XLII.

PROF. HUXLEY'S ARGUMENT, HOW MUCH MAY HANG UPON A WORD.

Argument from the Importance of Particles—Justification of God and Man by Words—Paul's Argument of the Resurrection 324
Prof. Huxley on the Epiglottis, and what constitutes Man—The Argument of Evolution applied to the Inspiration of Words—No such Thing as accidental or extempore Speaking.. 330

XLIII,—XLIV.

THE SPIRIT OF TRUTH WILL GUIDE YOU INTO ALL TRUTH. NOT DOUBTS, NOR OBSCURITIES, BUT CERTAINTIES.

Exactness of divine Information concerning Spiritual law—"If it were not so, I would have told you"—Regeneration, the greatest of Miracles, dependent on Words—Lord Bolingbroke on "Calvin's Institutes.".......................... 337
Verbal Inspiration and particular Providence—The Habit of Conjectures a Habit of Scepticism—Evil of turning Obscurities into Enemies, for Satan's Work—Anecdote from Dr. Witherspoon—An infallible divine Inspiration necessary for any right Reasoning... 343

XLV,—XLVI.

PROGRESSIVE ILLUMINATIONS BY WHAT THE SPIRIT SAITH UNTO THE CHURCHES. PRECIOUSNESS OF A CHILDLIKE FAITH.

Half Truths whole Errors—Absolute Safety only in the divine Record—Plato's Cave, and the poet Goethe in the Dungeon—Divine Certainty in all that the Spirit saith unto the

Churches—Necessity of a Fog-horn for mere human Language—Paul Speaking with Tongues, and Praying for the Power of Interpretation—What Men owe to God, a believing Heart—What God owes to Men, infallible divine Truth 356

Progressive Illuminations in God's Kingdoms of Nature and Grace—The Combinations of incalculable Minuteness and Grandeur in Word and Works—Illustrations from polarized Light and the Connections of the Physical Sciences—Necessary to Truth, a single Eye, a Child-like faith, a transparent spiritual Atmosphere, and God in Christ shining through it—The Climate of the Soul—Science itself demonstrates a verbal divine Inspiration................ 367

XLVII,—XLVIII.

THE WITNESS OF THE SPIRIT, THE HIGHEST HEAVEN OF SCIENCE.

Various Ways of spoiling and despoiling Preachers by Philosophy and vain deceit—The Bondage of Tradition and Doubt—Suspicion and Tickets of Leave—Archbishop Usher on the Witness of the Spirit 380

The Forgery of a spiritual Work impossible, the very ideas of Spirit and Foresight being unknown—Its Fulfilment and Proof as impossible as a Demonstration of Non-existence from Eternity—All scientific Truth the Servant of Christ, and Christianity the highest Heaven of Science........ 392

XLIX,—L.

ALL GOD'S WORDS CREATIVE FOR CHRIST'S REDEEMING WORK.

The Vesture dipped in Blood—The final Argument and its Perfection—Vision and Inspiration of the Word of the Lord to Ezekiel—The Divine-human and Human-divine, indisputable 399

The New-creating Life of divine Inspiration as Inhering in the incarnate Personality of Christ the Saviour—God's Words, Old and New Testament, creative Pencils of Light, employed by the Holy Spirit for Christ's redeeming Work. 404

LI,—LII.

DISCOVERIES OF THE SOUL IN PRAYER. THE BIBLE A CHILD'S BOOK FOREVER.

The Soul led and instructed by Supplications—Universal Truth discovered and recorded by Prayer—Testimony of ancient liturgies—Difference between living Branches and dead Clubs—The seven Sons of Sceva, their athletic Christianity, and its Results... 410

The Bible the most natural and supernatural of all Books—Divine Love its Substance, divine Light its Garment—Infinite in Mystery and Simplicity, microscopic in Intelligence and Care—A reason for the tiniest Flowers and Thorns in the Wilderness—A child's Book for all Ages........... 415

LIII,—LIV.

AN INFALLIBLE INSPIRATION THE ONLY TRUE HISTORIC FAITH. CONJECTURAL CRITICISMS GOOD FOR NOTHING.

Complexity, Minuteness, Infinitude and indestructible Unity of the Argument—Its Power of Anchorage the Same in all ages, but accumulating through all—Clouds and Tempests of Sin, Misery and Mystery, evolving in Rainbows of pardoning Mercy and sanctifying Grace and Love—Faith in the Word of God as infallible, the only true historic Faith—Internal Harmonies and Laws of Adjustment.................. 424

The Price of the Fabrication of Legends, Forgeries and Myths instead of the Divine Word—The Proverb of "the Devil to pay" illustrated—Bishop Hoadly on the Kingdom of Christ and of Conscience—Conjectural Criticisms and Clinkers of Thought—The Way to Doubting Castle—Consequences of the Fog within and Breakers without—Dr. Franklin's Vow to build a Lighthouse—Walk in the Light as Christ gives it, and go not out of the King's Highway—The Power that worketh in you, able to carry you through............. 433

INTRODUCTION.

The-Broad Church Translators, Revisers, Interpreters, and Progressive Theologians of our age seem disposed to retreat from the known severities of Divine Revelation, into what they please to call its " MERCIFUL OBSCURITIES." But is that a merciful process of revelation, which conceals from the vision of faith an actual danger? Would it be merciful in constructing a chart for an unknown sea, into which a navigator was appointed to enter, if the hydrographer concealed the known sunken reefs, the hidden sand-banks, the dangerous rocky coasts? Would it be merciful in a Lawgiver to render the penalties against crime so uncertain, and obscure, that the criminal might hope they would be infinitely smaller than the letter of the code ever intimates, or its strict equity permits? Is not the certainty announced, the greatest mercy, and the clearness and explicitness the greatest safeguard for the sinner? What is to keep a man from falling into crime, if the law itself is uncertain in regard to its guilt, or how can the Judge be justified in executing a penalty, both in degree and duration, unknown? He can go no further than the law allows; if he does it is iniquity. The perfection of law is its equity and clearness, and of government, its justice, benevolence, and stability. In the case of the Divine Government its foundations and its laws are just and right; but they can be neither, if concealed from the knowledge of the subjects of their operation, who are to be protected and guided by them.

Accordingly in God's Law-book the heaviest of penalties are denounced *against those who conceal the truth*. If they had stood in the gap, and been faithful to God's truth, souls would have been saved. They have concealed and falsified it, and theirs is the responsibility. "For THE WORD THAT I HAVE SPOKEN, THE SAME SHALL JUDGE YOU in the last day." It reveals God *now* to the knowledge of His creatures; it will justify God *then*, in the righteousness of His sentences. "Is God unrighteous who taketh vengeance? God forbid! for then how shall God judge the world?" If He may not righteously avenge the law, he cannot righteously reveal it. The question is tremendous and transcendent against all the false philosophies of sin and its penalty; in demonstration also of the infinite benevolence of the whole Divine Law, the justice, power and beatifying influence and intent of which are to make all creatures fit and worthy to glorify God, and enjoy Him forever. Laws cannot be cruel, the object and perfection of which are the foundation of a holy character, a divine nature, and eternal blessedness in God. Any thing less than that object, any thing different, would be impossible, if God is Love; and if He is not Love, He is not God. These are postulates of all right reasoning, from man to God.

"When will men learn,
The outward by the inward to discern,
The inward by the Spirit?"

Introduction.

THE SPIRIT OF JESUS THE WHOLE SOUL OF THE BIBLE.

The whole argument and demonstration of Christianity are in this, A FORGIVING GOD AND SAVIOUR; and for soul-satisfying assurance in this divine axiom of Eternal Life, and of conquering power by it, every man must make his own experiment, or he cannot believe, but abideth in darkness. Therefore "GOD HATH SHINED IN OUR HEARTS to give the LIGHT of the KNOWLEDGE of the GLORY OF GOD in the face of JESUS CHRIST": every word in that sentence being a law and progression of Light and Love, as the Eternity of God and Immortality of man are a key to the meaning of every thought in the Bible. "I know that whatsoever God doeth, it shall be forever: also He hath set Eternity in their heart, and hath made every thing beautiful in His time. And God requireth that which is past." Every instruction and command, every warning and promise, all deterring and alluring truths, bear the burden of God's mercy for man's good. The whole climate of the Bible is Eternity, and its atmosphere the Firmament of Love. The Lord God Almighty and the Lamb are its Temple; and the glory of God doth lighten it, and the Lamb is the light thereof.

All that is revealed is given THAT WE MIGHT BE SAVED. "The Lawgiver, ABLE TO SAVE, and to destroy."—James iv. 12. "I that speak in righteousness, MIGHTY TO SAVE."—Is. lxiii. 1. "And these things I say, that ye MIGHT BE SAVED."—John v. 34. "He that converteth the sinner from the error of his way shall SAVE A SOUL FROM DEATH."—James v. 20. "The Son of Man is come to seek and to SAVE THAT WHICH WAS LOST."—Matt.

xviii. 11, and Luke xix. 10. This very word SAVED demonstrates the peril of an everlasting destruction.

Let the childlike inquirer take simply his concordance, and study in their connection, the words for heaven and hell, darkness and light, salvation and perdition, saved, lost; life, death; reward and punishment; time and eternity; and everywhere he will find God in Christ, as at the beginning, so in the new creation, *dividing the light from the darkness*, commanding us to walk in the light, *as He is in the light*, declaring that we can *see light only in His light*, and pronouncing a woe upon them that put darkness for light and light for darkness. The pestilence and the fool "walketh in darkness," and the power of Satan's strategy and kingdom is the power of darkness, and its consummation the blackness of darkness forever. The Higher Literary Criticism, in its handling and circulation and endorsement of suspicions and doubts, is but a Doubting Castle kept by Giant Despair, even with Christian and Hopeful sometimes in its dungeons.

To remove the doubts of men by the certainties of Scripture, and not to measure or obscure the certainties of Scripture by the doubts and conjectures of men, is the work of a true, believing student of God's Word. From Genesis to the Apocalypse there is ceaseless progress in Theology, an infinite, ever-growing demonstration of the sinfulness and misery of man, and the loving attributes and saving mercies of the Almighty, till, as promised in Is. xxx. 6, and Zech. xii. 8, concerning the Holy One of Israel, and those that wait on His Word, "the light of the moon shall be as the light of the sun, and the light of

Introduction. xxi

the sun sevenfold as the light of seven days, and he that is feeble shall be as David, and the house of David as God." And so, "The isles shall wait for His Law, and His coming, who is the Life and Light of all nations; to open the blind eyes, and to bring out of the prison-house those that sit in darkness and in the shadow of death. I WILL MAKE DARKNESS LIGHT BEFORE THEM." "Then shall the deaf hear the words of THE BOOK, and the eyes of the blind shall see out of obscurity and out of darkness, and the meek and the poor shall rejoice in the Holy One of Israel, FOR THE SCORNER IS CONSUMED." Most mercifully consumed; for "when the scorner is punished the simple is made wise." "Smite a scorner, and the simple will *beware.*" "But a scorner seeketh wisdom *and findeth it not.*" A vast portion of human literature concerning the Bible is the literature of scorners, cavillers, evil surmisers, lawyers; taking away the key of knowledge, shutting up the kingdom of heaven against men, entering not in themselves and forbidding them that are entering.—Matt. xxiii. 13.

THE CERTAINTIES OF ONE DIVINE CODE, AND ONLY ONE, PROCLAIMED BY OUR LORD.

The criticism of conjecture and suspicion disorganizes the very faculty of spiritual discernment. It makes every miracle of truth run the gauntlet between lines of magicians with tractors of diabolic power to draw away the sacred magnetism, stealing from the soul the fire and faith of a divine inspiration. The progress of these critics across the sacred pages, denying the supernatural, is like that of snails over the leaves of flowers; their path is traced, and their work characterized, by the film of the slime left behind them. "*And as for my flock,*" says the Word of God in Ezekiel xxxiv 19, "they eat that which ye have trodden with your feet; and they drink that which ye have fouled with your feet." But the work of benevolence and truth is to make plain paths for the soul, "lest that which is lame be turned out of the way, and lest any man fail of the grace of God."—Heb. xii. 13, 15.

"And behold, a certain lawyer stood up, and tempted him, saying, Master, what shall I do to inherit eternal life? He said unto him, What is written in the Law? How readest thou?"—Luke x. 25, 26. The Law meant the Pentateuch, the books of Moses, the constant, unmistakable designation of THE LAW. "Did not Moses give you the Law, and none of you keepeth it." The lawyer knew this, and made answer accordingly, out of Deuteronomy and Leviticus; and our Lord said unto him, "Thou hast answered right." And so in Isaiah ix. 19, 20, "To the Law and to the Testimony! Should not a people seek unto their God? For the living to the dead? If they speak not according to this word, *there is no light in them.*" Here the reference cannot possibly be to any other authority than the Law of God by Moses. And so, eight hundred years later, "Moses of old time hath in every city them that preach him, being read in the synagogues every Sabbath day."—Acts xv. 21.

"Seek ye out the Book of the Law, and read." What Book, and what Law? Which of the codes, Elohistic or Jehovistic, and which of the Redactors

Introduction. xxiii

of Documents? "With whom took he counsel, or who hath directed the Spirit of the Lord?" "REMEMBER YE THE LAW OF MOSES MY SERVANT, WHICH I COMMANDED UNTO HIM IN HOREB FOR ALL ISRAEL, WITH THE STATUTES AND JUDGMENTS."—Mal. iv. 4.

Only one Law and Testimony was ever referred to by our Lord; one code, one covenant, one passover one atonement, one approach to God, *one law of Love.* The whole Law was fulfilled in that one word, given by Moses in Leviticus xix. 18, and Deuteronomy vi. 5, "Thou shalt love the Lord thy God; and thy neighbor as thyself;" and Christ's words illuminated the unity and Mosaic authorship of the whole, when He said, "*On these two commandments hang all the law and the prophets.*"—Matt. xxii. 40. The demonstration of the Mosaic era, and none later, was perfect.

CHRIST NEVER SANCTIONED ANY CODE BUT GOD'S ONE CODE OF LOVE, BY MOSES.

Christ never quoted any other code, nor referred to any other lawgiver than Moses. Neither did any of His disciples, or the Apostles. "This is that *Moses in the wilderness*, who received the LIVING ORACLES, λόγια ζῶντα, *to give unto us.*"—Acts vii. 37, 38. "Master, Moses said; Master, Moses *wrote unto us;* "—Matt. xxii. 24, and Luke xx. 28; and the writing was in DEUTERONOMY xxv. 5. If it had not been Moses, but a later authority, in a fifth code, somewhere down in the centuries of anonymous piety and fraud, the cavilling enemies of our Lord would have known it. If there had been even imagined a "*Deuteronomist,*" other than Moses, according to the nomenclature of the Higher Criticism, the Sadducees would have shuffled that card. If the texts quoted by our Lord had been in a document not of Moses' writing, or if there had been any suspicion or conjecture, not to say theory, of its not having been Moses, the Pharisees also would have fenced with that weapon.

But neither in the histories or prophecies of the Old Testament, or interpretations of God's Law in the New, is there aught of fact or reference from which the publication or existence of any code of divine laws, other than the Pentateuch, or after the time of Moses, or by any other lawgiver than Moses, can be proved, or even conjectured. The supposition of some half-dozen successive and separate codes, one for priests, another for princes, another for the people, another for or from the prophets, evolved in separate and distant ages, by anonymous voices of unnamed and unknown authors; codes supplementary, Elohistic, Jehovistic, with documents amendatory, as the contrivances or outgrowths of new patches on old garments, is no better than an atavistic utterance of Isaiah's "*wizards that peep and mutter.*" It is the ventriloquism of jugglers; an inspiration from the entrails; throwing the voice sometimes afar off, sometimes in the air, sometimes in a bog with marsh lights; it is Jannes and Jambres withstanding Moses, "*doing so with their enchantments,*" to obscure and adulterate, with second-hand imitative blood and frogs, the real miracles, and thus distress and daze the Pharaonic spectators. Cleavers of dead wood, themselves as dead to true spiritual life and meaning, as the punk-wood itself, out of which they split their torches.

The processes of this school of criticism, under the guise of free, fearless, scholarly expurgation and reconstruction, do but "*murder to dissect*" the Scriptures; disfiguring them almost as thoroughly beyond identity, as the slayer did the body of Dr. Parkman, so that the only proof of the *corpus delicti* was the jaw of his false teeth left in the furnace.*

NO PRIVATE OR ARBITRARY INTERPRETATION.

Sinful men are always suspicious of God, as if He had some private, selfish ends, like their own. This is a remarkable acknowledgment of the consciousness that a private, personal, self-seeking habit of character is wrong, is unjust to others; that such a character cannot co-exist with disinterested benevolence, which is and ought to be the ruling characteristic of holiness and truth.

Now, applying this conviction, which is just, to the revelation of God's will given us in the Scriptures, let the Sceptic ask himself, what possible private object can God have? The Creator of all beings and things, the Possessor and Governor of the Universe! "If I were hungry, I would not tell thee!." Can He do any thing but out of infinite love? out of a necessary regard to His own loving nature, not sacrificing one attribute to another, nor permitting one to contradict another; not justice to contradict love, nor love to be opposed to justice. Can He possibly conceal or mis-

* "The latest spiritualistic critical fraud, which has spread from Tubingen, through a part of the Evangelical Church;" "the patched-up legendary view of mingled traditions, with later compilations."—See Lange on Genesis, Scribner's edition, pp. 31, 99, 107, etc. "It reduces the Scriptures not only to fragments, but to *fragments of fragments*, jumbled in confusion." See Prof. Tayler Lewis, on the assumed Jehovistic and Elohistic distinctions, pp. 99 to 108.

represent any of His attributes or permit them to be misrepresented, or falsified, or dishonored?

And when a supreme regard to His own glory is described as the rule of Jehovah in all His dealings, can there possibly be any other just, benevolent, and righteous rule than this? For in the knowledge of that glory, and an active subordination to it, and rejoicing in it, lies the whole and sole possibility of order and happiness under the Divine Government. For nothing can be harmonious or blessed, that is not accordant with God's own infinite goodness and holiness, God's own self-respecting holy will, and the manifestation of it. Nothing can be blessed, or a means of blessing others, that opposes, or defies, or falsifies God's will; or that obscures His glory, or is not conformed thereto, or prevents it from being seen and understood, or causes it to be mistaken.

All the manifestations of God to His intelligent creatures are for their good, *that they may be partakers of His own holiness and happiness.* How can it possibly ever be otherwise? And the giving of His own Son to suffer and die the just for the unjust, that He might bring us to God, that we might be heirs of God and joint heirs with Christ, by the adoption of sons, is such a proof of love, such an infinite conquest of our suspicions, and such a winning of our confidence, that the very imagination of it could have come only from its reality as a divine revelation; and the revelation of it is a miracle of demonstration greater than the existence of the visible universe. Certainly, whoever confesses Christ before men will be filled with all the fullness of God's love and blessedness forever and ever; for in that confession from the heart consists the most perfect and glorifying service of gratitude and love we can ever render.

"*There shall this be told for a memorial of her.*" This, and the record of the offering of a poor widow among many rich men, and the mention of a cup of cold water by the Lord Jesus, are proofs of the infinite value of a very little faith and love, and how all the greatest things and creatures in the universe are put to their best service in the production of such love. Two mites that make a farthing! Scientific research discloses the fact that mountain ridges vast enough for the foundations of continents are the work of countless millions of invisible insects, ages on ages building up and fossilizing their substance and their habitations. Now suppose that every one of these animalculæ were intelligent, capable of thought, and animated in every part of its work by the single desire to bring an offering to God, to do something that might glorify God, and remain a manifestation of His goodness. The architecture would be an intelligent musical temple, vibrating within and without the melodies of love and praise. Every two mites of coral, and all the rising seawalls, atolls, and mountain ridges, would be as sacred as the thoughts of angels, would be more precious and glorious than continents of diamond and gold. Such will the whole universe of God be found forever, as the new-created work of His Divine Love, and of the faith of each regenerated creature, confessing and adoring that Love in Christ, when the whole people of God shall be delivered, every one that shall be found written in THE BOOK. "And they that be wise shall shine as the brightness of the firmament; and they that turn many to righteousness, as the stars forever and ever."

CERTAINTIES, NOT CONJECTURES, THE BUSINESS OF A TRUE CRITIC.

This therefore is the primal canon of a just criticism, imperative, obligatory, namely, to accept and press THE SCRIPTURES, just as Christ and His apostles pressed them; not doubtingly, but by manifestation of the truth; not apologetically, but aggressively; "to speak boldly, as we ought to speak;" not for a condescending patronage of divine truth, but for universal conquest. "Bringing into captivity *every thought* to the obedience of Christ; casting down every high thing that exalteth itself against the knowledge of God." "ALL SCRIPTURE IS INSPIRED OF GOD, and able to make all men wise unto salvation, through faith that is in Christ Jesus." ALL SCRIPTURE; for the righteous PREPOSSESSION of the Son of God is in it, for all mankind, from the cradle to the grave. "For all the promises of God in Him are YEA AND AMEN, unto the glory of God by us." Paul the Positivist wrote all these commanding, constituting, all embracing postulates, who wrote the fifteenth of First Corinthians, and the fourth, fifth, and sixth of the Second Corinthians. And he wrote these divine utterances, not as if there were any grounds of doubt in regard to them, or internal suspicions, whereby to ticket them, as perhaps bad bills, needing to be tracked back to the forgers; but for conquest, for payment in gold at the Savings Bank of Christ for sinners. It was the central power of LEGISLATING LOVE, by the Spirit of Christ, that coined these testimonies, with infinite confidence, not by permission or vote of "many authorities," but the One Supreme God, and by His oath, swearing by Himself, because He could swear by no greater, and would have all men justified by faith in His Son, and in none other way; that all should honor the Son even as they honor the Father.

The Word of God in Christ, is one and the same, equally, in the Old and the New Testament, having in it all the light, meaning, and purpose of human salvation, and all the instrumentalities for that work of regeneration in the soul, that the Divine Word, the Son of God, became flesh to finish:—all that was possible for the life of the soul, and therefore for its conviction of sin and its awakening unto prayer, and its spiritual resurrection from the death of sin, and its new creation in the image and nature of God in Christ; all that might contribute to the beginning or completion of that work; all the possible influences, suggestions, electricities, magnetisms, illustrations of God's attributes, and of man's dependence on God; God's holiness and man's sinfulness, God's mercy and man's despair and hope, God's thoughts towards man, and man's right way of thinking and believing and earnest striving after God.

COAL MEASURES IN THE OLD; INSPIRED MINERS IN THE NEW.

The boundless *coal measures* of Light, Love and Fire, in the Old Testament, were prepared for the working of companies of INSPIRED MINERS in the New. "The Lord gave the Word; great was the company of those that published it. Thou, O God, hast prepared of Thy goodness for the poor. The God of Israel is He that giveth strength and power unto His people." This 68th Psalm is of infinite Messianic grandeur. "Thou hast ascended on high, Thou hast led captivity captive; Thou hast received gifts for men; yea, for the rebellious also, that the Lord God might dwell among them." Compare Eph. 4: 8–16. "Unto every one of us is given grace, according to the measure of the gift of Christ, according to the riches of His glory, strengthened with might by His Spirit in the inner man, speaking the truth in love, to grow up in all things into Him who is the Head, even Christ."

Known unto God are all the workings of His Word from the beginning of the world. All the remotest flashes of light, and possible revelations of it, for the production of belief in God, and love to Him and adoration of Him in spirit and in truth;—all possible miraculous new creations by the Word, by what we call accidental fallings of it on the soul, meetings of the soul with any part of it, anywhere among savages or cultured infidels; in words and suggestions and unaccountable impressions, though seemingly driven like dead autumn leaves by the wind, and lost, yet carrying into the soil, possibly, some hidden seeds somewhere; and if any, then enough, in infallible aftergrowth and reproduction, for the life of some whole continent. Given, the Word of God from Genesis to the Apocalypse, for man's eternal life in God, and it is impossible to restrict any part of it, by men's canons of criticism, denying its infallible inspiration, or the possible intentions and applications of it, by the omniscient God that gave it, and His Holy Spirit that inspired and accompanies its thoughts and words, it may be for a hundred thousand generations, to the end of the world. God must foresee the action of its words, as well as its orbs of thought, as surely as He must have ordered and foreseen the atoms and action of the elements, the way in which light is parted, the velocity with which it travels, the power of every one of its rays, the chemical activities that it creates and governs, the laws of life it combines and executes; the organization of an eye to receive it, the creation of a mind and reason to adore its proofs and illustrations of the essence and attributes of God.

We say, from Genesis to the Apocalypse. The glory of the English literature of the 17th century is in the floods of light poured through its volumes of poetry and prose upon the spiritual meaning and Divine inspiration of the Scriptures, through the medium of the Authorized Translation in our language, and Luther's in the German. Bengel and Luther, Tyndale and their successors, made a Bible for the ploughboys, and therefore equally for the most cultured and self-applauding intellects, set together to the study of its pages, as little children to the syllables of earliest believing and imaginative thought for the saving of the soul. "A deliberate sad eye, with leisure," said the most illustrious of those Biblical scholars, John Lightfoot,* in his rules for a student of the Holy Scriptures, "might bring all the New Testament, both for words and sense, from the Old. AND THIS I EVER HELD THE SUREST WAY TO EXPOUND BOTH. God Himself hath taught us what is the best way to read, for He hath folded the two Testaments together; so that, as the Law begins, so the Gospel ends, and as the prophets end, so the Law begins; as if calling you to look still for the one in the other, Moses and Elias were Evangelists. And what did Christ ever do or suffer, which you may not see in the Law and Prophets, tracing Christ throughout the Old Testament."

* Lightfoot's Works, vol. ii. pp. 43–47.

THE PERFECTION OF OUR KNOWLEDGE AND DISCIPLINE GRADUAL IN CHRIST TO THE END.

In the gospels we are with Jesus; we follow Him in the way; we talk with Him, ask Him questions, hear His words, wonder at His parables of wisdom, His miracles of power. We behold the proofs of His divine nature, His deity as the Son of God, and one with the Father, His omnipotence, omniscience, the universe under Him, the kingdom of heaven His, the eternal world of being, and all its awards to the righteous and the wicked His. All these realities, these discoveries come out, as we travel with Him; we learn them gradually, just as His disciples did. The proofs of His divinity are as positive and plain as of His humanity; we behold one day, one hour, the Son of Man, the next the Son of God. The facts and seals of both natures drop out as artlessly, as spontaneously, as naturally, as the motions and prattle of a child. The most sublime and astounding announcements of His supremacy as Lord of all, Governor and Judge of mankind, possessor of dominion over all worlds, visible and invisible, drop from Him as by accident, unconsciously, in the midst of discourses not at all intended for a proof of His greatness, nor the argument instituted for that, but as it were unawares, under the form of man, a servant; the infinite God giving utterances, that no human being would put in language, but the moment they are spoken, and the mind at leisure to ponder them, God, not man, is seen in them. One of the earliest of such instances comes out at the close of the Sermon on the Mount. "*Many will say* TO ME *in that day*," etc., "and then *will I profess unto them, I never knew you;* DEPART FROM ME, ye that work iniquity. Whosoever heareth THESE SAYINGS OF MINE, and doeth them, I WILL LIKEN HIM," etc.

Then His dealing with the Decalogue: "Ye have heard that it was said, But I SAY UNTO YOU," etc. These avowals of His divine power and majesty were so frequent, and so natural, that the impression of them grew as a flower opens, as the sun rises; never startling or tremendous, as with the rending of the rocks, or the rolling fires around Elijah, or the bush of flame to Moses, but calmly as the falling of the dew; so does the vision, the sense, the conviction of a supernatural, superhuman Being, though in the form of man, the servant, in uttermost lowliness of life, even unto the crucifixion, go down into the soul. And so it carried the illuminated reason of the centurion, "TRULY THIS WAS THE SON OF GOD." And so the sight of Jesus on the cross, blameless, dying, praying for His murderers, *Father, forgive them, for they know not what they do!* removed the veil of darkness from the dying thief, and the Holy Spirit breathed in his soul that wondrous prayer of faith and love, "Lord, remember me, when Thou comest into Thy Kingdom!" So from the beginning, the vision carries us, and so we follow on, through the gospels, walking with Christ, beholding His glory, till we are not only prepared, but constrained to cry out with Thomas, "My Lord and my God!" And with Stephen, "Behold, I see the Son of Man standing on the right hand of God! Lord Jesus, receive my spirit." All this revelation, from the first verse of Genesis to the last word of the Apocalypse, is of the POWERS OF THE

WORLD TO COME, for life or death eternal, to the never dying soul; and of the Love of Christ, pleading with us, that we may not be self-banished, in a sinful immortality, from the presence of the Son of God FOREVER. "Amen, even so, Come, Lord Jesus, come quickly, and dwell within our hearts by faith, that death, and sin the sting of death, may be swallowed up in victory!"

GOD'S TIMEPIECE FOR MAN'S ETERNITY.

I.

CHRIST THE CENTRAL LIGHT, LIFE, AND PROOF OF THE WHOLE BIBLE—ALL OUR KNOWLEDGE OF IT DEPENDENT ALONE ON HIS DIVINE PERSONALITY —OUR BIBLE FOR ETERNAL LIFE.

THE BIBLE ITS OWN WITNESS, is a received proverbial expression, yet so little realized, analyzed, believed, acted on, that it might have been catalogued as among Coleridge's "bedridden truths in the dormitory of the soul." God can have no witnesses, but only confessors. "Where wast thou when I laid the foundations of the earth, when the morning stars sang together, and all the sons of God shouted for joy? Where is the way where light dwelleth? Wast thou then born?" Christ alone is the AUTHOR AND FINISHER OF FAITH, and His Word the substance and the evidence of things not seen. He receives not testimony or endorsement from man.

We learn from Him alone, and by His enlightening of our understandings, as to all things written *in all* the *Scriptures*, in Moses and the Prophets, and the Psalms, that the Word of God is a growth, by the Holy Spirit, and not a mere creation by Almighty Power;—that its living, growing evolution and progress, according to the necessities of man and the mercies of God, because of man's fall into sin, and his consequent hereditary progression in wickedness, are demonstrated in itself, even as the growth of an oak is registered and proved by the successive rings of its annual life, grown and recorded in the sections of the trunk. "Thou hast magnified Thy Word, above all Thy name."—Ps. cxxxviii. 2. "My name is in Him." Ex. xxiii 21. An incarnate personal prophesying Life and Light.—Deut. xviii. 18, and John i. 4.

The Word, thus begun, perfected, and finished in Christ, is in Him forever living and abiding, as manifest and complete as the I AM BEFORE ABRAHAM, the same yesterday, to-day, and forever; Emmanuel, God with us, Christ the Word, the Way, the Truth, the Life, the Revealer of God, the Creator and Redeemer of man; Christ inhabiting Eternity, investing Himself with humanity, in form and nature; born and manifested in the flesh, suffering, dying, rising, ascending into Heaven, and upholding all things by the Word of His power:—All this is THE WORD, all this union of impossibilities in Time, and yet indisputable Eternal certainties; a temporal Eternity, and an Eternal To-day; Christ the Letter and the Spirit, Christ the written Gospel and the unwritten glory;—All this in a visible, legible volume, a perfect oneness, "a whirlwind, a cloud, and a fire infolding itself"; loosed and opened by God at the beginning, sealed by Christ at the close; a volume, as known and perfectly finished, as the Virgin Mother with her Babe, by the Holy Ghost upon her, and the power of the Highest overshadowing her;—and afterwards the attendant ministries of worshipping and singing angels, prophets, priests, and devout inspired men, waiting for the Consolation of Israel, and beholding the Lord's Christ, by the Spirit, in the Temple. This is the Word, the Bible, the VOLUME WRITTEN OF ME, an Eternal Now, past, present, and to come, an Orb of Love, Light, Life, Power, and Law, self-existent, omnipresent, forever settled in heaven, forever on earth, OUR BIBLE; GOD MANIFESTING HIMSELF TO US, AND US TO OURSELVES IN HIS SIGHT.

All this supernatural overwhelming array of Eternities in Time, the Attributes of God, the Word, made flesh, yet in a record so natural and simple, so artless and sublime, so convincing and irresistible, that in the reading of it, in gazing at the glory, we can only exclaim with Thomas, "My Lord and my God!" and with Isaiah, "Mine eyes have seen the King, the Lord of Hosts!" and with John, "That which was from the beginning, which we have heard, which we have seen with our eyes, which we have looked upon, and our hands have handled, of the Word of Life!" and with Christ Himself upon the cross, "It is finished!" Nothing can be put to it, nothing taken from it. Heaven and earth shall pass away, but My Word shall not pass away.

This is that witness of God, which He hath testified of His Son, and that witness of the Son, which He hath testified of God the Father. God speaking to us by His Son demonstrates the Old Testament Scriptures as His Word; and the appearance and testimony of His Son throw the same God-given demonstration over the whole New Testament as over the Old. And so the whole volume is in all ages a finished spiritual orb and unity of divine inspiration, as indisputably the work of God as the sun in the heavens.

What infinite sublimity, and assertion of supreme, self-existent truth, authority and power, in all these introductions of the Saviour to the souls of all mankind! The openings up of divine revelation in the Old Testament, in the Gospels, in the Epistles, and in the Apocalypse, are as the successive breakings of heaven's seals of light and fire by the hand of God Himself.

Read and compare the first five verses of Genesis,

the 1st, 2d, and 110th Psalms, the first five verses of the Gospel of John, the first seven of the Epistle to the Romans, the first five of that to the Galatians, the first chapter of the Epistle to the Ephesians, and the opening chapter of "the Word of God and the Testimony of Jesus." in Patmos. And then, as a central instance, take the august and magnificent opening of the Epistle to the Hebrews: "God, who at sundry times, and in divers manners, spake in time past unto the fathers by the prophets, hath in these last days spoken unto us by His Son; whom He hath appointed heir of all things, by whom also He made the worlds; who being the brightness of His glory, and the express image of His person, and upholding all things by the Word of His power, when He had by Himself purged our sins, sat down on the right hand of the Majesty on high."

"IT IS THE SPIRIT THAT BEARETH WITNESS, BECAUSE THE SPIRIT IS TRUTH. He that believeth what the Spirit saith hath the witness in himself; for this is the witness of God which He hath testified of His Son. He that believeth not God hath made Him a liar, because *he believeth not the record* that God gave of His Son." "HE THAT HATH THE SON HATH LIFE, AND HE THAT HATH NOT THE SON OF GOD HATH NOT LIFE."—1 John v. 11, 12.

FORGIVENESS AND ETERNAL LIFE IN CHRIST are the purpose and fulfilment of God's record, in the Law and Gospel; the whole, and only Scriptures Prophetic and Historic, of "God manifest in the flesh, justified in the Spirit, seen of angels, preached unto the Gentiles, believed on in the world, received up into glory." The Scriptures demonstrated in Jesus Christ alone, as GOD OVER ALL, BLESSED FOREVER. And recorded in the Volume written concerning Him, Old and New, "that believing we might have life through His Name."—John xx. 31. "For whatsoever things *were written aforetime, were written for our learning*, that we, through patience and comfort of THE SCRIPTURES might have hope. ALL SCRIPTURE is given by inspiration of God, and is able to make thee wise unto Salvation, *through faith which is in Christ Jesus.*" For the law by Moses is not one thing, and grace and truth by Christ another; but both are equally the love and inspiration of the Father and the Son, by the Holy Spirit taking of the things that are Christ's, and showing them to the soul, for the assurance of Eternal Life in Him. "Being the AUTHOR OF ETERNAL SALVATION, He by one offering hath perfected FOREVER them that are sanctified; having by His own blood obtained ETERNAL REDEMPTION for us, that we might have ETERNAL LIFE IN HIM." The Testament of Life ends with the last words of God to man in the Apocalypse, "The grace of our Lord Jesus Christ be with you all. Amen."

II.

THE DIFFERENCE BETWEEN THE THINGS SECRET AND THOSE REVEALED—THE FIRST DISCLOSED ATTRIBUTES OF GOD, AND THE FIRST WORDS FOR GOD AND ETERNITY—EVERYTHING IN A DIVINE REVELATION DEPENDENT ON THEM—ALL THE FIRST THINGS CONCERNING GOD AND CHRIST AND THE SOUL'S ETERNAL LIFE AND DEATH FORESHOWN IN THE WRITINGS OF MOSES—GOD'S CHRONOMETER AND COMPASS FOR TIME AND ETERNITY.

"The secret things belong unto the Lord our God: but those which are revealed belong unto *us and to our children* FOREVER, *that we may do all the words of this law.*"—Deut. xxix. 29. It is from the outset a revelation from God, well known and admitted, of such a nature as to last forever, that *by means of it* we may keep God's law.

"For what the law could not do, in that it was weak through the flesh, God, sending His own Son, in the likeness of sinful flesh, and for sin, condemned sin in the flesh; that the righteousness of the law might be fulfilled in us, who walk not after the flesh, but after the spirit."—Rom. viii. 3, 4. The verse quoted from Deuteronomy is as a north star in our spiritual firmament; and the eighth chapter of Romans, and all the planets in the New Testament, are but as pointers to it, that we may do all the words of this law.

The Eternity of God and the Immortality of man in His image, the Holiness of God and the sinfulness of man after the fall, are as plainly revealed, with all the consequences, as a child's catechism. All the true principles of criticism follow inevitably;—the nature of a divine inspiration, the necessary infallibility of it for man's guidance, God's administration of His own government dependent on it, holiness and truth the foundations of it, and no true reasoning possible except from these postulates. They are summed up, after more than three thousand years, in the words of God to the prophet Ezekiel: "Behold, ALL SOULS ARE MINE; as the soul of the father, so also the soul of the son is Mine: THE SOUL THAT SINNETH IT SHALL DIE." That the solemn everlasting meaning and consequences of these words were accepted and known from the beginning by the Jews is manifest from Ez. xxxiii. 10: "If our transgressions and our sins be upon us, and we pine away in them, *how should we then live?*" Yea, and except God in Christ shall *give you life*, ye *cannot* live. There was never a question asked by an inquiring or an unconverted soul, that carried its answer more directly with it, for ourselves and for our children.

It is very remarkable that the first instance occurring of the word *forever* in the Bible (Hebrew, *olam*), is found thus expressly referring to the Eternity of God, and to the sin of man through the falsehood of the "LIAR AND FATHER OF IT FROM THE BEGINNING": "Ye shall not die, but be as gods." The dreadful comment of Jehovah instantly follows the crime; and then the first step is taken to save man from its eternal consequences. Thence comes the known infinite meaning of the word *olam;* it is the introduction of God's ETERNITY to the consciousness of sinful man.

After this, the first example of its use from God to Moses is in Ex. iii. 14, 15: "This is My name forever (*olam*); say to the children of Israel, I AM hath sent me to you." Thus was established, in the opening of Divine Revelation, the origin and spiritual meaning of the word, in God's own attribute of self-existence, ETERNITY. Then in Ex. xv. 18, in the song of Miriam: "Jehovah shall reign *forever*" (*olam*). Then in Deut. xxxii. 40: "I lift up my hand to heaven and say, I LIVE FOREVER" (*olam*).

These instances are postulates of the absolute infinitude of the word. All lower applications of it are figurative, in things and seasons of *time-worlds*, generations and limited periods. But the absolute Eternity of God is the governing and defining power for all the relations and responsibilities of the soul to Him, under all circumstances. And the Eternity of God is the background of all His communications, all His laws, judgments, institutions, provisions for mankind, "*that we may do all the words of this law.*"

This wonderful text foreshadows and ordains everything to come; the conclusion of the Book of Ecclesiastes, five hundred years later, is in it: "Fear God, and keep His commandments, for this is the whole duty of man. For God shall bring every work into judgment, whether good or evil." Here are Immortality, Eternity, and Eternal Life in God, for man, by the relations of the Divine Law, for the ETERNAL KEEPING OF IT. The whole of Divine Revelation is here, as when God said, "Let there be light, and there was light;" the same light at the beginning, and in the whole universe, as when reservoired in orbs, or prismatized in rainbows, for times and seasons, for covenants, emergencies, and successive enlarging dispensations, down to the coming of God incarnate in Christ. A more perfect description of a spiritual TIMEPIECE FOR ETERNITY could not be imagined than this verse of Moses. Chronometer and compass answering each to other in the conscience and heart of man, "*that we may do all the words of this law.*"

For, "He hath made everything beautiful in his time: also He hath set ETERNITY (*olam*) in their heart." Eccles. iii. 11, 17. Chronometer within, and compass without, for man's Immortality and Eternity; intended for and answering to the intuitions and ideas in man's original creation in the image of God. "So teach us," was the prayer of Moses, "to *number* our days, that we may apply our hearts to wisdom." "Lord, make me to know *mine end*," was David's prayer, "and the *measure* of my days, what it is, that I may know how frail I am," and may take action accordingly. The *measure* is for Life Everlasting, and so is the *number*.

A believing mariner under the teachings of Moses would know how to *box this compass* for Eternity. And so Christ told the Jews, after four thousand years' possession of it, and of the prophetic instructions as to its meaning and use, "Had ye believed Moses, ye would have believed Me, for he wrote of Me. But if ye believe not his writings, how shall ye believe My words?"—John v. 46, 47.

Within and without, God's Word and Spirit; Eternity in their hearts; chronometer, and compass! And such power and minuteness of inference, such infinite sweep round the whole horizon of our being, with indexes for Immortality and Eternity, *all the words of this law*, that we may know the Way of Life in God forever! This spiritual compass has more flaming lifelines and points, if the heart consulting it is steady toward God, as the needle to the pole, than the most experienced sea captain could ever trace, or commit to memory from the magnetic-figured circle, for the guidance of his ship. "Every one of Thy righteous judgments endureth forever. They stand fast forever and ever; His covenant forever. Concerning Thy testimonies, I have known of old that Thou hast FOUNDED THEM FOREVER."

"Jehovah, God, forever."—Gen. xxi. 33. "God of Israel from eternity to eternity."—Ps. xli. 14. "The glory of Jehovah shall endure forever."—Ps. civ. 31. "Thy righteousness is forever."—Ps. cxix. 142. "And forever all the *judgments* of Thy righteousness."—cxix. 160. "Blessed be the Lord God of Israel from everlasting to everlasting, from *olam* to *olam*."—I Chron. xvi. 36. And so repeated in Isaiah, Jeremiah, Ezekiel, Daniel, the word and its eternal significations are indisputable; always in reference to the attributes of God, and therefore unmistakable. "God, the GOD OF THE SPIRITS OF ALL FLESH."—Num. xvi. 22, and xxvii. 16.

In the historical and prophetic books these august declarations are equally and infinitely distinct and sublime. The attributes of the word always correspond with the attributes of God, and all things are ordered and established in unwavering deference to the Word, which is the one abiding certainty for the universe, and is so clothed with the divine authority and majesty, that the quality of piety acceptable to

God is just this: "To this man will I look, even to him that is poor and of a contrite spirit, and who trembleth at My Word. Hear the Word of the Lord, ye that tremble at His Word." For all things in Time and through Eternity are ordered by it.

Even if only the Pentateuch were before us, in connection with the gospels, we may see how the background of all God's dealings with man, and man's with God, is Eternity; how self and sin make man suspicious of God, and unfit to judge Him in anything; how self in view makes man intellectually blind as to God's purposes and ways; how suffering is the crucible of faith and the refiner of evidence; how God is supreme in all human history, and how an infallible divine inspiration is necessary to disclose God's thoughts, God's presence and plan, God's will and law, to judge rightly of which Faith must be the guide of Reason; for doubt and suspicion morally, darken a man's mind intellectually, and self-interest makes him almost unconsciously a perjured juror, a false critic.

We see how the history of the Hebrews is a tapestry of God's weaving, and must be either the record of infallible divine inspiration or a whole lie; for it could come only from God's plans in execution, and God only could reveal those plans, with their eternal meaning and issues; and could demonstrate, as in Isaiah,

Jeremiah, and Ezekiel, where and how the temporal events take up men's souls and run into eternity; and are proved by God's light, making every knot and line and crossline of the tapestry a prophet for the soul, and luminous as a transparency, revealing God and man together.

Moreover, in the study of these *key-words* of Eternity we learn to walk and work, with fear and trembling, because it is God that worketh in us; by manifestation of the truth commending ourselves to *every man's* CONSCIENCE IN THE SIGHT OF GOD, even as His attributes in Christ are plainly made known to us. And we see how a baptism with the infinite compassion of Jesus is necessary for the watchman of souls, and how Christ's own loving Spirit alone can deal with the doubt and despair of agonized consciences; how loyalty to God's Word, like that of Christ, can alone make a man true and faithful to man, and kind and tender and charitable and generous, just in proportion as he is true. God's patience reasons tenderly with the sinner, and wins him. Man's impatience strikes him and stuns him. The wrath of man worketh not the righteousness of God, but the righteousness of God restrains the wrath of man, and causes it to praise Him in many adorable ways of His Eternal wisdom and grace in Christ Jesus.

III.

THE RECORD OF CREATION IN THE PENTATEUCH OUR ONLY DIVINE AND DECISIVE AUTHORITY —THE SEEMING CONTRADICTIONS, AND THE MEANS OF UNDERSTANDING THEM, IN GOD'S WORD, FOR ETERNITY.

THE REVELATION thus belonging to us and to our children FOREVER, begins with the record of Creation *as God's work in successive periods.* It is therefore the first and highest decisive authority as to the questions which science is now agitating and investigating. The only element of uncertainty is in regard to the just interpretation of the language; but so far as we can ascertain that, it is the highest scientific as well as moral and theological authority that we possess, or can possess. Wherever there is any doubt, it is the revelation that has the rightful precedence, and must decide.

The question, what is the first book of this revelation? does not rest upon man's testimony, nor does the question, who was the writer of it? It begins as a light from God and eternity, with no announcement of any human scribe or reporter. Forever, O Lord, Thy Word is settled in heaven. It was reserved for Him who is the AUTHOR AND FINISHER OF FAITH to establish infallibly for the knowledge of all mankind what is the first book of revelation, by referring explicitly to Genesis, and quoting from it as the Word of God. Our Lord's references to it, and His quotations of its words as divine authority, demonstrate the manner of the Creation of Adam and Eve, as there reported, to be absolute and unquestionable truth. Those therefore who proclaim that account to have been a fable do most undoubtedly hold up to scorn the Lord Jesus Christ as an impostor and a passer of counterfeit money in the name of God. They do this in the face of an accumulation of demonstrative proof, both physical and moral, of the supernatural truth and divine personality of Christ, immeasurably greater than anything ever offered by scientific men as to their theories.

In the Word of God there are the same contrasts, diversities, seeming contradictions, and, applying the terms of natural science, "*faults*" (that is, "dislocations or disturbances of *strata*, interrupting the miner's operations"), as in His works. There are also analogous methods of the *differential calculus*, for finding and measuring the actual differences and their meaning; comparing spiritual things with spiritual, and the parts with the whole. In the large dictionaries we

God's Timepiece for Man's Eternity. 17

have illustrations given of "*faults*" in a mine, and there are engravings presented of the dislocated strata, before which the experimentalist or miner is *at fault*. So, both in the Divine Providence and Word, we are sometimes interrupted by seams and scars unaccountable, and depths unfathomable. Thy judgments are a great deep. In nature we have the mountain of granite, and quartz, and the gold, for which we must dig, and separate it from the quartz. But the granite and the quartz are as much God's work, and God's designs are in it, as the gold itself. We ourselves can mix mud and sand, and make our own quarries; but we cannot make the gold, nor the organizing principles and laws. We can convey, express, and modify thought in language, but we cannot make, nor successfully imitate or dissemble, a divine inspiration with its seals. None but God can create and demonstrate the inspiration. No human being could imagine the proofs, the methods of proof, and the irresistible power of conviction, with which God could and does establish *that*, in the intuitions of heart and conscience, the moment an immortal being looks down into the mirror of His Word, and sees both his own and God's image. He sees himself in God's sight, and the conclusion is, Thou God seest me! Then at length, when he sees himself in Christ's likeness, or longing after that likeness, the demonstration is, Thou my Divine Redeemer hast sought me, and found me, and brought me back to God.

I did not find Thee, nor accept Thee, nor acknowledge Thee, nor would I, nor could I, of mine own perverted will and reason; but Thou, against both, didst seek me, and new-create and save me, by Thy Spirit and Thy Word, laying hold upon me, within me, leading captivity captive, subduing my self-will, my carnal mind, the enmity of my heart, and drawing me by infinite long-suffering love, redeeming grace and dying love. And Thou makest me to comprehend this, only by Christ dwelling in my heart by faith, strengthening me for this, with might by Thy Spirit in the inner man.

Here it is that Jude, closing up the epistles in the New Testament, presents the *differential key* to the whole inspired Word: "Ye, beloved, praying in the Holy Ghost, building up yourselves on your most holy faith, keep yourselves in the love of God, looking for the mercy of our Lord Jesus Christ unto Eternal Life." Only thus, by discovering and using this *Divine Calculus*, can we bridge the gulfs, or accept with intelligent, grateful, adoring belief, the infinite mysteries of "God manifest in the flesh." PRAYING IN THE HOLY GHOST is the one element of scientific investigation in the Scriptures, without which all the textual criticism of scholars is presumptuous and vain. "PRAY-ING ALWAYS WITH ALL PRAYER AND SUPPLICATION IN THE SPIRIT," is Paul's watchword as well as Jude's.

God's quarries are infinite. The chronology, the history, the records, the workmen, the instruments, the stuff to be wrought, the purposes, the methods, the boundless suffering:—the very difficulties *to* us are God's methods *for* us.

>"Blind unbelief is sure to err,
> And scan His work in vain;
> God is His own Interpreter,
> And He will make it plain."

"He that formeth the mountains, and createth the spirit; and declareth unto man what is His thought, and turneth the shadow of death into the morning, and maketh the day dark with night. The thunder of His power, who can understand? O the depth of the riches both of the wisdom and knowledge of God! How unsearchable are His judgments, and His ways past finding out!"

Science and religion are the same infinitude and mystery of Godliness. All is of God from Eternity to Eternity. The truth and its surroundings, its settings, its background and foreground, perspectives and retrospectives, its origins, occasions, sources, elements, intermixtures, accidents and ends; all of God.

Nor will any one in his senses say, The gold indeed is of God, the mountain and its quartz, not. He that made the gold made the mountain to contain it, to enshrine it, and He that made the mountain made the gold. Both, and equally both, are of God, and could not have been without Him. All science is God's truth. And so, in all our scientific investigations we are but tracing the work and the footsteps of God's Presence and Power; so that an impelling faith in God is the very substratum of the possibility of science. And without this faith, the best university in the world, managed by the highest minds, is only a scientific treadmill, or a dissecting hall, with the positivism of the surgeon's knife the only thing credited in it.

IV.

THE GRADUAL PERFECTION AND INTERPRETATION OF WORDS FROM THE OLD TESTAMENT TO THE NEW—THE WORDS FOR "DEATH," "HELL," AND THE "GRAVE," AND THEIR ETERNAL SPIRITUAL MEANING AND TEACHINGS.

For the conveyance and understanding of God's plan of salvation, human language itself had to be rescued from the grasp of demonism, materialism and idolatry, and new created by the Holy Spirit. The words *sin* and *redemption* as well as HOLINESS, could be understood only by God's disclosing of Himself, in His infinitely holy and adorable attributes, and revealing in contrast, man's sinful heart, character, and ruin. These and other terms were more and more exactly and fully defined through the gradualism of inspiration, in institutions, laws, precepts, examples, appointed and expressed by divine wisdom and mercy, dealing with the necessities of sinful men, providing for and prophesying the coming Redeemer, that the world might know when, where, and in what character, and with what signs, to welcome Him for the salvation of their souls. The words *Sheol*, *Hades*, and *Gehenna*, regarding the unseen world, and the dwellings of men in that world, according to their character in this, have had a similar gradual perfection and interpretation, from the Old Testament to the New. The expressions heaven and hell, the kingdom of heaven, and of God, expiation and atonement, sacrifice and offering, as well as the righteousness of God, were seeds of eternal and infinite significance, gradually unfolded and illustrated, through eras of inspiration by the Holy Spirit, and in the life and experience of men distinguished for their piety. Coming up out of the darkness of Egypt, the relations and realities of the future life, as well as the duties of the present, and the right methods of God's worship, had to be redeemed from the doctrines of devils and clothed with divine light.

The AUTHOR AND FINISHER OF FAITH must Himself inspire the spirit of a loving trust, and teach its adoring language for believers. The Redeemer of the soul, coming to save mankind, must do everything for them, making all things new. His work was as that of a Missionary Angel among Dacotah savages, compelled to construct their written language for them out of the elements of their rude spoken dialects, never before reduced to writing. Their instructor must make their very dictionary out of their own rugged, imperfect conversational vocabulary.* He be-

* See the interesting history of the progress of the mission among the Dacotah Indians, and the making of a Dacotah dictionary and Bible, by the first missionary, Stephen R. Riggs, D.D., LL.D., and his wife. The volume is entitled, "Mary and I." Having translated the gospels into the Dacotah tongue, Dr. Riggs says: "We now addressed ourselves afresh to the work of teaching and preaching. In preaching I began to feel more freedom and joy. There had been times when the Dacotah language seemed to be barren and meaningless. The words for Salvation and Life, and even Death and Sin, did not mean what they did in English. It was not to me a *heart-language*. But this passed away. A Dacotah word *began to thrill* as an English word. *Christ came into the language. The Holy Spirit began to pour sweetness and power into it.* It became a joy to preach,—not exhausting as it sometimes had been."

Thus it was that Christ came into the language of our com-

comes the Inventor of an Electric Telegraph, who must arrange the posts and the wires, and contrive the alphabet of ciphers, and teach the operators and the postmasters how to manage the machinery, how to catch and interpret the signals, the dots, dashes, pauses.

If God taught Adam the language of Creation before the fall (see Gen. ii. 19, 20), how much more the language of Redemption for himself and his posterity after the fall. A Messianic language, and illustrations of the covenant by blood, such as in the Passover, and the sin-offerings, and purifications, must be provided, as well as the promised Messiah. A language not only of words, but of symbols and signs prophetic of His coming, and making known the needs of fallen men, and the spiritual heart-and-life-renewing nature of salvation by divine grace.

God early put mankind into the school of object-teachings, as children are taught by pictures, puzzles, ships, buildings, trees, animals, to draw lessons and make definitions from them. So with the lessons of

mon version of the New Testament from the first moment when Tyndale, guided by the Holy Spirit, and filled with love to souls, began his work upon it. The revisers of such a translation need something more than additional Greek MSS., and critical skill, to fit them for their work, and preserve its *theopneusted* beauty and sacredness.

religion, from the garden and its dressing and keeping, from the Trees of Knowledge and of Life, from Cherubim and the flaming sword, from worship by altars and incense, from ladders of angels between earth and heaven, pillars of cloud and fire, the burning bush, smitten rocks and fountains in the desert, figures, types, brazen serpents, tabernacles of witness, cherubim of glory overshadowing the Mercy-seat. All these things had an infinitely merciful divine meaning in their origin and use. And by as much as for the accuracy of a compass or a telegraph the utmost exactness in the signals is indispensable for any safety or reliance in the emergencies of our *temporal* life (and so in the science of our medicinal notations), infinitely more must the language of inspiration regarding ETERNITY be absolutely true and infallible, for our *Eternal* Life. It has been well said that an incarnate language is as necessary as an incarnate God; an infallible thought and speech, as an omniscient heart-searching Redeemer.

The first instance of the word *Sheol*, and the first mention of the grave in the Old Testament Scriptures, we shall find in the record of Jacob's grief for Rachel, in Gen. xxxv. 20, and for Joseph, in Gen. xxxvii. 35. "I will go down into the grave unto my son, mourning" (I will go down into *Sheol*). A hundred years before this, Abraham had purchased the cave of the field of Machpelah for the burial of his wife. "In the choice of our sepulchres," said the children of Heth, "bury thy dead." Their *Sheol* was a cave, and the *Sheol* of the Egyptians still earlier, a succession of caves, a tier of caves, with places for the *sarcophagi*, one above another, a kingdom of catacombs, the origin of the imagery in Isaiah xiv. 9, 11, 15, where the Hebrew is *Sheol* throughout, though translated *Hell* in verses 9 and 15, and *Grave* in 11. It was not yet rendered *Hades* (for the era of the Greek translation of the Hebrew Scriptures had not arrived), but *Sheol* from beneath, the kingdom of the dead, "is moved for thee to meet thee at thy coming. Thy pomp is brought down to the *grave*, *Sheol*. The worm is spread over thee, and the worms cover thee." Two hundred years later we find the same imagery in Ezekiel xxxii. 21, 27, "The strong out of the mighty shall speak to him out of the midst of *Sheol*, whose graves are set in the sides of the pit, the nether parts of the earth."

Gesenius thinks *Sheol* means by its derivation a hollow subterranean enclosure, but also suggests, what seems more likely, a derivation from the root *shaal*, to demand; being the *orcus rapax* of Catullus, the rapacious, all-remorseless *Hell* or *Hades*, never satiated with its victims. But as yet, in Abraham's day, Homer was not, nor Pluto, nor Achilles, nor the adventures of

Ulysses, nor any dreams or records of explorers or discoverers of the regions of the dead.

This Hebrew word then had a meaning of its own, several hundred years prior to the Greek mythologies. And its meaning, as to the extent and nature of the kingdom of the dead, grew, with every experience of death and its terrors as revealed of God. Thus *Sheol* gradually swept up all the death-judgments and pestilences of every age, from Sodom and Gomorrah, and Korah and his company, and the *Kibroth hattaavah* of the desert, to *Hinnom* and *Gehenna*, with their burnings and corruptions, growing into a more intense presentation and spiritual meaning, through successive floods of light in the Prophets and the Psalms; till in the gospels, in Mark, for example, ix. 43–48, it is Gehenna, "where their worm dieth not, and the fire is not quenched"; and in Luke xvi. 22–31, it is Hades, where the Sadducean, unbelieving rich man is in torment, beholding Abraham afar off, and Lazarus in his bosom. Death was always a judgment against the wicked, and the grave a kingdom of terror, never relieved of its terrors to the ungodly. The beggar died, and was carried by the angels into Abraham's bosom. The rich man died and was buried, and found himself in *Hades*, tormented in the flame. Definiteness, under the growth of inspiration and experience, took the place of uncertainty. Opinion of what was to be after death became more and more fixed, as the world drew towards the rising of the Sun of Righteousness. See the whole Book of Job, and its vivid references to the traditions and histories of the judgments of God, antediluvian and otherwise, against the wicked; "The heritage appointed unto them by God." "Hast thou marked the old way which wicked men have trodden? And the terror when God taketh away the soul; the portion of a wicked man with God, when the heavens shall reveal his iniquity?" It is the assertion of experience and truth by the Spirit and the Word of God; the common prophetic belief in a coming state of guilt and retribution in the unseen world, where the wicked will receive the due reward of their wickedness, and God will be justified in the sight of the whole universe.

Not only in Genesis and Job is there the concentration of these lightnings, but in Ecclesiastes and the Book of Proverbs. There is never the possibility suggested of any such thing as an Eternal Hope for the wicked, but the very contrary is affirmed; despair instead of hope. They that say unto God, Depart from us, for we desire not the knowledge of Thy ways,— they *have* their desire, their reward. This conviction of a righteous and eternal judgment is an atmosphere of sublime and awful consciousness over and within the whole human mind.

It was an early Hebrew proverb that "the wicked shall be *driven away in his wickedness*, but the righteous hath hope in his death." The consequence or effect of dying in one's sins was an increasing terror and burden on the soul, that nothing but the sense of forgiveness could remove. See Ezekiel xxxiii. 10, 11, and compare Ps. ix. 17, "The wicked shall be turned into *Sheol* (that is, a region and state of penal retribution) and all the nations that forget God." This receptacle and habitation of the wicked was not the grave merely, and could never have been so misinterpreted, but a condition of misery for evil men according to their character in this world, carried into the next. All men, all nations, go down to the grave, the house appointed for all living, good or bad, believing or unbelieving. But only the wicked are "turned into *Sheol*," as in Ps. xlix. 14, 15, 19, "never to see light." This word, in all such passages translated by the Greek Hades, is demonstrated by the context as meaning nothing less than what we call *Hell;* that is simply, the abode of the wicked who die in their sins.*

* Consult for ample proof the Exegetical Essays of Prof. Stuart on the Hebrew and Greek words relating to future punishment. Of this volume, reprinted in Great Britain, it was said that no investigation of the same terms, of like extent or equal ability, existed in our own or any other language.

But the ancient believer in God had a refuge and rest in Him, and in dying was said to have been *gathered to his fathers*. And the hope of eternal life continued to increase in intensity and brightness, till in Christ it assumed shape and lustre, as when carbon is crystallized into the diamond. This was the *progressive inspiration and Christian experience* in the Old Testament. *Forgiveness of sin* removed all the terrors of death, and quieted and comforted the soul in passing through *the valley of the shadow of death*. Across all the darkness, clouds, impenetrable sorrow and gloom of the grave, the Pilgrims under Moses, the Prophets, and the Psalms went direct to God in the belief of that life and immortality, which were not only brought to light, but reduced to sense, in Christ's resurrection and ascension. They had received that promise, and lived upon it by the power of faith, though they saw not its fulfilment; God, says Paul, having reserved that divine triumph, that better thing, that finishing thing, for us, that neither they without us, nor we without them, should be made perfect. But if there is truth in the eleventh of Hebrews, or religion in the life of the Old Testament saints, or the foundations of true piety in the Old Testament revelation, the old witnesses for God carried on all the processes of their spiritual life with the same respect precisely to the great recompense of reward in a better country, even a heavenly, as we. From what living well indeed did Christ's own piety flow forth, but those very Hebrew Scriptures? And by what was He nourished and sustained, but by every word of promise from the mouth of God, for the fulfilment of which He Himself was to be the Bread of God which cometh down from heaven for the life of the world?*

Had there not been, deep-grounded, those original fixtures of opinion and belief in the realities of heaven and hell, as states of happiness and misery contrasted

---

* Some learned expositors have maintained that the faith of the old Hebrews in God was higher and more remarkable and effective than ours ever could be, because they had set before them nothing but temporal expectations and rewards; and yet, knowing nothing about immortality, nevertheless rose to a more exalted piety and disinterested obedience, obeying God exactly as they were commanded, notwithstanding that they knew nothing about Him except as a temporal governor, for temporal ends, and never expected to know anything more of Him, or to have anything more to do with Him, after death. This is the absurdity with which Warburton, and a multitude of German Commentators since his day, have blasted the verdure of the Old Testament like a simoon, and rendered it a land of darkness and confusion, instead of an Eden of the Tree of Life, whose leaves were for the healing of the nations. The palsy and the poison of their speculations are on many books of so-called Christian exposition still.

and eternal, in holiness and sin; and axioms of reasoning from the character of incorrigible criminals with passions set on fire of hell, and habits fitted for no other abode, there could have sprung up neither such proverbs, nor such prophetic reproofs and threatenings, nor the endurance of them when proclaimed. They were believed and understood as God's incontrovertible representations of a future world, where the consequences of sin persisted in would inevitably be endured by men who had chosen to live and die in their own wickedness. We find a demonstration of all this in comparing our Lord's warnings to the Jews against the consequences of dying in their sins with the third, eighteenth, and thirty-third chapters of Ezekiel.

These moulds of thought, then, even if an omniscient Saviour had been restricted to the use of them, or could have contrived none others, were, with all their weakness and inexactness, abundantly sufficient for the conveyance of "the mind of the Spirit" in the gospels, and in the New Testament. And as to the eternal meaning, the eternal reality, vast, infinite, overwhelming, there is no room for doubt. It is not a dispute of words, nor any contradiction or uncertainty of thoughts, or durations, but existence itself, according to character; and character set a-going by choice, in Time, for Eternity.

So in the passage in Matt. xi. 23, "Thou Capernaum which art exalted unto Heaven, shalt be brought down to Hell" (*Hades*); the word cannot possibly mean the grave merely, for the issue immediately is defined to be that of the last judgment; and Capernaum with all the cities of the world will go down to death and the grave at any rate, irrespective of character. But Capernaum, and the other unbelieving cities wherein most of Christ's mighty works were done, and by which their inhabitants through possession of such light and mercy had been raised to Heaven, should in the day of judgment be "thrust down to Hell." Compare Luke x. 14, 15.

Now if we take only a few of the great shining passages of Old Testament Revelation on which the New was built,—the 16th Psalm, eighth to eleventh verses, and the seventeenth, "I will behold thy face in righteousness; I shall be satisfied when I awake in Thy likeness"; along with the 73d Psalm, "Thou shalt guide me with Thy counsel, and afterward receive me to glory"; and Job's shaft of supernatural inspiration, "I know that my Redeemer liveth," and the corresponding translation of these articles of Job's and David's faith into their daily life and experience; just there especially where a man's effective religious hope and belief are brought out most decisively, and demonstrated in the presence and suffering of disease and death; the conclusion is inevitable of a satisfactory knowledge of a blessed immortality. Take for example at the funeral of David's child, the words of the king, "I shall go to him, but he will not return to me"; this knowledge and prophecy of the future heavenly state, and the simple acquiescence of all the attendant and questioning people in David's behavior, as being perfectly accounted for and satisfactory, with that key of eternity opening the door! The logical faculty must be indeed blind, and unfit to disclose the treasures of a revelation from heaven to mankind, if it can make out anything other, or anything less from all this, than the knowledge of the certainty of life and immortality. The same may be said of the record of the translation of Enoch and Elijah, and the words, "He was not, for God took him," and the world-wide knowledge of such events by tradition as well as history, in the ages of divine communication.

Now then, plainly, when our Lord put into universal currency with His own image and superscription, as the real bullion of divine truth, in words of the Holy Spirit's coining, that infinitely solemn and concentrating parable of the rich man and Lazarus, and Abraham conversing in the Eternal World, as to the endless retributions for character and action in this world, He taught no new doctrines. But He did take up and open and illustrate the Volume of His Father's will concerning Himself, and the value and destiny of human souls, and concerning life, death, and Eternity, in the presence of Sadducean, Epicurean, unbelieving men. He depicted and dramatized for men what He knew to be divine realities, and what he came in infinite mercy and love to reveal fully for salvation of the lost; though taught already by Moses and the prophets so clearly, that if men would not hear and be convinced by such witnesses, neither would they, though one rose from the dead.

"Son, remember!" An affectionate, compassionate address! What could be more so? The very spirit of the Divine Saviour weeping over Jerusalem. Yet all the compassion in the universe could not bridge the gulf, or bring that man into Abraham's bosom, who in his lifetime had received his good things, and believed in and regarded nothing better, while Lazarus had received evil things with patient submission and faith in God.

It was infinite Incarnate Love, nothing less, in the Man of Sorrows and acquainted with grief, on whom God hath laid the iniquities of us all, that then and thus on earth was revealing, opening, expounding, for the instruction and salvation of the soul, these dreadful mysteries of self-will, and sin, and its eternal consequences. And the one truth of overwhelming power in all these warnings is that of the interminable and ever-accumulating weight of character, for good or evil, as long as the soul exists, with the attribute of a conscious, voluntary responsibility belonging to it.

It was the vivid dramatization of these realities of guilt, with the assurance of their eternal results, that made Christ, at one and the same time, the Incarnation of God's mercy, and the most terrific Preacher of His righteousness and justice that ever spoke. Never man spake like this Man, when, from the depths of Love Divine, He uttered the thunder of that awful text, "Ye serpents, ye generation of vipers, how can ye escape the condemnation of hell?"

Yet the whole of its awfulness was already in the proverb: "The wicked shall be driven away in his wickedness, but the righteous hath hope in his death." And in the prayer of Moses: "Who knoweth the power of Thine anger? Even according to Thy fear, so is Thy wrath. So teach us to number our days, that we may apply our hearts unto wisdom." Who now dare palter with the watchwords of Eternal Life and Death, adopted in mercy by the Judge of all the earth, that the inhabitants of the world may, in the time of their merciful visitation, learn righteousness?

V.

THE INFLUENCE OF CLASSICAL MYTHOLOGY AND GREEK POETRY UPON CHRISTIAN LANGUAGE AND BELIEF—STALACTITES OF HOMER'S GENIUS IN THE CAVES OF PLUTO—THE LIGHT OF DAVID'S PSALMS—THE INTERNAL EVIDENCE CARRIES EVERYTHING—THE GREAT SHINING PASSAGES DRAMATIZED BY CHRIST.

We certainly attribute too much authority and power to Homer and the Greeks, making him almost a teacher of inspired theology or *eschatology*, when we go to him for the meaning of *Sheol;* or especially if we go with the crowd of Indian path-finders to Babylon and the Oriental philosophers, to find either the details of the future, or the intermediate state, or any of the foundation stones or principles on which the Hebrew imaginations or beliefs of such a state rested.

The Hebrew words of spiritual instruction and warning, promise and legislation, were shafts of divine revelation at successive periods, Adamic, Noahic, Abrahamic, more and more resplendently lighted from God. It must be remembered that Herodotus and Homer did not begin to write till centuries after the Exodus of the Israelites when they came forth from bondage, full mailed in all the knowledge of immortality received from Abraham, Isaac, Jacob, Moses, and all that was possessed also by the Egyptians themselves. And when the Hebrew words or phrases concerning death, the grave, and the world to come were translated into Greek, those translations conveyed the full Hebraic meaning; thus transferring the breath and life of divine inspiration and knowledge even into the dialect of the heathen mythology. It was a baptism from the Nile of one language into the Jordan of the other.

It is more likely that the Septuagint translation carried the elements of heavenly light and teaching into the Greek mind, than that the Greeks carried and threw the vail of their philosophy and superstitions over the Hebrew mind.

Yet the droppings of Homer's genius have become *stalactites* to hold up the mythological caves of Pluto; and so we go in with our smoking historical torches, and admire the flashing lights, almost as if they were sunbeams. The true light to take into this awful and gloomy imagery of Styx and Acheron is that of David's Psalms, rather than of Ulysses' imagined experience and communications with the wandering desolate ghosts of *Hades*. For the Hebrew genius took the Greek captive for God's purposes of a wider and more perfect inspiration, not the Greek the

Hebrew. And so we have in *Hades*, as the adopted synonym of *Sheol* and the kingdom of the grave, not *Tartarus* and *Elysium*, still taught as if under divine sanction, but a kingdom of immediate spiritual forces and awards; not a running to and fro of shuddering ghosts, lamenting, as the great evil of death, that their bodies were never buried, but a foreshadowing of the departure of those eternal processions martialled at the word of the last Judge, "And these shall go away into everlasting punishment, but the righteous into life eternal."

The internal evidence carries everything, and we ask, What, on the whole, is the thought conveyed for our acceptance, belief, and practical usage and guidance? Over and above the particular words, there is a basis of known ideas which, if it cannot be exactly bodied forth in terms, still remains very clear in substance. Take for example the striking text in Proverbs, "The way of *Life* is *above to the wise*, that he may depart from *Hell* beneath."

This does not mean *what we call Hell*, say some of the critics, but only the grave, *Hades*, the house appointed for all living. Well then, what *does that* mean? It cannot surely mean the *grave merely*, the sepulchre or place of interment for the body; for no *wise* man or fool ever has avoided, or ever can avoid that, or depart from it, though in him were concentrated the science, philosophy, and life of all ages. And it cannot mean *death merely*, for it is appointed unto all men *once* to die, and *after that*, the judgment. And it cannot mean a mere *under-world* of departed spirits all alike in the same quality and condition; for it is contrasted with an *above-world* of the *wise*, by taking the way to which in this earthly existence, while the way of life is open, he departs from Hell *beneath*. The thought of the contrast is evidently eternal, and founded on character.

No matter then for the imperfection of human language, nor the ignorance or superstition of those who first used it, and made moulds of thought out of it. There remains, unescapable, inevitable, the great overwhelming thought or conviction of *a world of character beyond the grave;* and that character as eternal as the choices that began it, and the God that governs and hath appointed its retributions. It is *above*,—the way of life; *beneath*, the way of death; but each and both the way of our existence, conceived of as fixed and certain, *beyond the grave,* beyond the *death of the body.* So much, certainly, is included in the use of the word *Hell*, in this and a number of similar passages, so translated from the Old Testament into English.

It is plain that in these passages there was conveyed the assurance of a future state and place of retribution to the wicked, and reward and happiness to the righteous. Every man to whom these passages were addressed, every man who heard or read these words, knew that they described an indisputable reality and belief; they were elements of a commanding common consciousness, to which our Saviour Himself appealed, when He warned men against the destruction of soul and body in hell, and drew His teachings in regard to that hell—its nature, extent, and eternity—from the Old Testament Scriptures. The English reader has only to take Young's Analytical Concordance of the Hebrew, Greek, and English terms for Hell, and compare the passages, and the argument is irresistible.

Take them into the New Testament, and we find them dramatized by Christ with such vivid intensity in His own parables and interpretations, that the dead coming back into life could not have spoken more convincingly. It is impossible that our Lord's reasoning from such passages can rest on any other grounds than those of a Verbal Inspiration; the truths conveyed being of infinite importance, and therefore necessarily infallible, both in phraseology and meaning.

VI.

ABSOLUTE CERTAINTY OF GOD'S WORD, IN ORDER TO THE LIFE OF MAN'S SOUL, THROUGH FAITH IN CHRIST—TRUTHS FOR ETERNITY MAY BE AS WELL KNOWN BY INFERENCE, AS BY MIRACLE—CHRIST'S OWN METHOD OF REASONING AND BUILDING.

It is *absolutely certain*, if anything in this world can be, that God has given us the means of ascertaining all the truths necessary for our immortal well being, and of detecting and exposing the falsehoods that put us *in danger of eternal evil*. And yet, absolute certainty can, no more than goodness, exist anywhere out of God, or without Him in it, as its essence. It is with a *verily, verily*, that Jesus said to the Jews, "The Son can do nothing of Himself, but what He seeth the Father do, for what things soever He doeth, those also doeth the Son likewise; for the Father loveth the Son, and showeth Him all things that He Himself doeth." And to this end, "that all should honor the Son even as they honor the Father"; receiving His words and the words of His Apostles, as the Father's words. "The words that I speak unto you, they are Spirit and they are

Life. The word that ye hear is *not Mine* but *the Father's* which sent Me." "I have given unto them *the words which Thou gavest Me.* I have given them Thy Word. Sanctify them through Thy truth; Thy Word is truth. Them also who shall believe on Me *through their word*, that they all may be one, as Thou, Father, art in Me, and I in Thee, that they also may be one in us, *that the world may believe that* THOU *hast sent* ME."

If there be not here the truth and necessity declared of an infallible verbal inspiration *in all things necessary to the knowledge of God in Christ*, where can the assertion or the idea of it ever be found? But still it all hangs by the great prophetic covenant in Moses and Isaiah: "A Prophet shall the Lord your God raise you up; and I will put My words in His mouth, and whosoever will not hearken unto MY WORDS which HE SHALL SPEAK IN MY NAME, I will require it of him." "My Spirit and My Word," are pronounced inseparable. They certainly are as much so as the spirit and the words of Socrates and Plato, or the soul and body of the Lord Jesus Himself.

There are things as well known, as absolutely certain by inference, as they ever could be by a present miracle. So Christ reasoned. There are truths as absolutely known to be true, by correspondence between the external voucher and the inward experience, as if they were a minie-ball, shot through your heart, and taking you in a moment into the world of spirits. It is a thing to be wondered at; the majesty, profoundness, and far-reaching and minute application of the certainties, by divine inference from God's Being, driven down into the human mind, through these sentences of the words of Christ; recorded on purpose that the believers in God may build an Eternal City of Truth upon them.

After they are thus given, each individual soul must be the builder of his own house of worship out of them; for they are given and settled for the whole world; for the foundations of faith in God, that men may receive salvation from Him through Christ as the gift of eternal life, the salvation from eternal death. The eternal consequences, and a belief in them, become collateral assurances, inferences, and seals, for every mind that possesses the governing idea and conviction of an eternal existence and responsibility to God. On this possession, as the indestructible foundation of His own appeal to the human mind and on this desire of everlasting happiness Jesus Christ built, with infinite persuasion, for a divine eternal reality. These were the spiritual ringbolts in the substance of the soul, as made originally in the image of God, by which to fasten the very constitution of the mind of every believer to the anchor of Hope, "entering into that within the veil, whither the Forerunner is for us entered. Jesus, our High Priest, consecrated for evermore, and ever living to make intercession for us."

And so did Moses, by divine appointment and inspiration before Christ, build and intercede;—Moses, who was also, like Christ, "faithful to Him that appointed him, in all his house, as a servant, for a testimony of those things which were to be spoken after."—Heb. iii. 5.

VII.

THE TEACHING OF THE HEBREWS BY THE SILENCE OF GOD—A DIVIDING FIRMAMENT BETWEEN FALSEHOOD AND DIVINE TRUTH—THE REALITIES OF SPIRITUAL WICKEDNESS IN HIGH PLACES.

It has been undeniably proved by modern research and discovery that the Egyptians possessed the knowledge of immortality and a future state of retribution, and had their own Book of the Dead, with trials and verdicts and judgments in the world to come. Every Hebrew in the time of Moses must have been familiar with the particulars of their *last things*, their ideas of what was to be beyond the grave, as well as the rites of their bestial worship in this life. But all their system was so inextricably corrupted and depraved by the most degraded of all idolatries, mythologies, and superstitions, demoralizing the very moralities of life, and consecrating its immoralities, that the God of the Hebrews did not permit Moses even to refer to the *actual truths* connected with the vast system of the Egyptian priesthood; for this would have been to bind falsehood and truth together as a compound power upon the reason and conscience, even toward God.

God constrained Moses to set His clock of human conduct and belief by the attributes of God as revealed to Adam, Enoch, Noah, Abraham, Isaac, and Jacob, with never a reference to any divine truths learned from the Egyptians. This accounts for the reticence as well as the minuteness and exacting precision of the inspired records. The reticence, to indicate the unsearchable wisdom and holiness of the invisible Jehovah, not to be set forth by graven images or personifications; the minuteness, to expel and forbid the horrid cruelties, abominable practices, and imbruting will-worship of idolatry; and to enthrone instead thereof, for the conscience and heart of the worshipper, God's own appointed system of sacred rites, full of the symbolism of divine meaning, and prophetic of the Saviour to come.

Men have therefore needlessly perplexed themselves

with discussing the possible reasons why, if the truths of immortality and a judgment to come were known to the Egyptians, God did not more definitely appeal to that very knowledge, when He proclaimed the Decalogue by Moses, and prepared His people in the wilderness for the Promised Land. It was because the Egyptian heaven was like Mohammed's, nothing but earth, no heavenly horizon. ⸢The Hebrew heaven was "THE ETERNAL GOD, THY REFUGE, and underneath thee the Everlasting arms." And God, in His new creation of a people by divine truth and the divine Spirit, would make an infinite transparent void and variance between all that the Hebrews knew in and from Egypt and its priests, and all that God had revealed of the history of creation, and the fall of man, and the antediluvians, and Noah and the Patriarchs, for the worship of the true God in spirit and in truth. He made a separating firmament in the midst of the waters, and said, "Let there be lights in the firmament of heaven, to divide the day from the night."

The clouds of falsehood and corrupt example to which they had been accustomed in Egypt were so heavy with sense and sensual imagery and passion, that if shut up to that medium of instruction they could neither have seen God through it, nor have formed to themselves any righteous conceptions of the spiritual and never-ending existence of the soul. And therefore God, for their own good, restricted them in His own Word to the revelation of Himself as the Eternal and infinitely holy Jehovah, the only wise God; and made the disclosure of themselves to themselves, as capable of knowing God only by loving Him, and of living forever only in His blessed likeness.

Immortality was so well known to the Hebrews, coming up from Egypt, that it was an atmosphere of light and consciousness, surrounding alike the evil and the good. But the Egyptian beliefs and habits of a brutal transmigration (souls possessed and carnalized and thus demonized by sense), and their rituals accordingly,—and the corrupting power of sensuality carried into all their speculations concerning Eternity, must be carefully and utterly exterminated from the Hebrew rules of a divine service. The Eternal God was to be revealed in His infinite oneness and holiness; and the nature of sin against God was to be made manifest, and Jehovah was to be brought near to them in His Eternal Love, and in His present holy providences. And therefore all the regulations of life, social, political, economical, in work and worship, in earthly business and duty, were to be totally disentangled from idolatry, in abhorrence of its customs and its teachings; and in obedience to God's statutes, were to be interwoven in God's service, " unto the example and shadow of heavenly things and good things to come," in assured trust for God's eternal Mercy and Grace.

God Himself, and the forgiveness of the soul, and the blessedness of His never-ceasing presence and love ("if Thy presence go not with us, carry us not up hence"), were what He did and would bestow forever; but the things that He gave now, even the promised land, and prosperity in this life, were only *earnests* of the future, things by the way, provisions of a pilgrimage. This was Abraham's grand and glorious theology, "I am they *shield* (in Time), and thine *exceeding great reward* (in Time and Eternity);" and Moses and the Hebrews knew this, as well as the great Patriarch, their ancestor by covenant with God. For godliness had then, as now, the promise of the life that now is, *as of that which is to come;* and both together.

From the eternities of mud and materialism God raised believers in Him up to a life of practical obedience, under the clear, austere firmament of a law and precepts requiring from them a character of holiness as God is holy, and *because* He is holy, that they might be fitted to live FOREVER with Him. The promised land was but the frame of an invisible future, the telescope of faith for bringing near that "*better country*," alone suited to their immortal nature, brought into communion with God; and by reason of their belief in that, and their living for it at God's Word, *as* strangers and pilgrims on the earth, "God was not ashamed to be called their God, for He had prepared for them a city."—Heb. xi. 13, 16. And so Jehovah disciplined them with precepts and observances, connected with the Decalogue of Love to God and man, and protected them as with a coat of mailed fire from the monstrous lies of the Egyptian mythologies.

He had set them apart, as in a standing-stool of parental care, with the symbolism of Jacob's dream-ladder before them, let down from heaven, trodden by ascending and descending angels. He delivered them from the tyranny of Pharaoh, and carried them across the Red Sea, and through the deadly desert, by miracles of His own divine power, holiness, and love, and taught them that man doth not live by bread alone, but by every word that proceedeth out of the mouth of God.—See Neh. ix. 13, 14, 20. He instructed them, and the whole world through and after them, that man hath a higher life and holier needs of immortality, than those of the body, for which life God's grace, forgiving sin, must fit him.

The very reserve of a divine revelation, leaving them alone with God, with the heart and conscience directed towards Him only, because He alone was Jehovah, their God, and no God or Saviour besides Him, and because their true life consisted in loving Him and keeping His commandments out of gratitude and love, was a spiritual discipline of infinite solemnity and power. The silence of God, and the thought, *Thou God seest me*, taught them more concerning the realities of Eternity and Immortality, and did more to wean them from Egyptian superstitions and fables, and to educate their souls for heaven, than if there had been given a schedule of contrasted eternal felicities and tortures more definite than those of Pagan, Mohammedan, or even baptized Papal falsehoods.

In the books of Judges, Samuel, Kings, Chronicles, Prophets, there is demonstrated a closeness and fury of the life-and-death grapple between the principalities and powers of heaven and hell, a startling nearness and reality in the shock and flame of battle-life, unknown in our day, in the proximity and mixture, the confusion and *melée* of Pagans and Christians, idolaters and worshippers of God. Take Elijah's life of deadly conflict with Ahab, Jezebel, and Baal for illustration. But the literature of Devil-despotisms before the flood (τὰς μεθοδείας τοῦ διαβόλου, as Paul calls them, Eph. vi. 11), has not come down to us, whatever of that nature there may have been then.

Nor is there any indication in the Hebrew beliefs or literature sanctioning any compromise or indifference between truth and error, or any nullifying of the forever widening gulfs and consequences between holiness and sin. It is manifest that there had ever been a party of materialists, whose pleasures, aspirations, and beliefs were restricted to this world; but that, in the literature of better instructed spirits there was always the known reality of entirely another life, and that life a revelation from Jehovah, the written Word of God, directing all souls to Himself in faith and prayer, and to a reliance on His merciful and forgiving love forever.

VIII.

DEMONSTRATIONS FROM THE FIFTH CHAPTER OF JOHN'S GOSPEL—PRESENCE OF THE SPIRIT WITH THE WORD—OBJECT AND EVIDENCE OF MIRACLES —PERSONAL EXPERIMENTS AND PROOFS REQUISITE FOR ETERNAL LIFE.

The fifth chapter of John's Gospel is a demonstration (1) of the unity and divine inspiration of the Scriptures both of the Old and New Testaments, and (2) of the unity of God in Christ and Christ in God, as the same in person, attributes, authority and power. And yet how remarkable that the whole train of argument and instruction grows out of the healing of the impotent man at Bethesda, *followed by the persecuting fury of the Jews against Christ*, because He had wrought that miracle of divine mercy on the Sabbath day; and had justified His work by such an assertion of His oneness in power and being with the Father, as "*made Himself equal with God.*" Then followed Christ's affirmation of its being really God's will "that all men should honor the Son even as they honor the Father," and His offer of the gift of eternal life to every believer in His own Word. Here are some of the great connecting links of this vast and mighty argument. "My Father worketh hitherto, and I work. He that heareth My Word, and believeth on Him that sent Me, hath everlasting life. But I receive not testimony from man. The Father Himself which hath sent Me hath borne witness of me. But these things I say, that ye might be saved. Search the Scriptures, for in them ye think ye have eternal life. And *they are they that testify of Me.* And ye will not come to Me, that ye might have life."

The axioms of thought and belief so announced are themselves a demonstration from Christ, comprehending these conclusions, namely, 1. No testimony admitted or possible from man. 2. Then God Himself must give it. 3. God hath given it. 4. The Scriptures are God testifying. 5. Their testimony is concerning Christ. 6. It is for eternal life. 7. Life only in Christ. 8. For this, men are to search the Scriptures, for they alone testify of Him. And, 9, All men who hear Christ know what the Scriptures are.

These Scriptures, being the testimony of God, were not a vague or doubtful quantity, when Christ was speaking on earth, but absolute, and absolutely known, and referred to as containing the indisputable postulates of all right reasoning in regard to God, Christ, eternity, and the destiny and duty of the soul. These Scriptures, known then as the Word of God, are Christ's credentials now of divine testimony and authority solely from God. In them God's Word, infallible, neither asks nor receives man's sanction or support, any more than God the Creator can ask or receive authentication as God from man the creature.

In that Word itself which is demonstrated by Christ, we are informed that the Holy Spirit of God who gave it is attendant on the Word, and is a divine witness and interpreter in the heart of the believer. Comparing Isaiah lv. 8–11, and lix. 21, we have the infallibility of the Word of God, along with the ever accompanying presence and witness of the Spirit of God; a presence and witness which could never be given to an erroneous or fallible utterance or record. "As for Me, this is My covenant with them, saith the Lord. My Spirit that is upon thee, and My Word which I have put in thy mouth, shall not depart out of thy mouth, nor out the mouth of thy seed, nor of thy seed's seed, saith the Lord, from henceforth and forever."

This presence of the Spirit with the word, is in like manner assured by the Lord Jesus to every believer in Him, as constituting a sure, sufficient and perpetual guide, no matter whether there be any other external testimony or not. The evidence of the Word is in itself, by the Holy Spirit that inspired it; known as God's light, not by man's testimony, but by its own, which is God's. God speaks and it is done. The volume of the Book, from Genesis to the Apocalypse, is for all time, to all souls, an omnipresent, omniscient voice and spirit, for ever.

Miracles are as the ringing of God's bell, to call men to hear God's voice; as the burning bush made Moses turn aside to see that great sight; and when men begin to attend and hear, then the inward witness of the Spirit goes with the outward utterance, which itself becomes an inward breathing of the way, the truth, the life, carrying the same conviction of spiritual verity, as the consciousness of voluntary motion does of physical existence and reality.

God's Word being thus inbreathed, and demonstrated by a new spiritual creation and life of the soul, the possession and consciousness of its power are dependent on individual faith and experience, by the Holy Spirit; and its knowledge possesses this superiority, above all pretences and *antitheses* of science, falsely so called, that it is placed so entirely at the command and disposal of every believer, that the wayfaring man though a fool need not err in regard to it, nor ever be without its saving light.

All the miracles are wrought for us as truly as for those who first beheld them; and the Word of God is spoken to us; just as Christ said to the Jews, Moses wrote *unto you;* and the Sadducees said, Moses *wrote unto us;* and Christ said, Have ye not read that which was *spoken unto you by God,* saying, etc. (Matt. xxii. 31). Thus the Word is a present utterance of God to all mankind in all generations, as personal and direct *as if now first spoken;* and so the miracles are present miracles. And we ourselves are co-workers with God of them, as well as believers in them, the greatest of them being that of a personal regeneration. When we have read enough in the Scriptures to begin to understand their object and plan, then we perceive that the miracles recorded necessarily grow out of the revelation itself, in its life and nature, and are natural to it. Supernatural in themselves, they are natural to God's Word, which could never, with its provision and gift of life eternal, and its assurance of forgiveness, be established, be made credible, without them. The spiritual purpose of the book requires and justifies them, and its success demonstrates them. Forgiveness of sin is its object, and to get men to believe and accept forgiveness, its mightiest work, the greatest of all miracles; and common miracles, works of supernatural power, vouchers of omnipotence, are essential to prove that God offers forgiveness, and is capable of it, to the greatest of sinners.

But here we have to remember that the only possible self-satisfying test and proof of the Word of God in each man's case is personal. When we have fulfilled the commands given as to its use, then we shall KNOW. For God's own directions, with which His Word is committed to our trust, for ourselves and others, are not to be mistaken—being in every man's power. They are Christ's instructions, as the all-wise and merciful Physician of the soul, and are plainer and more precious than ever were given to accompany any medicine of sovereign and life-restoring energy. God provides, commands, and works the miracle; we demonstrate it. Herein is the combination human and divine, as in the text, "Work out your own salvation, for it is God that worketh in you."

The demonstration of its efficacy consists inevitably, first, in its being used; second, according to the directions. For it is confessedly a *spiritual* medicine, for the healing and forgiveness of the soul; good for *nothing else*, proved by *nothing less*, but ordered and administered by the Divine Physician, who would neither prepare nor send it without His own teachings how to take it, nor could it be efficacious without being taken according to those instructions.

Suppose your physician prescribes a medicine to be taken by the tablespoonful every three hours. The demonstration of its efficacy is in taking it in that way. If it were applied to the temples, instead of being swallowed, it would fail. Suppose the accompanying direction to be that the patient, every time he took it, should name over it the name of the physician, and ask him to accompany it with a blessing by the spell of his power. That, you will say, would be superstition. But suppose the use of the Bible to be, as directed by its Author, with inward prayer to God for the presence and blessing of His Spirit, He having given His Word with that essential qualification. That would not be superstition, but a perfectly reasonable and infinitely valuable and blessed condition and proof, because it brings the inquiring soul, that is seeking for healing and forgiveness, directly to God, in communion with God's own love, God's own Spirit. But, superstition or not, reasonable or not, in a man's judgment, if that were the direction, no man could be supposed to know the truth without minding that rule; or to prove the value of the medicine without seeking God in it. But, minding that rule, taking the medicine with prayer, he needs no other evidence. The divine power goes with the divine word. And so, the science of divine truth is the most perfectly experimental of all sciences, for every man is independent of every other man, and of all power but God's, and comes instantly and directly to the Author and Master of all science and life.

It is the experiment of a medicine for *eternal life*. Plainly, the word ETERNAL conveys the whole worth, importance, and necessity of the medicine, and of the *experiment* with it. Either is worthless, except with the other. The living knowledge and regenerating power of the Word, as life eternal, are to be wrought in the soul, only by personally knowing Christ, and trusting and loving Him *as He is*, and obeying His Word *as God's Word*.

Without this, if any one should ask you, Can you tell me whether this proclaimed specific is genuine, whether it is good for mine or any disease; what could you say, but that you know nothing about it? But if you yourself had taken it, and found it an elixir of life, if it had restored you to health, if you had found the nature of it, and the manner of its power, in your own case by experiment, then could you answer, with the conviction of your own renewed existence, that a divine power was in it, and a divine blessing upon it. This was David's certainty. "Restore unto me the joy of Thy salvation; then will I teach transgressors Thy ways, and sinners shall be converted unto Thee."

Now then, the evidence of the Word of God, incomplete and worthless without Christ, is infinitely perfect and fulfilled eternally in Him; and satisfactory in the personal experiment of the soul coming to Him, even if only with, "Lord, I believe, help Thou mine unbelief." The central proof-light is Christ in the gospels. The light and the life flow from Him as the fountain; and from Him also radiates all the light, which, falling upon other beings or things, both *reveals them* and constitutes *in them* a species of demonstration in regard to *Himself;* an effulgence of testimony coming from Him originally, and reflected back to Him, pointing to its source. Not more certainly does the tracing of a stream conduct you to its fountain, its spring, than the pursuit of real evidence in regard to God's Word brings you always to Christ. The old painters were wont, in their representations of the Holy Family to make all the light in the painting issue from the Babe, Christ Jesus; by the light flowing from His form all things else were seen, and all persons were beheld gazing towards Him, and doing Him homage. All the potentates, all the wise men, all the nations of the world assembled together, could give no testimony as to this Babe being the incarnate God and Saviour of mankind, nor how this mystery came to be revealed. No man ever saw or knew it, any more than any man could have beheld or imagined God's creation of the universe. And such is the reality of the Word of God.

IX.

CONSEQUENT INFALLIBILITY AND INDEPENDENCE OF THE WORD ABOVE ALL HUMAN TESTIMONY—ILLUSTRATION FROM THE WATCH.

Man can no more be a witness that God spake this word, that this word is God's Word, than he can that God created the sun, or that this sun is God's sun. And what one man cannot do, ten thousand men cannot, in whatever form, or with whatever assumption of authority they might be combined together. No church, nor all the churches on earth, can give God's Word its authority, or prove its infallibility; but the Word itself judges the Church, tries the Church, proves the Church; just as the testimony of man cannot make the sun shine, nor give authority to the light; but the sun itself discloses men, and they see one another only by that light, and could read one another's evidence only by that light.

The men that lived three thousand years ago might tell us that then the sun was shining, and could describe how the world looked in its light; but such testimony is no evidence to us that God made the sun, no ground of our belief that God made the sun. We know *that*, by the sun itself, which is a greater testimony of and for God, than any word of man, or of the whole race of men can be.

And just so, we know from Jesus Christ, that it is God's own Word, and not from any word or witnessing of man. If all recorded history, all books of men, all knowledge of our race from human testimony apart from the Scriptures were annihilated, that would not diminish the truth and power of those Scriptures, testified by Christ to be God's Scriptures; so that, if God's Word were as completely separated from all human testimony as the sun itself is separated from our globe, we knowing it only by its shining, that would make no difference as to its being God's Word, nor as to the power of its light, the clearness of its shining, and our knowledge of its being from God.

This then is the sole, sovereign, independent fountain of Living Truth, a perpetual heritage of life, that, " by every word that proceedeth out of the mouth of God, man may live." Here it is, and God's covenant of His Spirit forever co-present with it. It must be definite and stable, to be *matter of such a covenant*, and it must be *infallible*, to be a covenant *forever*. It was never recorded or discovered elsewhere on the earth, nor ever committed in trust, nor gathered in by traditions or fragments from any other sources. It was never given to the diviners of Babylon, nor to old Mesopotamian astrologers or astronomers, nor to the soothsayers or fire-worshipping magi of the east, nor to Chinese moralists, or Indian mystics, or self-torturing or self-indulgent idolaters of Baal or Ashtaroth in any age or nation in the world. The inspiration of the Almighty is only here, and here only for the redemption of guilty and lost man, only for the revelation of a SAVIOUR.

This is the Divine gift and inspired description of that anchorage for the soul, "which is sure and steadfast, and entering into that within the veil." Let us endeavor to illustrate this blessed and life-giving independence of THE WORD ALONE, our Timepiece for Eternity, by an argument from the watch, which every man carries with him, for his knowledge of the time of day.

THE WATCH IS; no matter where it came from.—If you found a watch by the way-side, or under the crag of a mountain, or in a cave by the sea-shore, or in an excavated subterranean sepulchre, and it were the first watch ever known, or of which there was ever any record in the world that had come to your knowledge, and if, after much study by many minds upon it, you had found out its use and meaning; would you have any doubt that it was made for that use, or that one mind designed it? And if you found the name of the maker inscribed upon it, should you have any doubt that he made it? Would you need any vouchers, any witnesses, except the watch itself? Would the absolute vacuum of testimony elsewhere in regard to the watch prevent you from believing that it was a watch, that it was made to keep time, and that it was made by the person declared to be its artificer?

On examination, you would find that it was not all made at once, that it was made in parts, and put together, and that some wheels were made to strike into other wheels, and set them a-going. You would find, moreover, a mainspring, giving motion to the whole. You would find balances, levers, compensations, and a most curious, involved, and accurately calculated adjustment of mechanical powers. You would find prophetic assurances and designs in one part of the watch fulfilled in another part. You would find that it could be taken asunder, and each part laid by itself. And you would find some parts made out of materials which you had reason to believe were discovered and brought into use much earlier than the materials employed in other parts; and you would find some parts that seemed older in their construction than other parts. But would any of these facts prevent you from believing that all the watch came from one maker, from one design, comprehending and giving unity to all?

Furthermore, you would find portions of the watch that might appear not absolutely essential to it, and some things that might be taken away from it, without preventing it from going, or hindering its practical use; just as some persons imagine that certain chapters in the first or second book of Chronicles, or both, or perhaps the whole book of Canticles, or some catalogues of names, might be dropped out from the Bible, without any apparent injury, and without diminishing its usefulness. And you would also find portions of the watch, of which, at first, you would not be able to discover the use,—portions indeed that you would be ready to set down as mistakes, or ignorances of some one who did not know his business. In the regulator you might discover proofs of imperfection or intimations that the watch was to be confided to the care of persons who must daily wind it up, and guard against its gaining or losing time.

But would *this* discovery, or rather this want of a perfect intelligence on your part, lead you to the conclusion that those portions were not made by the maker of the watch? You would find some

God's Timepiece for Man's Eternity. 65

parts without the name of the maker on them, or any indication in themselves that they came from his hand; just as you may find chapters in the Bible without any such indication, the whole Book of Esther without mention of the name of God; but would that ever suggest the imagination that He did *not* make them, or did not mean them, or that some one else added them without His intention? Is there a single wheel in the works, or pin in the machinery not there by plan and purpose of the maker? He may not indeed have made the watch-case with his own hands, but it was certainly made for his work, and so made under his direction, by his will, as to be a fit and proper covering and protection for the watch, though not an essential part of it.

Finally, there might be parts of the watch, in regard to which you might have, or might find, some testimony elsewhere, in some part of history, in some art or science, in the historical record of some age, by a writer regarded as a competent witness; some testimony showing that those parts had existed, though affording no reference to the whole watch, and giving no indication, from such writer, of his knowing that there *was* a watch. Thus there may be quotations in very ancient Pagan writers from particular books in the Old or New Testament, without any reference to the whole volume of Divine Inspiration. Could you take those particular parts of the watch aside, and feel that you had any better evidence in regard to them, as being the work of the maker of the watch, than in regard to the whole watch?

Would you for a moment imagine that the proof of the whole watch being from the maker, the person declared as the maker, depended in the slightest degree upon that human testimony as to the former existence of certain parts of it? Or if all human testimony as to the watch, and every part of it, were blotted out, if no being and no age could be found with any record or vestige whatever in regard to it, would *that* in the slightest degree shake your confidence that the watch was really made, and made by one man, that is, with one master's design and direction, however many hands may have been employed in perfecting its separate parts, and preparing them to be put together in the one designed whole. You would find that the watch keeps time; you would feel perfectly convinced that that was the object of it; you would find the hours and the minutes marked on the dial in it; and you would have no doubt in regard to its purpose, its value, its wondrous ingenuity, its unity of design and construction. You would regard any man as a fool, who should tell you that it sprang forth as a natural product of the evolution of forces, by the cohesion of natural selection.

And though there is not a particle of evidence, except in itself, who the author was, nor the least trace of any external testimony in regard to such a person ever having existed in the world, yet you would have no more doubt as to his being the author, than you would have as to the existence of the watch itself. You would have no reason for doubting, nothing to suggest a doubt, nothing in the watch, nothing out of it. It is a unity of art and skill, design and wisdom, unaccountable and incomprehensible on any other supposition than that of one and the same purpose and authority in all the parts and authorship of its being.

THE ARGUMENT OF CHANCE.—But now suppose that some one should tell you that after all, this wondrous compound product of forces never had an author at all, but that it did really grow of itself by correlation and conversion of energy; that that particular species of time-keeper never had a creator, never was constructed by special authority or action of an intelligent designing mind, but that it was evolved from a preceding construction not so perfect, and that from another preceding machine still less accurate, and that from one quite clumsy and savage in the comparison, and that from a mere elastic spring in the bore of a barrel, or a bent bow struggling to get loose. Thus you would have the great-great-grandfather of watches, and the great-grandfather, and the grandfather, and the father and the son, and then the grandson, and so on, in a regular evolution of force with differentiation by directive agency of natural selection, till you have at length evolved the convenient and perfect little creature that you carry in your vest pocket.

But you are hardly yet convinced. And now suppose your scientific demonstrator could show you an old Dutch clock, or a mediæval clock, found buried in a bed of sandstone far below the altitude or locality where the watch was found, and should assure you that that particular clock was one of the preceding genealogical links through which the parentage of the watch was demonstrated by natural evolution from a microscopically discovered bit of antique protoplasm; so that the landing-place of the clock might occupy a position relative to the preceding and succeeding developments much the same as the marsupials or great-grandfathers of the monkey tribes occupy, between men and the first worm; so that the hypothesis of a special construction either of the watch or the clock, but especially the watch, was a mere miserable assumption, such as no one but a savage, content to gaze at phenomena without tracing their connection, would for a moment entertain. Would you dismiss your belief in a designing mind, that you are sure must have contrived and constructed the watch, on any such authority or testimony as that of such reasoning? Would you not rather dismiss the reasoning itself, as the uncoiling and stagnation or dropping loose of the nerves of a shattered brain, the beginning of a return of the mind into chaos?

But suppose, as in the case of the watch, you had found the rough clock of the Old Testament preceding the finished watch of the New, in an evidently lower stratum of the universe far backward from this present era. Suppose you had found the Old Testament, as a record of God's dealings with primeval man, ending at four hundred years interval from the New Testament and no other known connection between them, save only the manifest belonging of the one to the other, and the playing of the one into the other, so that the last could not possibly be accounted for, or be of any use without the first, and the first would be proved an unmeaning riddle or convicted falsehood without the last. Would not that discovery absolutely demonstrate to you the authorship and creatorship of both volumes, as being from one and the same designing and benevolent intelligence? Would that discovery persuade you that neither of these volumes had any designing special creator, but that both were merely products of the force of evolution in strata of existence and of thought, eocene, miocene, primary, secondary, tertiary, glacial, and post-glacial, succeeding one another by process of natural selection from a practical eternity?

THE ARGUMENT FROM GOD.—Now we apply all this to the existence of the Word of God, and its entire independence, as His Word, of all external testimony. Suppose you should find the whole volume of God's Word, just as we have it, buried in a dry well. Or suppose it should have been found in the heart of Abyssinia, or beneath a crag in the Andes, or under a rock on the summit of Mount Washington, and men should take it forth and study it, and find out the coherence of its parts, its nature and purpose as the law of human duty and salvation, its record of the creation and history of the human race, with the fall of man, and God's sovereign wisdom, will, and merciful pleasure revealed in the government and redemption of the race so fallen; its authoritative address to mankind, its revelation of the nature of morality and religion, its adaptation to the conscience and condition of humanity, its heavenly benevolent design and unity, with its announcement of God as the Author. And suppose that all records of human testimony save this only, and what can be gathered from its study, had perished. Suppose that no volumes or traditions or chain of witnesses or evidences from man remained, in regard either to the construction or authorship of such a volume, or of any part of it. Yet the volume itself carries its own evidence, declares and proves its design, unity, and Author.

That it is the Word of God and not man, itself is enough to prove. There are things in it beyond the compass of the human mind to originate. It is as clear that man could not have made it, as that man could not have made the sun. And if it has God's authority, it stands on God's authority alone; nothing else could support it. No human testimony could make it God's Word, or make it powerful as God's Word, if it were *not* God's Word. A forgery would *detect itself*, even as the genuine reality *demonstrates* itself.

In the process of this examination you find, as in the watch, wheels striking into other wheels, and setting them in motion. You find prophecies and their fulfilment. You find, as in the watch, part answering to part, the Old Testament playing into the New, and the New Testament answering to the Old, especially in the incarnation, character, divine claims and demonstrations of the Lord Jesus, as God manifest in the flesh, Christ revealing God, Christ the Author of eternal life. You find the elements of that life, the nature of true holiness and love, the hour hand and the minute hand, of duty to God and duty to man, in this chronometer of immortal character; and you find the mainspring of all virtue, God, and His love, and the seeking of His approbation and glory.

You find the prescribed duties for man's acceptance with God, and obedience to Him, set not in human authority, by human precept and law, nor taught by the fear of man, but forbidden to be so taught; nothing forced, nor basely motived, nor ostentatious, but sympathizing, disinterested, every thought an offering of grateful love, every hole jewelled, every pivot turning in love and reason, on principle, everlasting, immutable. You find a moral time-keeper and regulator for the conscience, and a guide to everlasting life. You discover the design of this wondrous volume, and you find that on obeying it, it sets you right, but you never were right before, and it shows you the error of your way, and the direction of the only right way. You find its descriptions of yourself, and its predictions as to yourself fulfilled in yourself. The more you study it, the more you discover its wonderful coincidences, its irresistible power of demonstration and conviction, its network of internal evidence, both telescopic and microscopic.

Although it seems a small casket in the letter, yet it diffuses a flood of light. The nature and glory of that light are enough to prove to you that it is from God, and the evidence of the whole human race could not add to its authority. The mere evidence of man, fallible man, would be a doubtful element in that which otherwise is irresistible. Therefore external testimony is admitted only as a gateway, a *propylæum*, an avenue of sphinxes, in order that your faith should not stand in the wisdom of man, but in the power of God, in demonstration of the Spirit and of power within the temple of the Word. Human learning, external research, is good to clear away rubbish, to prevent prejudice, to gather out the stones, to prepare the way of the Lord, to disentangle difficulties. Good sometimes, as Mr. Berridge used to say, to silence scorners, or as a stone to throw at a dog to stop his barking, but the power is within. For it is written, "I will destroy the wisdom of the wise, and bring to nothing the understanding of the prudent." Where is the wise? Where is the scribe? Where the disputer of this world? Hath not God made foolish the wisdom of this world? Because the foolishness of God is wiser than men, and the weakness of God is stronger than men, and in no conceivable way could man testify that the Word of God is God's Word, unless you find God's own authority evident in itself, apart from man's testimony.

And if you find and feel *that* (which is indeed the witness of the Spirit), you can neither mistake nor doubt it; nor do you ask for any endorsement of it, nor indeed will you submit to any such supposition as that it is not in itself all-sufficient and divinely authoritative. No creature shall patronize it, or put his seal upon it. It needs no candle, neither light of the sun, nor of the moon, to shine in it, for the glory of God doth lighten it, and the Lamb is the light thereof. When you are sensible of that presence, all the questions as to canonical or uncanonical, as to whether particular books have been received by the Church, or not received, go for nothing. When the Spirit that inspired the Word inspires your heart to behold and adore its glory, the disputes of outside traditionists as to antiquities, seals, councils, are of little moment.

Just so, in a watch, to determine its merit and its maker you would pay no attention whatever to

God's Timepiece for Man's Eternity. 75

any questions or conflicts as to the time when rubies or diamonds were first discovered, or cogged wheels first invented, or the elastic power of a steel spring first put to use. No matter for all that. There is the watch, a perfect watch, declaring its maker. A party of metaphysical or mechanical wranglers might contend that the watch had no authority or design, because there was no proof of its ever having been made at all, or of certain parts of it ever having been in existence as mechanical applications. But that is nothing to you; there is the watch, and it could not have grown there, as an apple or an orange grows. And just so, a party of theological or anti-theological controversialists may tell you that the Bible has no authority, unless you can find a church that can give you some account of its origin, or a set of literary or scientific witnesses that can give you some history of such or such a book, or of all the books.

But there is the volume, God's own Word, and you see how its parts are inwrought together, how the whole coheres, how it keeps time, how it is entirely superior to human evidence, how it would not work one whit better, if it had the literary and historical evidence of all ages. And further, you see how, if its wheels did not play with infinite accuracy, if any wheel or tooth ran against the cogs of any other, it would stop, and prove itself useless and powerless, even though all the writers, witnesses, and corporations of all time conspired with unbroken testimony to establish its divinity.

We see at once how impossible to demonstrate its divineness, if God Himself did not establish it, if the volume itself did not rightly reveal God, and establish its own authenticity as from Him. And if God Himself has really stamped it as His Word, all the vouchers of all humanity are needless. As the Timepiece of humankind for eternity, it can go alone; it does go alone; it does not go any better for the testimony of all Christendom. All Christendom must go by it, or Christendom is not Christianity. It keeps no better time for the certificates of all generations, whether of Christendom or heathendom. It judges mankind, not mankind it. It is the ultimate everlasting authority, the court of last appeals.

X.

CHRIST'S TESTIMONY COVERS ALL THE SCRIPTURES—
MAN'S PERSONAL EXPERIMENT IN PRAYER—CONSE-
QUENCES OF PROTESTING GOD'S DRAFTS.

The testimony concerning Christ in the Scriptures extended over the whole range of those Scriptures, from Genesis to Malachi. Its infallibility was grounded in the fact that all those Scriptures were the Word of God. They could not be the Word of God merely in those passages which Christ selected for exposition, and the testimony of man, and fallible, in the whole course of providential and historical narrative, any more than the sun, moon, and stars could be the work of God in their primal elements, their light and life-giving energy, but the work of man in their orbits and periodic motions.

If you believe that God made the light, He made all things, He made the correspondences of all things with the light. If you believe that the utterances of the Old Testament concerning Christ were the truth of God, all the correspondences and roots of that truth were of God likewise.

Carry this Divine Word to the Sandwich or South Sea Islands and pour its light upon the savages there.

Do they know or care anything about canonicals, authenticities, churches, witnesses? Not one word of all this shall be mentioned, but the Word of God shall stand separate and apart from every human record and endorsement, and they shall feel it and know it to be God's Word when simply preached by God's messengers with His Spirit. The Divine Watch goes as well, when they use it, without a solitary voucher as to its manufacture, as if it had the applauding roar of all generations. It is God's Word, and it needs no witness whatever *from* man, save God's own witness by His own Spirit, *in* man. It would have just as much divinity and power now, though all the stream of history were cut off from it, as it ever had, or could have, with all the libraries, councils, and conclaves of the whole world attached to it. If it were reduced to the solitary isolated condition we have imagined, and were discovered without a hint in regard to it anywhere else in the world, either of tradition or of history, it would go forth conquering and to conquer.

It no more needs man's testimony, than a watch needs a chain of seals dangling to it in order that you may believe that it is a watch, or know that it keeps time. God's light in His Word is as independent of man's authority, as the sunbeams themselves are independent of the certificates of the Stock

Exchange. Poor, puny, miserable witlings (if that be your reliance), with your winking tapers of Church authority held up to prove God's Word, to shine before it, like farthing rush-lights in the noonday! And yet, the papists presume to tell us that the testimony of *their Church* is the only thing that can sanction God's Word, or prove it truly divine. We might as well take the testimony of Pilate as the only proof and sanction of the veracity of Christ. And yet, not only the papists, but the supporters of a hierarchical establishment under other forms will tell men that we cannot support and defend the Bible, unless we take it on their authority, and their Church polity, dominion, and government along with it.

Such are the foundations of our faith, impregnable, unchangeable, eternal. This being the case, one cannot but marvel at the facility with which skeptical minds and books can produce a sensation almost as wide as Christendom by the reconstruction of infidelities and errors ten times exploded, but again strutting on the stage, and challenging fight as Goliaths, in such shapes as the books of Strauss and Kuenen, Renan and Colenso, or of men who, denying a divine inspiration, demand that you come down to their plane, and contend on their premises.

Others, scoffing at prayer, and dogmatizing without spiritual experiments, demand a demonstration to every man's senses, which would leave no room for faith, trust, submission to the divine will and wisdom. The natural man receiveth not the things of the Spirit of God, neither can he know them, because they are *spiritually discerned*, and he does not apply his spiritual faculties in the methods suited to them and required by them, but only the methods and the powers of sense. It is just as if a man should undertake to see the heavens and study astronomy with a tube of sheet iron instead of a telescope. Our mere senses, and men's scientific judgments according to sense, are as inadequate for the higher truths of the soul, and of the world for which it is destined, as the brass and iron, the pullies and screws of Lord Rosse's great telescope would be for the discovery of the stars, without the converging lenses and the reasoning mind. The mere natural man is no better than a cunningly devised brass tube, with Babbage's calculating machine attached to it, and subservient to its machinery. The mere natural man, rejecting the spiritual, puts himself out of court, disqualifies himself as a witness. He cannot even make a single spiritual experiment, any more than a man despising and rejecting the telescope could see the star Sirius at noonday with a piece of smoked glass.

God's covenant and method in and with the telescope of His Word is of PERSONAL PRAYER; and without faith, exercised in prayer, it is impossible to please Him; for he that cometh to God must believe that He is, and is a *rewarder* of them that *diligently seek Him*.

We must all conduct our own experiments, depending both for our facts and our methods, upon God. If we intend to acknowledge and believe only by experiments with acids and sub-acids, retorts and crucibles, accompanied with the lectures of scientific chemists, we can see nothing. We are shut up to personal prayer, at the same time comparing spiritual things with spiritual. That is science in theology, true science everywhere; and science without that is science falsely so called, intruding into that which it hath not seen, and vainly puffed up by a fleshly mind, whose dogmas are more dogmatic and unreasonable than any theologian's.

The Word of God is put into our hands as a note of promise, on the back of which we are to put our own name, and carry it to the bank, that we may receive the money. The only absolute certainty to us, the complete evidence that the note is genuine, is our own presenting it. It is drawn for us by the Lord Jesus Christ, the Word Incarnate, and it runs, " Whatsoever ye shall ask the Father in My name." If we carry it to God, this is the process of faith, and the condition of salvation. We must ourselves present this draft in prayer.

Now then, if we refuse to believe beforehand in the genuineness of such a draft, if we deny that it is from God, and so refuse to present it, we can neither receive its benefit, nor have any personal evidence or belief in regard to it. If we deny the possibility of such a note, and the existence of such a bank, and if we can make believe ourselves, or make others believe, that the whole thing is an imposition, and the note of hand of no more value than any other piece of paper, we cut off all that we thus persuade, from the possibility of ever receiving the boon. If we succeed in making men believe that this is not the Word of God, and that this merciful Being, who offers to us eternal life in and by that Word is not a Divine Saviour, we thus exclude the whole race, so far as this unbelief extends, from the possibility of salvation.

But we have not done with this protested draft, when we thus dismiss it as worthless with our own warning against it. The most profound and careful scientific tests and experiments will avail us nothing, by which we have attempted to justify our unbelief, and on which we have thrown ourselves for defence in our rejection of *Justification by Faith*, despising as unreasonable and unscientific that cardinal revealed rule and method of the soul's business with God for eternity. See the extraordinary illustrations of such scorn in the volume of Prof. Huxley's "Lay Sermons."* But he that rejects and protests this Word, as *not a Divine Authority*, will have to encounter that protest itself again, as certainly as Christ Himself is Divine. God's note of hand, with Christ's name at the bottom of it, but the name of the unbeliever across it, protesting it as a falsehood, is to be examined in the final settlement of the soul's account with God. Every man will be judged by that Word and its acceptance, or that Word and its rejection. The dishonored draft of God will be all that is needed to convict the criminal. "He that rejecteth me, and receiveth not my words, hath one that judgeth him. THE WORD THAT I HAVE SPOKEN, THE SAME SHALL JUDGE HIM IN THE LAST DAY."

* Example, page 18: "The man of *Science* has learned to *believe in justification*, not by faith, but by *verification*," etc. But how shall the hundreds of millions, *not of science*, but of *ignorance*, believe? Whose experiments shall *they* accept as authority? Or whose *asserted verifications* can *they* trust, to guide them safely into Eternity, concerning which, no scientist has ever yet made an experiment?

XI.

THOUGHTS OF NAPOLEON CONCERNING CHRIST—THE SOUL AND ETERNITY, CHRIST'S OWN KINGDOM—TIME DISREGARDED, ETERNITY GOVERNING ALL—FORGIVENESS AND THE POWER OF MIRACLES IN CHRIST THE DEMONSTRATION OF A GOD.

One of the most remarkable judgments of the human mind anywhere recorded in history is that of the Emperor Napoleon concerning the character and kingdom of Christ, as God manifest in the flesh. It seems to have been the result, at St. Helena, of a profound discernment and conviction of the spirituality of that kingdom, and of the work of Christ its Lord, in man's immortality and redemption; the eternity of man dwarfing every other consideration into nothingness. Thence arose, in conversation with General Bertrand, a demonstration of the Word of God and of the Deity of Christ, rarely if ever expressed in more imperative form, even by Christian theologians.*

* Compare the celebrated paragraphs of Rousseau concerning the life and death of Jesus and of Socrates. Both these instances, of Napoleon and the French philosopher, show most impressively how near the human mind can come to a full perception and acknowledgment of divine truths, in regard to which there is no evidence that the beholder of them ever received and used them as the means of a personal possession of Eternal Life.

"Truth," said Napoleon, "should embrace the universe. Such is Christianity, the *only religion* which is *purely spiritual.* I know men, and I tell you that Jesus Christ is not a man. Christ proved that He was the SON OF THE ETERNAL, BY HIS DISREGARD OF TIME. ALL HIS DOCTRINES SIGNIFY ONE AND THE SAME THING, ETERNITY. He had but one single end, THE HOLINESS OF THE SOUL. He came to reveal the MYSTERIES OF HEAVEN, AND THE LAWS OF THE SPIRIT. He *commands* that we *believe them*, giving no other reason than the declaration, I AM GOD! There is between Christianity and all other religions whatsoever, THE DISTANCE OF INFINITY. What an abyss between my deep misery, and the ETERNAL REIGN of Christ, which is proclaimed, loved, adored!"

"For the things seen are *temporal*, the things unseen are ETERNAL." This axiom accounts for all. The mind of Napoleon, the discipline of whose life was battles, and his habit the concentration of energy, foresight, means and opportunities, for mere transitory earthly empires, was arrested by this divine Nihilism of the temporal, and Omnipresence of the Eternal, as an overwhelming demonstration of God manifest in Christ, the God of the Scriptures, the Redeemer of the soul, the Lord of the kingdom of Eternal Love.

The Son of the Eternal, and the new Creator in His own image, of immortal beings, fallen, ever falling, and needing forgiveness and eternal life; a forgiveness made possible only through His sufferings and death; Time disregarded, Eternity governing all; therefore, Christ, Divine and Human, the Way, the Truth, the Life, the Author and Finisher of Faith.

For, indeed, the whole intent, interest, and use of the Old and New Testament,—the purpose and work of God in the Covenant of mercy with man just fallen, and of "God manifest in the flesh," fulfilling that covenant, depend on the revealed immortality of man. God's oath by Himself in the Old Testament, "I live forever, and change not,"—and Christ's in the New, "BECAUSE I LIVE, ye shall live also," hold by this co-eternal duration of man with God. And the disclosure of it in the grand Messianic Psalms, "In the volume of the Book written of Me," applied with such fulness and glory of consolation in the Epistle to the Hebrews, constitutes an illuminating demonstration of infinite power. "Thy years are throughout all generations. The earth and the heavens are the work of Thy hands. They shall perish, but Thou remainest. As a garment they shall wax old and be changed; but Thou art the same, and Thy years shall not fail. AND THE CHILDREN OF THY SERVANTS SHALL CONTINUE, AND THEIR SEED SHALL BE ESTABLISHED BEFORE THEE. Thy remembrance is to all generations. And therefore, THIS SHALL BE WRITTEN *for the generations to come,* and the people which shall be created shall praise the Lord."

Therefore, these three things, (1) life eternal; (2) the object, the work, and the worth of life, to glorify God, and enjoy Him forever; and (3) the means provided for accomplishing this, viz., the promises of God in Christ, the inspired Scriptures for all generations; these three things are paramount and manifest everywhere; and the providential government of God is demonstrated through the whole history, carrying out these objects. So that the whole book of which these things constitute the staple is as manifestly the work of God as the heavens that declare His glory. It could no more have been inspired or created by man, than the solar system, or the starry universe.

It would have been equally impossible for the human mind to invent the *predictions* of such a Being, as the Christ of the Old Testament, or the manner of His *incarnation,* or the qualities by which He could be *demonstrated* as the Saviour of mankind from their sins. A hyena among animals might more easily invent the bass or treble to accompany the tenor of one of Handel's Melodies. Or, given the predictions of the existence of a new planet, to create it in the required form, and set it in the required sphere, without interference with any other orb in the universe.

The solution of the Old Testament Scriptures was *wholly* in Christ's divine and human nature. Both were foretold in the Old Testament, both are demonstrated in the New. At the same time that nature was such, that none but the most divinely disinterested souls on earth, by the Spirit of God, at the coming of Christ, could discern it, and none but such would desire it. It would at once destroy the Jewish imagination of a kingdom of this world, and the Gentile imagination of any possible salvation through the pretended revelations of the heathen mythology. The impossible *beginning* of such imposture, in *prophecies* of the coming of such a Saviour, and much more in their *realization*, is manifest. The moral qualities requisite are impossible, co-existing with the duplicity of such a cheat. It would require a height of spirituality, and a marvellous discernment of the human heart, and of true piety, and a jealousy for the divine glory, impossible to be counterfeited for a good purpose, impossible for a bad. There was no motive, nothing to be gained, by the invention of the idea, or construction of the reality; no such perception of the universal corruption of doctrine and morals, as would endure such effort against that corruption; no such sad, indignant sorrow or despair for the departure of the heart from God; no such severity of hatred against popular and prevailing sins, no such imagination of a heaven whose blessedness demanded and consisted in the utmost purity of the soul, excluding forever from God's presence the sensual and proud, the ambitious and warlike, the worshippers of idols or of saints.

XII.

POWER OF MIRACLES AND FORGIVENESS THE UNANSWERABLE ARGUMENT OF A SUPREME DEITY—GOD THE ONLY SAVIOUR—THE DEMONSTRATION OF CHRIST PROGRESSIVE, IN THE MYSTERY OF HUMAN AND DIVINE.

The argument resulting from the prerogatives of forgiveness and miraculous power united in Christ is incontrovertible. It is the combination of attributes and names *applied* to Christ and *claimed* by Him, both in the Old and New Testaments, belonging only to Jehovah, and that cannot be assumed or received by any man without blasphemy. Yet so absolutely are they ascribed to Jesus the Saviour, that the whole plan and reality of salvation are necessarily and inextricably interwoven *with them in Him;* and indeed are wrought out *from* them, and fulfilled by them, *only in Him.* "My Father worketh hitherto and I work" (John v. 17), the indwelling and outworking of all the fulness of the Godhead bodily; so that the whole Bible is simply the prediction and fulfillment of GOD MANIFEST IN THE FLESH; a demonstration of Christ's Deity and Humanity that can neither be evaded nor denied.

The very BEING OF GOD is attested and sealed to men by such a Saviour as the Son of God, one with God and addressed and worshipped as God, forever and ever; so that, if He be not *God our Saviour*, there is no God. This is that profound all-comprehensive declaration in Hosea xiii. 4, "Thou shalt know *no God* but Me, for there is *no Saviour* beside Me," compared with the exact correspondences in Isaiah, chapters forty-two to fifty-five. "No God else beside Me, a just God and a Saviour, none beside Me. This is My name; and My glory I will not give to another. Look unto Me and be ye saved, all the ends of the earth; for I am God, and there is none else."

What can be more positive, more intense, comprehensive and undeniable, than this demonstration of the Godhead?

The creations, revelations, statements, predictions, results, are a battery of divine reasoning and omnipotence; and the very focus of the power, and the manifestation of it to the whole universe, are solely in the personal oneness and sameness of God in Christ, bearing our sins, forgiving our iniquities; forgiveness being impossible but from God, and the pretence of its prerogative a blasphemy in any creature, and salvation of the soul impossible without it. But this very Christ is Himself the hearer and answerer of prayer unto salvation; the same Lord over all, and rich unto all that call upon Him; for whosoever shall call upon the name of the Lord shall be saved; the only name under heaven given among men whereby we *can* be saved. "Ye shall call His name Jesus, for He shall save His people from their sins:" and the calling upon Him and His name for that salvation is the highest act of faith and worship, and the acknowledgment of supreme divinity and power.

But all these mysteries were shadowed forth gradually like God's gradual processes of illumination and growth in the natural world from the beginning. All in God's progressive light out of darkness, in the whole revelation of Deity and Humanity, shining into the heart, "to give the Light of the Knowledge of the glory of God in the face of Jesus Christ." "Prepare ye the way of the Lord, and the glory of the Lord shall be revealed, and all flesh shall see it together. And the eyes of the blind shall see out of obscurity and darkness," when at length the vast majestic *steppes* shall have been successively travelled to the completion; the Son of Man, the Son of God; God over all, blessed forever; the human first, a child is born; then the divine, the Lord our righteousness; seen and adored of men and angels; crucified, buried, ascended at the right hand of the Majesty on high; the Lamb of God upon the throne of God, adored forever as *God the Redeemer.*

The disciples themselves were taught as little children, first in the standing school of Christ's humanity, playmates as it were with the young Nazarene; then gradual gleams of His divinity; then the Autocrat of nature, walking on the sea; then the healer of lepers; then Lord of the Sabbath; then raising the dead, and exercising the most exalted divine attribute of the forgiveness of all guilt; an attribute never imparted to man, and never possessed by any pretended "Vicar of God" on earth.

The human and divine are in one; either without the other, a falsehood; if one accepted, but the other rejected, a rejection and invalidation of both. Take the great promise in which the two are first united in Isaiah ix. 6, 7. "For unto us a child is born, unto us a Son is given, and the government shall be upon His shoulders: and His name shall be called Wonderful, Counsellor, The Mighty God, The Everlasting Father, The Prince of Peace. Of the increase of His government and peace there shall be no end upon the throne of David and upon his kingdom, to order it and to establish it with judgment and with justice from henceforth even forever. The zeal of the Lord of Hosts will perform this."

Now turn this infinite divine medal, and we have, on the other side in the whole 53d chapter of the same prophet, a solid mass of prediction, history, reality, the extreme realism of humanity, humiliation and suffering, in this same Wonderful Everlasting Being; the uttermost sorrow and disgrace, suffering and death for others, for the guilty, the poverty-stricken and lost in sin, and despairing of mercy; as the very means of fulfilling in Himself the triumph of forgiveness and eternal glory; and in them, the blessedness and peace on earth, and good-will to men, conferred by the Supreme Lord of the throne and kingdom of David.

We have what seems to a proud and patriotic race, descended from Abraham by God's own covenant, and to aspiring minds and hearts, such as John's, Paul's, and Peter's in their own blindness, an infinite contradiction and denial, to be repudiated with scorn and hatred as an impossibility. And yet it must be true and fulfilled to the extreme, in the letter and in the spirit, or the divinity and the glory and the salvation can never be verified.

In order to be a Saviour for sinners, who are immortal in sin and misery without Him, this Being must be able to say, I and my Father are One, in the same self-existence through eternity. He must be a High Priest *forever* after the *power of an endless life*, not the mere *law* of a carnal commandment, but the right and power of bestowing on us *a life in His own life*, His own indwelling in us, by which we are made partakers of the Divine Nature, and forever draw nigh unto God. He must be able to save *for evermore* all that come unto God by Him, because He is *consecrated for evermore*, made higher than the heavens, and *ever liveth to make intercession*, which itself is the peculiar attribute and prerogative of His own *human and divine majesty*, in all the fulness of the Godhead bodily.

This is the compound circuit of the magnetic trains of divine and human attributes and realities meeting on earth and in heaven, for the destruction of sin and death through the sufferings and sacrifice, the death and resurrection of the Son and Lord of David, when the Lord should have laid on him the iniquities of us all. The circuit could not be sundered, nor its terms altered, and anything of truth remain. For a Saviour is predicted, who is to be Jehovah our Righteousness, God with us, both in name and nature, infinitely holy, all-powerful, all-wise, a self-existing Being from eternity; but at the same time human, of the seed of David, in the form of man, so assuredly, and for such a purpose of human salvation, in such a way of expiation for sin, by such a sin-offering in Himself, fulfilling all the types and promises of the divine law, that the very divinity of His nature could be certified only through His perfect and infinitely holy humanity, as the Holy One of God. These infinite truths and phenomena of the divine existence are impossibilities to mere human reason without faith; yet they are as clearly foretold in the Old Testament, and demonstrated in the New, as the eternal power and Godhead of the invisible Creator are declared and understood by the things that are made.

Jehovah, our righteousness, the Messiah of God, was to transact all these mysteries, and put all these apparent impossibilities and incomprehensible contradictions into actual demonstrations, known realities, the practical working of which should be visible to the whole universe; and they were to be powers experienced and lived out in daily life and obedience. They were to be the things, "which we have heard, which we have seen with our eyes, which we have looked upon, and our hands have handled, of the Word of life."

The *laws* of the Decalogue, as contained in that Word, Christ took into His own human and divine life and interpreted them by obeying them, by fulfilling them in love. The *institutions*, as the Passover, and the Sabbath, and the Mercy Seat, and Prayer, and the blood of Atonement, were His alone, to make them in Himself a perpetual power of life, in love and duty, in holiness, in gratitude and joy, by His own authority and inspiration, as Head over all things to the Church. Other Head and Lord there never should be, never could be. The attempt would be a revelation of "THAT WICKED, ὁ ἄνομος, the Man of Sin, the Son of Perdition, whom the Lord must consume with the Spirit of His mouth, and destroy with the brightness of His coming." *

* And now to think of the amazing profanation, denial, subversion of these things, by the power of Satan among men, through the same blind, self-worshipping despotism, under which he had vainly endeavored to subdue even the Saviour! To think of a system of this world's power and glory being established among men, and accepted as the Church of Christ; which takes the forgiveness of sin out of Christ's hands, and puts it at the disposal of a priestly hierarchy for money; and takes the infallibility of God, and puts that also in the power of a man, as God, sitting in God's temple; which steals from Christ the keys of hell and flings them at the head of every believer in Jesus, who denies the authority and power of a priestly absolution; which takes the very doctrines of the gospel by name, and makes out of them by cruelty a torture of the Inquisition; and teaches in all things the worship of God, not by the Word of God, but the commandments of men. And at the instigation of such a Church, this Book of God given to be the guide of our souls from infancy

On this assurance of the authority and work of forgiveness residing only in Christ, and untransferable to any living creature, or agent, vicegerent or corporation of church or state, hangs all our security of pardon and eternal life, against human impostures and despotisms, against false religions, arrogating God's power.

XIII.

CHRIST OUR LAWGIVER AND KING, CREATOR, JUDGE, ADVOCATE, AND FORGIVING SAVIOUR; IN HIMSELF OUR ETERNAL LIFE—THE SUCCESSIVE TERRACES OF THESE GLORIES IN THE PROPHECIES OF ISAIAH.

"For the Lord is our Judge, the Lord is our Lawgiver, the Lord is our King; He will save us. And the inhabitants shall no more say, I am sick; the people that dwell therein shall be forgiven their iniquity." This passage in Isaiah xxxiii. 22, 24, is a profoundly interesting and most suggestive example

through life and into eternity, is to be expelled from our common schools, from the education of our children, from its supremacy over the family, and the state, and the world! And this tremendous apostacy we are required to receive as the Church of Christ, because its priests baptize in the name of the Father, Son, and Holy Ghost!

of the manner in which the Scriptures are constructed as an Observatory winding upwards, carrying the observer and believer, the Pilgrim to Eternity, constantly nearer to God: constructed with landing-places and revolving windows where the soul may rest and gaze forth illimitably. It is a Jacob's ladder up and down which God's angels are ascending and descending, even as they are beheld doing by steps, life-lines, and holdings on the Son of Man, whose Incarnate Majesty and self-existent glory are the medium of communication between the creature man and the Infinite Creator; who is before all things, and by whom all things consist, and by whom in His humanity bearing our sins, and so becoming the way, the truth, the life, we sinners, the guilty and the lost, come to God; and by the love of Christ dwelling in our hearts by faith, are filled with all the fulness of God, receiving the end of our faith, even the salvation of the soul. For as that is the end and object of faith, so the manifestation of that and the training of mankind for it, are the object and work of the whole divine revelation.

The culmination of all blessings, and the worth and security of all, were in this one thing, the forgiveness of sins. Without that, good were it for every man if he had never been born. And it is wonderful to see how this great truth is found incessantly lifting itself up in power and glory, with warning mountain beacons, all through the Old Testament, but especially the Psalms and the Prophetic portions, coming after the arrangements and figurative provisions of the law, and in a primal sense fulfilling them, even before the coming of the Saviour. The whole benefit and blessedness of the law, its object and instrumentality, as appointed of God, were first of all, the impression upon mankind of a sense of their guilt; and then the education and training of the wounded conscience to the search after forgiveness; that is, after the appointed Christ, the promised Saviour, to the fountain of whose blood all the legal provisions for the remission of sins conducted mankind. That was God's method of teaching, and for that He gave the law to be to us a schooolmaster to bring us to Christ, for holiness, forgiveness, and eternal life.

Ever and anon, all along the stream of divine revelation we come upon such a table-land, a terrace piled for the advantage of such a commanding view. So a Word like this at the close of the thirty-third chapter of Isaiah is like an open door through which, at the end of a dark vista or tunnel, our sight is conducted forth and opened upon a prospect of interminable space, and indescribable beauty and glory. It is like the vast range of landscape sometimes suddenly seen through the side closings and infolding slopes of the Swiss Mountains. The glory is all the greater for the pains we have taken, and the long reaches of fatigueing ascent up which we have toiled, to gain such a commanding point of vision.

You are sometimes amazed at the genius and skill with which some great painter has been enabled, by the intermingling and crossing of light and shade in great masses at the right intervals, to carry forward the whole attention and admiration, the whole power and enjoyment of the mind, to the opening at the end of this perspective; and the splendor of the distant view, which you know, if you could see far enough, would be revealed, is half made up by the training and excitement of the imagination in the foreground of the picture. Every step and circumstance, every tree, precipice, and rising bank, have made you expect, look out for, and prophesy some great development, and have prepared you to meet it with belief and appreciation.

And such is the training of the mind of a believing person, travelling along the record of the Scriptures. Sometimes gloomy dark mountains shut you in, entirely locking up your vision and sense to a present desolation and terror. But you come to an opening; there is always an exit to a wider world. The prophetic intuition with which you began is sustained and deepened, as a mountain brook is increased at length to a river in its passage to the open sea. Sometimes a valley is traversed and watered like a garden of Paradise, as if that particular thing were the final cause of the stream that is carrying such verdure and refreshing beauty through the world. But always there is the warning and uplifting sense of a mighty conclusion to which you are advancing. "Arise ye, and depart hence, for this is not your rest." It is but a pilgrimage to a better country, even a heavenly, up to which all God's discipline, rightly interpreted, conducts the soul. Everywhere, as in some magic land of dreams and portents, the awakened spirit sees or feels the invisible warnings.

> "I see a hand you cannot see,
> That beckons me away;
> I hear a voice you cannot hear,
> Forbidding me to stay."

It is wonderfully like the intimations of immortality from the recollections of childhood as traced in the Poet Wordsworth's celebrated Ode; only in this case the intimations are increasing with the progress of the believing Spirit, and instead of seeing them mournfully obliterated, or shaded and dying away, till at length they fade into the light of common day, the believing soul arrives at Christ by means of them, and in Him knows, even by the ministration of His Spirit, vouchsafed to the heart that is following on after Him, the reality of this predicted life, and something of its glory beforehand. Such is the operation of the successive shafts of light in the Old Testament Revelation, continually broadening and deepening in unity and glory, till as ministering angels they bear us on their wings into the presence of the Saviour, where Moses and Elias retire, and leave the soul satisfied in Christ's love, assured of His likeness.

XIV.

THE INTUITIONS OF THE PEOPLE AND THE TEACHINGS OF THE LAW COMBINING WITH THE DIVINE LIGHT OF PROPHECY—DEATH SWALLOWED UP IN VICTORY BY OUR FORGIVING LORD AND GOD—FORGIVENESS THE GREATEST PROOF OF DEITY AND OBLIGATION OF GRATITUDE.

Now from the twenty-fourth chapter of Isaiah to the thirty-sixth there is a very striking example of this divine light of prophecy combining with the experience and intuitions of the people, and the teachings of the divine law, and leading them to God as their Great Physician, and to Heaven in the enjoyment of His presence as their home. It is promised that God "will destroy in the mountain of the Lord's House the face of the covering cast over all people, and the veil that is spread over all nations, and will swallow up death in victory, and will wipe away tears from off all faces. And it shall be said in that day Lo, this is our God; we have waited for Him, and He will save us; this is the Lord; we have waited for Him; we will be glad and rejoice in His salvation. And therefore will the Lord wait, that He may be gracious unto you, and therefore will He be exalted, that He may have mercy upon you; for the Lord is a God of judgment; blessed are all they that wait for Him." "Moreover, the light of the moon shall be as the light of the sun, and the light of the sun shall be sevenfold as the light of seven days, in the day that the Lord bindeth up the breach of His people, and healeth the stroke of their wound."

"Thine eyes shall see the King in His beauty; thine eyes shall see Jerusalem a quiet habitation. There the glorious Lord will be unto us a place of broad rivers and streams. The Lord is our King,

He will save us. And the inhabitant shall not say,
I am sick; the people that dwell therein SHALL BE
FORGIVEN THEIR INIQUITY." *

* See the magnificent description, in Wordsworth's Poem of
the "Excursion," Book II., of such a Mountain Revelation from
the Eternal God.

"Through the dull mist, a step,
A single step, that freed me from the skirts
Of the blind vapor, opened to my view
Glory beyond all glory ever seen
By waking sense, or by the dreaming soul.
 The appearance, instantaneously disclosed,
Was of a mighty City,—boldly say
A wilderness of building,—sinking far
And self-withdrawn into a wondrous depth,
Far sinking into splendor without end!
 Fabric it seemed of diamond and of gold,
With alabaster domes and silver spires
And blazing terrace upon terrace, high
Uplifted; here, serene pavilions bright,
In avenues disposed; there, towers begirt
With battlements that on their restless fronts
Bore stars,—illumination of all gems!
By earthly nature had the effect been wrought
Upon the dark materials of the storm,
Now pacified; on them, and on the coves,
And mountain steeps and summits, whereunto
The vapors had receded, taking there
Their station under a cerulean sky.
 O, 'twas an unimaginable sight!
Clouds, mists, streams, watery rocks and emerald turf,
Clouds of all tincture, rocks and sapphire sky,
Confused, commingled, mutually inflamed,
Molten together, and composing thus,

Now beyond question this portion of the prophecy of Isaiah is an example of God's method in foretelling, first of all, the coming and reign of the Messiah upon earth, and ultimately the glory and blessedness of the result in everlasting heaven of the

> Each lost in each, that marvellous array
> Of temple, palace, citadel, and huge
> Fantastic form of structure without name,
> In fleecy folds voluminous, enwrapped.
>   Right in the midst, where interspace appeared
> Of open-coast, an object like a Throne,
> Beneath a shining canopy of State,
> Stood fixed; and fixed resemblances were seen,
> To implements of ordinary use.
> But vast in size, in substance glorified;
> Such as by Hebrew Prophets were beheld
> In vision,—forms uncouth of mightiest power,
> For admiration and mysterious awe.
>   Below me was the Earth; this little vale,
> Lay low beneath my feet; 'twas visible,—
> I saw not, but I felt that it was there.
> *That which I saw* was the revealed abode
> Of Spirits in beatitude: My heart
> Swelled in my breast,—I have been dead, I cried,
> And now I live! Oh! wherefore do I live?
> And with that pang, I prayed to be no more!
> The apparition faded not away,
> And I descended."—

But never to forget this vision, having been caught up by it to the third heaven, and better fitted to say, "Now I know in part, but then shall I know, even as I am known. There shall be no night there, for the Lord God giveth them light, and they shall reign forever and ever."

forgiveness of sin from God through Him. The forgiveness of sin is the one blessing on which the heart of man is taught to set its desire, and the importunity and urgency of its seeking. God's course of disciplinary education with men and nations is ordered with reference to this seeking; even as it is stated in Paul's discourse to the Athenians, that God hath made of one blood all nations of men for to dwell on all the face of the earth, and hath determined the times before appointed, and the bounds of their habitation, that they should seek the Lord, if haply they might feel after Him, and find Him, though He be not far from every one of us.

They that seek Him shall find Him, and in the forgiveness of sin by His mercy shall find and shall receive all things that pertain unto life and godliness through the knowledge of Him that hath called us to glory and virtue, and hath given us those exceeding great and precious promises, by which we may be partakers of the divine nature. And this very promise in Isaiah, as being the Sun at midnoon of the heavenly revelations from God in the Old Testament, we may take; and as a navigator at sea, in taking his reckoning, brings the sun down with his quadrant to the sensible horizon, and makes his calculations and determines his position, even so, we may bring this central light, this concentration of all light from heaven concerning the soul's forgiveness and the blessedness resulting from it, down to the appearance of our Lord on earth, to the incarnation of Him Who went about doing good, healing our sicknesses, and bearing our infirmities, and forgiving our sins. We may bring it down to a particular point in the horizon of the gospels, where our blessed Lord appears as the healer of all the sicknesses and pains both of soul and body of our ruined race.

Our Lord's manifestation on earth with this claim for this purpose, as the searcher and healer of hearts, proves Him divine, and is a seal irresistible of both volumes of divine revelation, the Old and the New, the Old discovering sin, the New, redeeming from it. No such Being, no such revealer of the innermost nature and ruin of mankind, no such pretended physician had ever appeared from the beginning of the world; no divine messenger had ever opened his lips with that claim of having come on such a mission. No one had ever made the discovery of men's universal, unexceptionable need of such a salvation.

The misery of man had been known, but not as sinful, and therefore inherent, inevitable; not the acknowledgment made of the state of man as in himself incurably sinful by his own will and fault, and consequently, if immortal in sin and guilt, forever miserable. Yet the cure of human wretchedness had been tried, and quacks had made their experiments and played their tricks. But for a man to stand up before his fellow-men, and offer, as the only hope for them, and as being Himself without sin, to heal their souls, to forgive sin, to make men holy and thus happy, in and with God as their Father and Friend forever and ever, was a manifestation never known, and would have been, in man, a superhuman audacity.

For a man to rest his whole authority, and his claim to be heard, and the worth of his teaching on that, on the right to say, "Thy sins be forgiven thee," and to venture the performance of a miracle to test *that;*— openly calling God to witness both the power and right; not merely as Elijah once did, proclaiming that he was a prophet of the true God, a messenger commissioned against all idolatry, but that he was invested, by God Himself, on earth, with the very highest prerogative of divine sovereignty in heaven, the power and right to forgive sins; this was either God, or blasphemy against God.

And here the intuition of the Scribes and Pharisees was perfect, for it was trained by divine revelation itself, and in accordance with it. None can forgive sins but God only. Their theology on this point was axiomatic, incontestable, unmistakable. Expiations, priests, altars, sacrifices, temples, nothing on earth, nor any creature of the race of man, could forgive sin, but God only, God, against whom all have sinned. All we like sheep have gone astray: God had revealed that, and man could so discover it, and feel it; but none could ever by any means redeem or forgive his brother, or give to God a ransom for him, or say on earth, as God, I forgive thee, or, "Thy sins be forgiven thee." How could any but the Omniscient God know what any man's sins were, to be forgiven?

And this it was, when our Lord Jesus stood and said, in the court of a Jewish house, with the crowd gazing on the man sick of the palsy, let down into the midst at the feet of Jesus, and the Scribes and Pharisees watching every motion, every word, "Son, be of good cheer! Thy sins be forgiven thee!" This it was that arrested the thoughts of all, and carried them up to God, as if a cataract had been stopped in its fall, and flung back towards heaven. Not an individual expected it, and all but the sick man himself were thunderstruck by it, and overwhelmed with astonishment and awe. And no wonder that the Scribes and Pharisees, with all their prejudices against Christ, and the purely spiritual and heart-searching nature of His teachings, and all their jealousy for the God of Moses and of the Jews, and all their knowledge of what blasphemy in a mere mortal might be, accused our Lord of blasphemy. For their theology was just, was indisputable, and the conclusion inevitable; who can forgive sins but God only? And what else is this, but the claim of being God? And this Nazarene, this carpenter, makes it!

It must be noted and remembered all along, that this claim comes in at the very beginning of Christ's ministry, that it struck the key-note of all His teachings, that it is grounded in the infinite and eternal value of the soul, that it implies the profound truth of all the sense that can be drawn from the warnings of God in both the Old and New Testaments, to flee from the wrath to come, and to secure the salvation of the soul; its redemption from the death of sin, being the one great object alone worthy the effort of an immortal being. It was the subject of Christ's first sermon, and the burden of His last prayer. It was the reason for His own endurance of the dread, intolerable misery of being forsaken of God, and the reason why He would not pray, amidst the trouble of His own soul, that God would save Him from that hour; because for the sake of that very suffering, and the glory of redemption to be gained by it, He came into the world, and met the conflict of that hour, having become voluntarily partaker of our flesh and blood, that through death He might destroy him that had the power of death, that is, the devil.

Now we can neither understand the gospels nor the character of Christ, but with this key to the study of them, taken from His own words, and from His own estimate of the value of the soul, and of His own work in coming into the world as the Physician of the soul. Forgiveness of sin, and the gift of the Life Everlasting! "I am come that they might have life, and have it more abundantly. I am the Good Shepherd: the Good Shepherd giveth His life for the sheep."—John x. 10, 11. "For the Son of Man is come to seek and to save *that which was lost.*"—Luke xix. 10, and Matt. xviii. 11.* In infinite mercy our Blessed Lord has caused this declaration to be repeated in the midst of an argument of compassionate warning for both Jews and Gentiles, and for all man-

* The modern revisers of our English translation have thought fit to strike out utterly from the Gospel of Matthew this shining and gracious light; thus destroying from that part of the New Testament one of the brightest evidences of Christianity, and one of the most comforting assurances of the Holy Spirit against despair. Let the reader compare the passages in the New Testament explanatory of this word *Lost;* few, but comprehensive; absolute, and infinite in compassionate warning. Compare, also, Acts xiii. 46, where the contradicting and blaspheming Jews are said to have *condemned themselves as* being unworthy of Everlasting life.

kind. In Matthew, for the whole world of sinners, to warn them of the danger by sin of being in their temporal and eternal guilt, unrepented of and unforgiven, cast into everlasting fire; and to invite and persuade them to take refuge in His offered forgiving grace, that they might never find themselves among the souls thus lost.

If not thus lost, then no need of ever being found; if not thus lost, not lost at all, so that the very word before God would be a falsehood. And again, as the Sadducees and materialists argued, if not immortal, then nothing forfeited; if a mere material physical organization for this world only, but neither spirit nor a future life, then no more sin than a machine, nor any need of pardon, nor anything to fear, nor need of any Saviour, nor any other blessedness or glory but to eat and drink, for to-morrow we die. Nothing, either of quality or circumstance, could have any reality or power beyond the grave, for creatures not immortal; nor could anything be made to appear of any importance, except only in this transitory life.

XV.

HOW THE APPEARANCE OF CHRIST IN THE WORLD WAS ACCORDINGLY FORESHADOWED—ON WHAT HIS APPEAL TO MANKIND WAS GROUNDED—THREE REALITIES OF EXPERIENCE AND FOREWARNING —KNOWLEDGE OF EXISTENCE AND RESPONSIBILITY BEYOND THE GRAVE THE GREAT DISCIPLINARY, INSTRUCTION AND EXPERIENCE OF MANKIND, —TWO EXTREMES OF TEMPTATION AND GUILT CORRESPONDING, AND TO BE PROVIDED AGAINST BY CHRIST—WHO SHALL LEAD HIS ARMY OF WITNESSES?

Now then, with the slightest adequate sense of man's sinfulness and darkness, with the least obtained result of wisdom from all preceding light, and from the whole course of God's discipline with mankind, a reasonable man would feel and say that the appearance of such a being as Christ on earth with such claims and such demonstrated power supporting them, must be the promised Emmanuel, God with us, the God incarnate, God manifest in the flesh, seen of angels, believed on in the world; the manifestation of Almighty power and mercy, demonstrated by works that none but the Almighty Creator and Preserver of men could perform. If such a person appears, working miracles, and referring all things to God as His Father, it will prove Him incontestably to have been sent from God. If this person appears saying to guilty men, conscious of their transgressions against God, and burdened with remorse and terror, Thy sins be forgiven thee; claiming to be a person in His own right forgiving sins, having that prerogative and power, He must be divine, if in attestation of the truth of that prerogative He really performs a miracle; He must be the present God incarnate, for none can forgive sins but God only, and God would never sanction such a pretense by conferring upon such a person the power of working miracles.

There are three realities, or possessions of knowledge and experience in the soul of man, upon which the Appeal of Christ, when He came unto His own and His own received Him not, was grounded; the sense of immortality, the sense of guilt, and the fear of death.

But the moment an existence and accountability beyond the grave are introduced, and the power of a guilty nature and its consequences in another state are made known (especially of that nature as giving the law *there*, if carried *unchanged* there, establishing character *forever* there), *that moment* a Saviour becomes the very first requisite and demonstration of divine revelation, *a forgiving God and Saviour*.

Indeed there can be no such thing as a revelation from God without this, nor any possibility of anything that really reveals this, not being God's own revelation.

The revelation both of sin and its eternal consequences having been gradual, so has been the revelation of a Saviour, continued and accumulated till the fulness of time should come, the fulness of demonstration, the all-sufficiency of the redemption, and the cure, and the preparation of an army of redeemed witnesses, to certify and proclaim the cure to all mankind.

And therefore comes the Gospel of our Lord, with the grand central assurance in the "faithful saying, and worthy of all acceptation, that Christ Jesus came into the world to save sinners," "Of whom," says Paul, "I am chief." I who have gone further than even Cain went, or any other sinner that ever lived, having claimed God's forgiveness for myself as being a son of Abraham and a keeper of the law, but denied it to all others, and especially to all believers in the Lamb of God Who taketh away the sin of the world; and I being exceedingly mad against them, murdered them as intruding on my birthright; which Cain never did.

Of the whole army of experimental witnesses of the forgiving power and grace of Jesus Christ as God manifest in the flesh, Paul was to be the leader, and therefore was permitted, with all his claims of an unsullied morality and patriotic piety, to fall into this great guilt of the murder of the saints; and was lifted out of the gulf of consequent unbelief and despair, to be the world's foremost preacher of faith, hope, justification through Christ, peace with God and grateful, all-constraining love to Christ as the life and joy of redeemed souls forever and ever.

There being these two extremes of falsehood and error growing out of human guilt and unbelief, first, My sin is greater than can possibly be forgiven; second, My sin is so little that it needs no forgiveness at all, or, the forgiveness is as certain as the sin, and therefore the sin itself shall occasion no separation between me and God;—there was needed the enthronement of this other principle or attribute in the Divine nature and administration, *There is forgiveness with Thee that Thou mayst be feared.* If there were no eternal evil in sin, nor consequence of evil from it, then there would be no occasion for fear; but if no forgiveness of sin possible, then no possibility of a returning, repenting, loving fear, no possibility or room for anything but despair and perpetuity in guilt. Now then, for the sign of the Cross, the assurance written in the blood of Jesus Christ, the Lamb of God, who taketh away the sin of the world, that there is forgiveness with God, and eternal redemption, that He may be both feared and loved forever.

Of all these truths of revealed theology, and of man's nature and God's as demonstrated in the revelation, human experience, vast, indisputable, and from age to age accumulated, has become the witness. You cannot put it to death, as the Jews sought to put Lazarus. It rises again out of the tomb, and accompanies you all through life, a presence that you cannot bury, whether Jew or Gentile; and you yourself in every circumstance and period of your own being, do but add to the testimony, whether you regard it or not. So we see how on all sides not only is the sense of sin, the consciousness of its guilt and misery, necessary to the first adequate perception of the evidences of Christianity, but also a sense of forgiveness, and of peace with God, through Christ dwelling in the heart by faith, is equally necessary to constitute a witness of Christ's infinite willingness and power to save whoever will.

"Go therefore to Decapolis, and tell how great things the Lord hath done for thee." Like David of old, "Publish with the voice of thanksgiving, and tell of all His wondrous works." The earnest of the Spirit in the heart, the comfort of the Holy Ghost, the joy of salvation, is given for this very purpose. "Restore unto me the joy of Thy salvation, and uphold me by Thy free Spirit; then will I teach transgressors Thy ways, and sinners shall be converted unto Thee. Open Thou my lips, and my mouth shall show forth Thy praise." "Thou hast brought up my soul from the grave, and girded me with gladness, to the end that my soul may sing praise to Thee, and not be silent. O my God, I will give thanks unto Thee forever!"— Psalms 51 and 30.

Without the provision of a succession of such living forgiven witnesses, the proofs of Christianity from God would die out, notwithstanding all miracles, and the world would be left in darkness. But God, by the very operation of the truth as it is in Jesus, acting in men's hearts, by the power of the Holy Spirit, provides the succession of such witnesses; and in the nature and development of His kingdom they never can be wanting. That inalienable sense of sin, which is the ground-wave of the tide of human consciousness, makes a man see and feel the truth of the system revealed by Christ the Saviour, the truth of all revelation from Adam's sin downward, the truth of the fall of man, and of God's interposition for his redemption.

The accumulating consciousness of every age, and the breaking surge and roar of every novel tide of resisting, unwilling, unbelieving philosophy, prove this. Self-will in conflict with God's will, once chosen, once committed, and the creature, by his own choice committed to it, can no more be returned from, by mere discovery of the consequences, than a remorseful murderer can bring back his victim into life. The embrace of crime changes the soul, and its relations with God and the universe. Cain could no more have changed his own nature, after the killing of his brother, and the adoption of the savage rule, "Am I my brother's keeper," than he could have given again, at a wish or a word of remorse and sorrow, the sacred life and form of immortality to the ashes of his buried victim.

And then the man so changed begets a self-will in his own likeness. Physiological science tells us with a terrible emphasis and solemnity how injuries of the embryo, and hereditary disturbances, beginning in the outline of the substance of the egg, may be produced and perpetuated in successive generations; and a man's or mother's will may carry down the constitutional propensities of the drunkard to a far posterity. Geological science tells us that a bone of Cain's skeleton, could it have been found in the strata of a prehistoric world, would have demonstrated him to have belonged to this present human race; and certainly a nerve laid bare of Cain's moral experience is enough for demonstration that such is the normal experience of like human guilt through the successive ages of its descent as a characteristic of self-willed humanity.

Without supernatural intervention, how *can* it produce a species above itself, or nearer to God than its own image; nor can it have power to change itself, any more than the skeleton of a megatherium could by natural selection rise out of death with its forelegs expanded into wings as of angels, and its hind feet provided with muscular attachments, enabling it, by pulleys in the vertebral column, to stand upright as a man. Only God, who made man upright, can raise him up after a voluntary renouncement of that uprightness. Only the Creator can new-create His own work. Man cannot possibly have the power to be one day God's friend, another, God's enemy,—one day His enemy, another His friend,—to change from one condition and character to the other at His pleasure, and no lasting consequences. The permission of such a creature, the sustaining of such a machine, would be an anomaly subversive of all our ideas of wisdom and holiness in the governor of a universe of moral beings.

The existence of man as a witness or indicator of the will of God would be impossible. Of what use could a watch be that stopped whenever it chose, and went again whenever it chose, once or a dozen times in the twenty-four hours, and not a notice given or possible, of the point of change or stoppage. Stopping once for five minutes or a quarter of an hour makes the watch false all day long, without your knowing it. You never can tell the time. And if you discover the stoppage and set it right, yet it may occur five minutes afterwards in your watch pocket, and in the course of an hour start again, so that, when you have occasion again to look at your watch, you might as well be looking at the sparrows on the house-tops, for any note of time to guide you.

You are sure to be false with a watch that stops when it pleases and gives you no notice; goes again when it pleases, and you know not that it has stopped. It is good for nothing but to lie. And such would man be, even as a mere machine, with the faculty and habit of stopping and disobeying God at pleasure, denying Him one day and confessing Him the next, without lasting consequences of misery from the denial, or gain of happiness from the confession. It is impossible that such a state of things can exist in the universe. The friend of God, the man that would testify truly of Him, or receive testimony, or the confirmation of it by miracles from Him, must be one doing the will of God.

XVI.

TREATMENT OF THE CLAIMS OF CHRIST BY THE JEWS JUDGED ACCORDING TO THEIR OWN LIGHT AND KNOWLEDGE—THEIR POSSESSION OF THE POWER OF CORRECT REASONING FROM THE PHILOSOPHY OF THE SCRIPTURES—FORGIVENESS OF SIN IMPOSSIBLE BUT BY GOD ONLY—IF THIS MAN WERE NOT OF GOD, HE COULD DO NOTHING—EVERY MAN HIS OWN LABORATORY, AND THE POWER OF HIS OWN EXPERIMENT LAID AT HIS OWN DOOR—BUT ANY EXPERIMENT BEYOND THE GRAVE, IMPOSSIBLE, AND THIS MEN KNOW BEFOREHAND.

Here the good sense of the Jews was manifested, in some remarkable instances of their intercourse with Christ, and their treatment of His claims; and there is to be noted the evident national possession of a power of correct reasoning, derived only from their long heritage of the Scriptures of divine truth, and their familiarity with them. They were the best philosophers, with all their faults, the least carried away by mere speculation, in the world; that is, the common people, who heard Christ gladly; for they had a rugged and shrewd common sense that might have made each of them, touched with the foresight of their coming Messiah, and humbled in the sense of their need of Him, a Plato or a Socrates, combining the qualities of Peter and John. The ninth chapter of John's Gospel is a wonderfully graphic representation of their characteristics.

"Give God the praise," said the carping Pharisees, "but this man is a sinner."

"Whether he be a sinner or not," said the victim of their cross-examinations, "I know not; but one thing I do know, that whereas I was blind, now I see; and another thing I know, that He healed me. Now we all know that God heareth not sinners, but if any man be a worshipper of God, and doeth His will, him He heareth. If this man were not of God, He could do nothing."

And this is the very climax of demonstration and belief to which the world needed to be brought; in order to such a trust in God, such an approach and return to Him on the part of sinful creatures, as a God inviting men to be forgiven, a God with whom is forgiveness that He may be feared, a God whose attribute, as well as right and power, is that of a forgiving God. Because, manifestly, with none other God can we have anything to do; for if we cannot be forgiven, there is nothing for us but despair; so that the demonstration of a **forgiving God is our one, vast, indispensable requi-**

site. A forgiving God, or none, is what the soul of man must have, what it cries out after, what the whole world's schoolmaster in the Old Testament reveals and mercifully urges, and what the whole possibility of repentance and grateful trust and love and obedience from the heart is grounded in.

This manifestation is in Christ, and in Him only, correspondent with the preparations and promises set forth in the only religion that ever pretended to meet the wants and longings of the world of immortal beings burdened with sin;—the religion of the Old Testament. And the appearing of Christ, in the fulness of time, with these prerogatives, demonstrated by every species of evidence that a sane and humble mind requires, is the divine, irresistible, and perfect demonstration of a present God.

His appearing as the Physician and Healer of the sin-sick soul; His coming and preaching to lost sinners as such, not to condemn them, but to seek and save them; His announcement of having come not to call the righteous, but sinners to repentance; His assurance of having left the bosom of His Father for that very object, and for nothing else; His grasp of the greatness and urgency of that object; His cardinal question for the whole race of mankind, What shall it profit a man, if he gain the whole world, and lose his own soul? His unveiling to all men their innermost character, and their one universal need; His proclamation of Himself, not as King of the Jews merely, nor of any earthly race or kingdom, but as man's Redeemer from sin and death accordant with the divine name bestowed at His coming into the world, "Thou shalt call His name Jesus, for He shall save His people from their sins":— All this is the manifest deity of "Him that loved us and washed us from our sins in His own blood; to whom be glory and dominion forever and ever. Amen."

But all this is so utterly superhuman, supernatural, impossible to mere nature even in conception or imagination, and in execution, in performance, still more impossible, that for any man to arrogate this as his mission would be to set himself forth in the stocks of a world-wide madness and falsehood, to put himself in the grip of a demonstrated insanity; only, that the conception and announcement of the mission would of itself be proof of inspiration and superhuman truth.

But here it is; and the very claim makes the imposture incredible, so that before its shining the clouds and darkness flee away, and it is as the light out of darkness, or as the sun shot forth into chaos. And Christ's putting Himself, His character, (which of you convinceth Me of sin?), His claims, there in the very focus of that concentration of divine light and previous demonstration in the Old Testament Scriptures, and

in the corresponding experience of all mankind;—
there under the test of that combined telescope and
microscope in one, the telescope of faith, prophecy,
and foredrawn characteristics, and the microscope of
human nature, jealousy, acuteness, enmity, unbelief,
scrutiny of resistible claims—all this was a movement
incapable of being supported, except by the divine
reality; a movement of which every attempt at support
would only have involved a more desperate failure.

The God who is the object of worship and thanksgiving in the Old Testament, is a God forgiving men's iniquities and healing their sicknesses. When His Representative on earth should come, He was to come with those two qualities and powers of divine benevolence. "Bless the Lord, O my soul, and all that is within me bless His holy name. Bless the Lord, O my soul, and forget not any of His benefits. Who forgiveth all thine iniquities!"

That, and not health or wealth merely, is the first thing, the first characteristic of a God of infinite mercy and love; the first obligation of gratitude is there; the first and only real need of the soul, and of man's life, is there; and that is, in one view, the main view, the *whole of divine revelation*, the thing without which there would have been no revelation at all, nor any blessedness in it, nor any use for it. Who healeth all thy diseases, is a secondary claim of grateful worship and love, growing out of the first. And the one grand reality for men to believe, is the first, that they may come to God in assurance of His forgiving mercy; and feeling their need of such mercy, all knowledge and all discipline may be a divine pathway to lead them to God for it; that being the only possible condition of blessedness and life eternal.

But this once gained, all was gained. The quality of being forgiven is that of being thoroughly redeemed and cleansed from sin, from its power and its consequences, from its misery-making, sickening, deforming, soul-destroying terror and desolation. A soul forgiven hath all its transgressions removed, the love, the habit, the disease of sin extirpated, as a leper was wholly cleansed, the blood purified, the flesh restored as clean and fresh and sweet as that of an infant, when once the miracle of divine healing was performed. No man was ever forgiven, or ever will be, but was taught to hate sin and love God and holiness; no man was ever forgiven, to return to his iniquities, and take back and bear again the burden, of which God had first made him heart-sick even unto death, and then had taken it away and restored him to life. Now the indestructible consciousness of mankind, once awakened and quickened by the knowledge of sin, feels and knows that a deliverance from sin, and a restoration and new-creation of the purity of

God within the soul, carries with it all needed blessings, all happiness, all grace and glory.

If men are once made to feel this, and in the freshness and strength of this conviction can be made to believe in a forgiving God and Saviour, and to come to Him for such mercy;—*that* is the work of salvation, that is the kingdom of heaven on earth, that is Christ's mission from the Father. Here then we see the object and end of the divine miracles of healing, and every other exercise of Almighty power wrought by Christ on earth, to convince men of His power to forgive, and to persuade men to come to Him for such forgiveness. Here is the Orb of that lightning of God's Love, brighter than the sun, turned upon Christ's works, "That ye may know that the Son of man hath power on earth to forgive sins; then saith He to the sick of the palsy," —to whom He had before given the soul-cheering assurance, "Thy sins be forgiven thee,"—" Arise, take up thy bed, and go to thine house." That ye may know that there is such power from God on earth; that it inheres in Me, your Saviour; that I have come to be your deliverer, your Redeemer from sin and death eternal, which alone can make sickness and death dreadful; that ye may know that there is on earth the Divine Being promised in your Scriptures, to seek and to save that which was lost; that ye may know such glory, such mercy from God your Father, and may be encouraged and induced to apply to Me for it, and receive from Me the forgiveness and eternal life which I offer.

Now let any man read in this connection the tender and inimitably pathetic and encouraging seventh chapter of Luke; our Lord's free forgiveness of the woman of the city that was a sinner, and His own loving appreciation of her grateful penitence and love in washing His feet with her tears, and wiping them with the hairs of her head; and the astonishment and indignation of the Pharisee that had invited Christ, and of the guests that were partakers of the feast with Him; and he cannot fail to see a new proof of the Deity and divine compassion of the Saviour, as our High Priest and Advocate with God, touched with the feeling of our infirmities, tempted like as we are, yet without sin, who was Himself to taste even the misery of despair in the soul forsaken of God, that He might know how to succor, in the last extreme, the souls that are thus tempted. Despair of forgiveness in this life, is the terror of death and hell beforehand.

And not one of these words of mercy can be spared, nor the significance of any of them diminished. The seventy times seven in Matt. xviii. 22, are truer to the text and context, and to the character and work of Christ the Redeemer, than the seven times to which "some authorities" would reduce them; and the words, "to save that which was lost," infinitely more likely to have been repeated in two of the gospels, than interpolated in any.

Luke's Gospel and John's, are pre-eminently the gospels of forgiving mercy and love; and not one of the instances or illustrations of Christ's exercise of the divine attribute of forgiveness can we afford to give up; especially such as are contained in the seventh chapter of Luke, and the eighth of John, and the eighteenth of Matthew; jewels of inspiration beyond all price, each of them affording a combination talisman, or key, to unlock the mysteries of redemption in the whole Bible.

XVII.

THE CENTRAL EVIDENCE OF CHRISTIANITY IN THE CHARACTER OF CHRIST, AND THE EXPERIENCE OF FORGIVENESS, FROM HIM—COMBINATIONS OF PROMISES AND WARNINGS, EACH CO-EXTENSIVE WITH ETERNITY—GOD'S ALARM-BELLS OF DEATH, AND JUBILEE CHIMES OF SALVATION—THE PILLAR AND GROUND OF THE TRUTH IN THE CHURCH OF GOD'S WITNESSES.

This is, beyond question, the mighty central evidence of Christianity; namely, the character of Christ in this one respect of the ability to take away sin, the authority and power in Himself to forgive sin; and therefore His coming from the Father, according to the promise in the Old Testament Scriptures, for this one object, the forgiveness and sanctification of mankind. To this demonstration, so much needed in the greatest possible clearness and power, all Christ's miracles were turned; for this object He and the Father worked them together, the Father in attestation of the Son, the Son in proof of His divine oneness with the Father. He takes in hand the greatest outward and inward proofs of human misery, and manifestations of the dreadful power and consequences of human guilt in the body and the soul. He takes the leper, banished from society, and the palsied and bedridden, and those possessed of evil spirits, and wandering in the congregation of the dead; sometimes at their own prayer, sometimes at the prayer of others; but always for this one compassionate and merciful purpose, to lead the souls of the lost in confidence to Himself, to draw them into that faith, and so bring them back to God. The object of all miracles from the beginning of the world and its human apostacy, is just this, to turn men's hearts from sin and Satan unto God, to induce them to apply with faith to Him, for the *greatest* of all miracles, and the most necessary of all blessings, even the forgiveness of their sins.

To make that forgiveness the covenanted inheritance of all believers in God was the object of Christ's assuming our nature, Christ becoming incarnate, and living a *divine-human* life on the earth. But for that, there were no need of His coming, nor justification of His dying, if there were no eternal death in sin beyond the grave, and therefore no need of forgiveness; if men without forgiveness were not lost forever, or if they could have been forgiven without His death. For what reason for His coming, to seek and to save that which was never lost? What reason, if that which was lost was only temporarily mislaid, and sure of a final recovery in the natural working of things, there being no such reality or possibility as that of the eternal death and ruin of a soul in God's universe, but all souls as sure of coming at last to the glory and happiness of God's eternal kingdom, as of having begun their existence? Therefore the demonstrations of God's law, the preparations for Christ's coming, the array and continuance of miracles, the sudden rush and glory of them at His advent, as witnesses of God for Him; and the combination of awful warnings, and infinite seraphic promises and assurances contained in them.

They were God's alarm-bells and Jubilee chimes

of salvation; the red lights of warning, and the trumpets of the watchmen, as in Isaiah, Jeremiah, Ezekiel. The soul that sinneth it shall die! God's *tocsin;* the axe laid at the roots of the tree; the whole universe astir with flames, and vocal with messages, to awaken the soul, and call it from the reign of death to Him who alone gives life; to hear Him, to believe in Him, to be healed by Him, and restored to eternal health and blessedness. They were the convergency of all trains of knowledge and demonstration, and all modes of God's providential discipline, upon that infinitely blessed message, set vibrating in men's hearts, consciences, and reason, from the very beginning of sin and death in human nature: "Behold the Lamb of God that taketh away the sin of the world!"

"Good and upright is the Lord; therefore will He teach sinners in the way of Life;" nor is there anything that can or could be done for this purpose, that He has not set in motion, to make men see, feel, and know their need of such divine intervention.* The intervention promised was the be-

---

* Consider the exquisitely beautiful condensed description in Herbert's Sonnet, of the warning, loving, and inviting, redeeming discipline of God, in the Word and its institutes, for the good of all mankind:—

  "Lord, with what care hast Thou begirt us round!
  Parents first season us; then schoolmasters

ginning of the proof; the intervention completed and experienced is the completion and fulfilment of the proof, brought down for every man's trial or experiment, and laid as it were at the threshold of every man's soul as of old at Cain's, a sin-offering at the door; or as at the escaping of the Hebrews from Egypt, the sprinkling of blood upon the doorposts; an experiment for every family and every man to make by themselves, by the exercise of their own faith. This experiment was what Christ demanded, and still demands, of each person, because each person can make it. Each man is his own scientific laboratory, for himself, with all the means requisite for investigation and satisfaction of the truth. Religion is most perfectly of all things the science of experiment and demonstration. There is no uncertainty about it, and all radical doubt in regard to

> Deliver us to laws; they send us bound
>   To rules of reason; holy messengers—
> Pulpits and Sundays; sorrow dogging sin;
>   Afflictions sorted; anguish of all sizes;
> Fine nets and stratagems to catch us in;
>   Bibles laid open; millions of surprises;
> Blessings beforehand; ties of gratefulness;
>   The sound of glory ringing in our ears;
> Without, our shame; within, our consciences;
>   Angels and grace; eternal hopes and fears:—
> Yet all these fences, and their whole army,
> One cunning BOSOM-SIN blows quite away!"

it is just merely a consequence of not trying the experiment for ourselves.

But after all, experiment is only an aid to our faith, only a servant, not the master. Experiment beyond the grave is impossible in this world; all our knowledge of what takes place there, must be from God's testimony, on God's authority, received from Him by faith in Him, without which faith it is, in the nature of things, impossible to please God. This faith, followed by its consequences through the invariable attendance and grace of God's Spirit in the soul, produces witnesses that the most rigid science can have nothing to object against. This faith wrought these qualifications of a witnessing demonstration in our Lord's apostles and earliest disciples, by the working of truths drawn from the only divine revelation ever given from Heaven, and put beyond dispute by the transformation of their own characters from common human nature and life into the character and life of Christ, as formed in them the hope of glory, and they themselves changed into His image from glory to glory, by His Spirit dwelling in them.

The Church of such witnesses is THE PILLAR AND GROUND OF THE TRUTH, holding forth the Word of Life, lifting up on high, in the sight of heaven and earth, THE VOLUME OF THE REVELATION OF GOD IN CHRIST, RECONCILING THE WORLD UNTO HIMSELF; a life-giving demonstration of the Scriptures, acting them out, teaching, interpreting, dramatizing, attracting; constituting, in visible immortality, from generation to generation, such a living temple and *Shekinah* of Christ's spiritual power and glory, that the gates of hell can never prevail against it.

XVIII.

DEMONSTRATION OF A SPIRITUAL ETERNAL KINGDOM OF GRACE AND GLORY—ALL NATIONS SHALL CALL HIM BLESSED, AND THE WHOLE EARTH SHALL BE FILLED WITH HIS GLORY.

All this is divinely-revealed prediction and fulfilment with thousands of years of growth and preparation between the first announcement and the Pentecostal result. Then proceeds, with miraculous power and glory, the ministry of the witnesses, in "the preaching of Jesus Christ, according to the revelation of the mystery made manifest by the Scriptures of the Prophets, and by the commandment of the Everlasting God made known to all nations for the obedience of faith." "That in the ages to come, and unto principalities and powers in heavenly places, might be known by the Church the manifold wisdom of God; that the name of our Lord Jesus Christ may be glorified in His saints, and they in Him, according to the grace of our God and the Lord Jesus Christ."

All this is the reality of a spiritual Eternal Kingdom of believing regenerated souls; a kingdom of witnesses by experimental knowledge; the nature of which kingdom is openly illustrated in the character and conduct of its new-created subjects and citizens, and by facts seen and known, and holy principles, eternally active through the operation of divine truths breathed within the soul by the Holy Spirit; truths first postulated as infallible for man's guidance, and then presented for voluntary trial and belief, that there may be a free, heart-felt, unbiased reception of them; and then and thus, with open appeal to every man's reason and conscience in the sight of God, demonstrated both by individual experience and external testimony.

And so accords our Lord's own announcement beforehand: "Ye shall receive power after that the Holy Ghost is come upon you; and ye shall be witnesses unto Me both in Jerusalem, and in all Judea, and in Samaria, and unto the uttermost part of the earth;" witnesses unto Me, for this purpose, to open men's eyes, and to turn them from darkness to light, and from the power of Satan unto God, "that they may receive forgiveness of sins, and inheritance among them that are sanctified by faith that is in Me." Witnesses to Me through experience of the same new-creating life given unto you that ye may transmit it unto them, and they unto others. This divine testifying power and magnetism of faith in Christ was to pass down through the whole Church of witnesses to the last day; and for one and the same mighty purpose of divine benevolence it was sealed to a certainty of fulfilment by our Lord's wondrous prayer: "Neither pray I for these alone, but for those who shall believe on Me through their word; that they all may be one, as Thou, Father, art in Me, and I in Thee, that they also may be one in us, that the world may believe that Thou hast sent Me. And the glory which Thou gavest Me I have given them, that they may be one, even as we are one. I in them and Thou in Me, that they may be made perfect in one, and that the world may know that Thou hast sent Me, and hast loved them, as Thou hast loved Me."

So, then, the perfection of Christian evidence, that which God's reason in God's Word and in man's mind demands as the ground of absolute knowledge,—that the world MAY KNOW, that it may be put beyond reasonable doubt by such knowledge from such testimony—is the visible immortality on earth, from generation to generation, of such a witnessing church as was predicted and described in the Old Testament, and assumed and established by Christ in the New, against which the gates of hell should never prevail. Let any man connect and compare some of the battalion passages in Moses and the prophets and the psalms, with those in the gospels, Acts, and epistles, and he will see realized the sublime imagery in Ezekiel, of "the whirlwind of fire infolding itself, and the living creatures running and returning as the appearance of a flash of lightning, and the noise of their wings, like the noise of great waters, AS THE VOICE OF THE ALMIGHTY."

Let him take such psalms as the 22d, 45th, 48th, 66th, 68th, 72d, 78th, 89th, 102d, 110th, 145th, along with Isaiah, chapters xlix. to liii. and lv., lix. and lx., lxi. and lxii.; and then in connection in the New Testament, Matt. xvi. 18; John xv. 26, 27; xvi. 13; xvii. 20, 21;—Eph. i. 17-23; ii. 19-22; iii. 8-10; iv. 12-16; —I Tim. iii. 15, 16. The comparison is overwhelming; the succession of proofs is drawn out, from generation to generation, and was concentrated by Peter in his first sermons to Jews and Gentiles, beginning with Abraham, Moses, and all the prophets, as in the following passages in chapters iii., v., and x. of the Acts of the Apostles: "The Word which God sent unto the children of Israel, preaching peace by Jesus Christ; He is Lord of all; how God anointed Jesus of Nazareth with the Holy Ghost and with power; and we are witnesses of all things which He did, and of

His death and resurrection, having eaten and drunk with Him after He rose from the dead; and He commanded us to preach unto the people, and to testify that it is He who was ordained of God to be the Judge of quick and dead."

"To Him give all the prophets witness, that through His name whosoever believeth in Him shall receive remission of sins. Him hath God exalted, a Prince and Saviour, to give repentance to Israel, and forgiveness of sins. And we are His witnesses of these things; and so is also the Holy Ghost, whom God hath given to them that obey Him."

Now there is no break in this reasoning, nor any possibility of forgery or mistake; for it is grounded on experience, and is open to the examination of all persons willing to make trial of that faith that is challenged in all rational creatures, and invariably produces the assurance of eternal life. "And this is life eternal, that they might know Thee the only true God, and Jesus Christ whom Thou hast sent."

Nothing less than this can be the perfection of heavenly and earthly science united. It is infinite, celestial, Christian evidence, leaving no loophole or excuse for unbelief; the very method of proof, which God's reason, in God's Word and in man's mind demands, as the ground of absolute knowledge. It is the Lord of all, the Author of Eternal Salvation, the

Author and Finisher of Faith, who begins and completes in Himself, as God and man, this science for the universe, this demonstration of all power in heaven and on earth.

This, and nothing less, is the infinitely glorious conclusion of the 72d Psalm; even the fulfilment of that promised celestial and eternal glory, wherein "the prayers of David, the son of Jesse, are ended." "He shall deliver the needy when he crieth, He shall redeem their souls. Prayer also shall be made for Him continually, and daily shall He be praised. There shall be a handful of corn in the earth on the top of the mountains; the fruit thereof shall shake like Lebanon. He shall have dominion also from sea to sea, and from the river unto the ends of the earth; His name shall endure forever; His name shall be continued as long as the sun: and men shall be blessed in Him. All nations shall call Him blessed. And blessed be His glorious name forever, and let the whole earth be filled with His glory. Amen and amen."

XIX.

THE TEMPTATION IN THE WILDERNESS THE FIRST EXPLANATORY NARRATIVE IN THE GOSPELS—ITS CONNECTION WITH THE ACCOUNT OF THE TRANSFIGURATION, AND THE WALK TO EMMAUS—THEN THE CULMINATING NARRATIVE OF THE CRUCIFIXION, OUT OF THE SAME DIVINE NECESSITY—"IT IS WRITTEN."

The Temptation is *the first grand self-demonstrating narrative in the Gospels*, presenting Christ, acting for us, in our nature, and giving the normal example, the principles, the grammar of life and the germs of motive and of feeling, to guide and inspire us in all our conflicts with evil, and the Evil One. It is the method for our intelligence and heart. As Christ did in the wilderness, when tempted of the devil, so must we do, whose whole pilgrimage, in consequence of sin within us, is that of a temptation through life, by the world, the flesh, and the devil. But having a present God to appeal to as our refuge and strength, and the example of a friend and Saviour who was in all points tempted like as we are, yet without sin, the outstanding lessons and example in this narrative are found in Christ's incessant use of the Word of God, as His only authority and weapon; in the exercise of faith in God as His overmastering, sustaining, inspiring principle and vital power.

The next grand narrative is that of the walk to Emmaus, with the same Scriptures that Christ used for Himself against Satan in the temptation, now disclosed in the full glory and majesty of their significance and purpose in regard to Himself as the Saviour of mankind, and for the complete instruction and arming of believers in Him, to be His witnesses and God's, in and for the work of redemption, in the preaching of the Word, in the publication of the Gospel, in the lifting up of Him upon the cross, whom the Word presents for our salvation, and who has given us to know that if He be so lifted up, He will draw all men unto Himself. Now if our strength for ourselves, in all our personal conflicts, is in the knowledge and use of God's Word by a personal faith, equally or much more are such knowledge and use necessary, and certainly with need of a much wider and more fully instructed comprehension of the same, in our work in and upon the world, as Christ's agents in behalf of others, for the planting, encouragement, and instruction of their faith; and all because, IT IS WRITTEN.

Between these two narratives, there came the vision, and there stands the account of the Transfiguration, which is a double example of Christ's communing with and recalling the Old Testament and His Father's prophets in it, both for His own comfort and strength advancing to His sufferings and death, and for the instruction and confirmation of our faith, when He should have fulfilled in Himself all things testified beforehand in Moses and the prophets. In the temptation in the wilderness, Satan appeared to Him, and proposed that He should save His own life from suffering and death by miracles. In the Transfiguration, Moses and Elias appeared, and spake with Him of His decease, which He should accomplish at Jerusalem. It was Christ communing with the dead but living prophets of the Old Testament, in regard to His own dying and rising and kingdom of glory, even his inheritance of the saints in light, the purchase of His sufferings and death. Peter, James, and John, the representatives and leading spirits of those who were to be the living prophets of the New Testament, were alone admitted to behold His glory and listen to that conversation, in order that they might be the better prepared to bear witness and to preach. Admitted to hear the thunder of the voice of God from heaven, the same that fell at His baptism; but warned that they should submit even this majestic utterance to the Old Testament inspiration; that surer word of prophecy, according to which all procedures were evolved, As IT IS WRITTEN.

The reference to this testimony in the second of Peter's Epistles is in this view very wonderful, as to a thing well known, an event recorded, full of divine glory, and indisputable, and yet of secondary importance to the utterances of God in the Old Testament AS IT WAS WRITTEN. "For we have not followed cunningly devised fables, when we made known unto you the power and coming of our Lord Jesus Christ, but were eye-witnesses of His majesty. For he received from God the Father honor and glory, when there came such a voice to Him from the excellent glory, This is my beloved Son, in whom I am well pleased. And this voice, which came from heaven we heard, when we were with Him in the holy mount. We have also *a more sure word of prophecy*, whereunto ye do well that ye take heed, as unto a light that shineth in a dark place, until the day dawn, and the day star arise in your hearts. Knowing this first, that no prophecy of the Scripture is of any private interpretation. For the prophecy came not in old time by the will of man; but holy men of God spake as they were moved by the Holy Ghost."

Two of the foremost of these holy men of God were now present on the Mount of Transfiguration, permitted to break through the impassable barrier between the Eternal World and this, in order that they might renew their testimony, direct *from* heaven, to the glory of that Being, through the foreseen efficacy of whose blood, shed for the remission of sins, they had already enjoyed a thousand years' *experience of* heaven. They appeared with Him now in glory, and *spake of His decease, which He should accomplish at Jerusalem.*

It was a re-personation of the Word, IT IS WRITTEN, in august living personages, adoring and talking with the Word Incarnate; a crystallization to the spiritual and physical sense of the beholders, of a portion of the heavenly unseen world, with its living glorious inhabitants, and the themes of their absorbing interest. If there had been any doubt or questioning of the resurrection, or future life, of departed human beings, as living on in another world, this would take all that doubt away; but the death and rising again of the Lord Jesus could not be understood by that, save only *in mysterious prediction.* And therefore Christ sealed in them the vision for perfect silence, not to be broken even to the dearest and nearest of the disciples, till His own resurrection *had been seen and known.* "You have seen *these transfigured beings in glory, along with Me, as really living beings as I am.* They, you well know, died, and have not been seen on earth for a thousand years. You have heard the voice of My Father in heaven. I, whom you have seen and known as yet only living, but to-day transfigured, am Myself to be put to death, but *to rise from the dead, the third day*, from the grave in which I shall be laid among you. Tell the vision to no man, *till I am risen from the dead*, when you will know its whole meaning and power, and can relate it, *along with the event of My resurrection*, in your presentation to men of My glory."

So He charged them that they should tell no man what things they had seen, till the Son of man were risen from the dead. And they kept that saying with themselves, questioning one with another *what the rising from the dead should mean.* Peter, James and John had that secret subject among themselves, all the remaining time of their education with Christ, and ever and anon were studying it. But Christ, to their minds, Christ, the Messiah, Christ, the person of Peter's confession, Christ, the Son of the Living God, was *always living*. How should He die? How should He rise again? He who said to Martha, I am the Resurrection and the Life, He who Himself called Lazarus from his grave, how should He die? How *should* death ever have any power over Him?

Because He had power to lay down His life, and

power to take it again. Because this commandment He had received from the Father, and thus in His Father's Book it was written of Him, I delight to do Thy will, O God. It must be fulfilled, *as God had written*, not because the fulfilment was necessary, and must be brought about, in order to save the credit of the prediction, but because *it was God's prediction*, and could not be broken; because heaven and earth might sooner pass away than one jot or tittle of God's Word be unaccomplished. And because, by His voluntary dying, in obedience to God's will, and bearing our sins out of infinite divine compassion, having Himself become a partaker of our flesh and blood, in order that He might do this in body, soul, and spirit in our nature, He, through death, destroyed him that had the power of death, that is the devil, and delivered the life-time subjects of the devil's bondage.

Ought not Christ to suffer these things, and to enter into His glory? The first thing requisite for them to know was, that CHRIST OUGHT, in obedience to His Father's Will, and because IT WAS WRITTEN. The other eternal reasons they should see and know, even in their knowledge of Christ's own glory, by experience and participation of the same. For the present this must suffice—IT IS WRITTEN.

In the walk to Emmaus the receivers and representatives of the information and the glory were not apostles, not of the twelve; and therefore the record possesses an importance, as disclosing an affluent of the great river of inspiration from the Lord Jesus *before it was put in writing*, and showing whence they derived the materials and the illuminating power of their testimony who *spake the Gospel as from the lips of the Lord Jesus, as He Himself gave to them the Word of God with His knowledge of it, and His authoritative interpretation*. This witness is for us, and for all men directly, not through what is called the Apostolate, or any apostolic succession, but as an open reservoir, *that we know to have been set open before our Lord's Ascension*. And we are at liberty to put all the elements in it, which we can discover through the Gospels or in the Epistles to have been drawn at any time by our Lord from the Old Testament Scriptures, or communicated concerning Himself by after inspiration.

In the walk to Emmaus we are ourselves with Christ as our teacher, and are taken by Him into the Word of God entering with Him into the depths, unfathomable, to see the sunken pillars of God's redemptive architecture, and how the new world wherein dwelleth righteousness must rise upon them and out of them, and how every builder and every believer that would possess the infinite honor and happiness of being a co-worker with God in

Christ, and would be prepared for such a glorious ministry, and be successful in it, must work and build upon *that Word as it is written*, and according to it, and to the directions of Christ, everywhere pointing to the plan divine, and giving the specifications. Here was Christ, taking some of the master-builders of His kingdom into His secret studio, and unrolling before them His plan and God's plan, ground plan and upper story, in the Old Testament Scriptures, as God took Moses up into the Mount, and revealed to him and made him understand the plan and specifications of the Tabernacle, and said to him, "See that thou make all things according to the pattern showed thee in the Mount," so also in the same manner He instructed David, and David Solomon, for the building of the Temple. See Ex. xxv. 40, xxvi. 30, and Num. viii. 4, compared with I Chron. xxviii. 11, 12, 19, and Heb. viii. 5.

In the narrative of the Crucifixion, to which every preceding path travels, and without which the Gospels would be vain, and our faith vain, we have everything advancing by divine foreknowledge and plan, transpiring in the same method, by reason of the previous revelation, now coming to its conclusion, with the same divine necessity, As it is written. That is the one thing regarded. There is the same invariable exaltation of the Word in its written exactitude, as the Judge and Determiner of all things. But we have this narrative also recorded by the witnesses, just exactly as its scenery passed before the minds of the disciples, still veiled and darkened, looking on in astonishment and despair, only one person admitted to the full understanding of it, and that, THE THIEF UPON THE CROSS, whose faith was the first triumph and reward of the Redeemer's sufferings.

As yet, that Christ should suffer death they no more knew the meaning of, than that He should rise again from the dead; for with that rising they could as yet connect little more than the idea or belief of continued existence in another world; and it would necessarily take Christ away from this world as the King of glory, and from all their hopes and expectations as Hebrews, of a glorious empire on earth under His Kingship.

They knew not the meaning as yet of any part of the great tragedy; and so it went on, and so the whole is related as to them its events were developed, under that veil. Every step in the history, every betrayal of the victim, every insult, every agony, the scenes of Gethsemane, the words of prayer, the bloody sweat, the desertion of the disciples, related with such inimitable simplicity and severity; not one word or mark of exaggeration or of effort at display; not a shade of coloring put in for effect, but just the hue of living truth, circumstance after circumstance; and the admission, so freely made, that all this was done *that the Scriptures of the prophets might be fulfilled*, but that the disciples did not understand it, and that there was an inexorable necessity of such fulfilment, by which the Son of God Himself was bound. "Thinkest thou that I cannot now pray to My Father, and He shall presently give Me more than twelve legions of angels? But how then shall the Scriptures be fulfilled that thus it must be?" IT IS WRITTEN; and that is My divine necessity, even the written Word of My Father, and that Word as He meant it, without one attempt to vary or escape its meaning or its consequences.

XX.

THINGS TO BE NOTED AS ILLUSTRATED IN THE TEMPTATION—FIRST THE OPENING POSITION OF SATAN, AS THE ACCUSER AND ENEMY OF MANKIND—SECOND, THE DIFFERENCE BETWEEN SATAN'S METHOD, AND THAT OF MODERN INFIDELITY—THIRD, OUR LESSONS FROM HIS EXAMPLE AND THAT OF THE SAVIOUR, "THUS SAITH THE LORD."

We now carry this general survey back to our Lord's history of the Temptation in the wilderness, on our behalf, and continuing our argument, we note first, that the very first temptation of Adam and Eve by the devil was of *doubt as to God's Word;* had He given any word at all, any divine revelation? If He had, was it true? Literally true, or to be taken *cum grano salis,* with conjectures and asides, according to the needs of our self-seeking interpretation? He may have issued the command; but as to the penalty—is that to be taken literally?

By no means, is the answer of the Tempter. There is concealment of the truth under it. For God doth know that ye shall be as gods, knowing good and evil, but not as demons suffering the vengeance of eternal fire.

The form of temptation for the fall of the second Adam was neither of concealment, nor denial, nor misinterpretation of the Word, but the very contrary; ambitious and self-exalting presumption in the application of it; self-seeking as the right rule of blessedness.

Had the Son of God really come? Was this He? Let me try His own belief in the Old Testament Scriptures as the Word of God. Is He sincere? Or can He be tempted to put those Scriptures to use, not in His own sufferings, but for His own ease and grandeur.

The Satan of the temptation is himself a believer in God, but at war against Him, and an unbeliever in the reality of any such thing as true piety, disinterested love, in man. He is the accuser of mankind; he would fain be the accuser with proof against

Christ. If he can succeed in moving Him one hair's breadth from His integrity as the servant of God, to put self in any way, with whatever fair pretence, above God's will, or still more, by pretended conformity with that will, he will gain the whole victory; and even after all the manifestation of heaven at John's baptism of Christ, he will be able, as hell's prince of detectives, to convict Christ as a forger and false prophet; a sinner against God, and therefore by no possibility a Saviour of mankind.

It is remarkable, and full of instruction, that the temptation by which he intended to expose Christ as a forger and false prophet, consisted in this crucial trial of His character, as to His disinterested *loyalty to God and love to man*. Had He really come on earth, as the Son of God, to bruise the serpent's head by dying for sinners? He hoped, as in his torturing work upon Job, more than a thousand years before, to prove that there is no such thing as a self-denying piety on earth, but that all seek their own reward in pleasure and glory, in this world. He hoped, and attempted, to turn Him aside from a supreme regard to the will and Word of God as His law, and from an unchangeable sympathy with God's purposes, and submission of His own to God's will; preferring self-indulgence and power to the cup of death, which the Father had given Him to drink. And the temptation being addressed to Him as a man, and not as God, the superiority, safety, victory of Christ consisted not in His being one with God, but entirely, intensely, infinitely, unchangeably, in body, soul, and spirit, consecrated to God's will, *as made known to men in God's Word;* having no other will but God's, and no possibility of ever preferring His own will in anything whatever, even for an instant. It was not incarnate God-ship merely, but human nature and divine in one perfect, consistent, immaculate manifestation of character; the God-man indeed, but the man Godlike, God-perfect, absolutely, unchangeably, infinitely holy, *as man;* and though in all points tempted like as we are, as man, yet without sin; as man, without one breath or shade of human self-seeking. As man, our infinitely perfect example; as God-man, our Saviour, God in Christ reconciling the world unto Himself, having borne our sins in His own death, at God's will; the iniquity of us all being laid upon Him, as our propitiation, our redemption, through His blood.

Consider, in his use of Scripture, the unexpected testimony of the devil as to what is written in the Old Testament being the true and undisputed Word of God. Any evidence extorted from a criminal, which criminates himself, is of all things most undeniable. It is not, however, extorted, for Satan gives it willingly, and in the most natural way, admitting particular texts of the Old Testament, *drawn especially from Deuteronomy*, as the Word of God. He dares not now, as in the method of the devil with Eve, even ask the question, *Yea, hath God said?* The whole Volume of the Hebrew Scriptures, the Oracles of God, from Genesis to Malachi, had become, by the Will and Providence of God, a possession and prepossession of the whole Hebrew people; and the known designation of that Sacred Volume, as God's own, THE SCRIPTURES, was as limited and definite and certain in its meaning, as any algebraic sign is to-day to the mathematician. The devil no more thought of disputing the Hebrew Canon, as if it were unknown or mistaken, than the formula that two and two make four. IT IS WRITTEN is accepted by the devil himself, as an unquestionable axiom and standpoint of perfect reasoning from God to man. He admits the authority of all that our Lord had quoted from Moses, as divine, and as meant for all mankind. And most remarkable it is, that our Lord's three quotations from God's Word, in this primal and all determining conflict and conquest, were *only from Deuteronomy;* the devil accepting the same, and not the shadow of a suspicion or contradiction permitted to fall upon the book, or the texts, or Moses as the writer.

There is a vast difference between Satan's method in this conflict against the Lord Jesus, and that of modern infidelity against both inspiration and Christianity. Satan not only did not attempt a denial of the supernatural, as impossible, or of verbal inspiration as incredible, but availed himself of the truth and certainty of both; himself, following Christ's method and example, quoted the 91st Psalm, and proposed that Jesus, *if He were the Son of God*, should make experiment of its inspiration accordingly, and justify, in the sight of the whole world, His own confidence in God's protection by it. He attempted neither evasion nor denial, either of Moses' inspiration or authority; but, first opening his batteries of temptation on the ground that *a voice from heaven had declared* Jesus to be the Son of God, he continues the conflict on the admitted grounds of divine inspiration, and receives our Lord's appeal to the Old Testament Scriptures, *without the least question that they are the Word of God*. He does not even interpose that most common form and apology of unbelief, that even if inspiration be admitted, it is in so general a sense, that you cannot assert of any particular phrase or sentence that that is the Word of God; for the words themselves are not inspired, and at best it is only a human historic record of things supposed to have happened.

This is an easy refuge for any man against the

divine authority of any and every part of the Scriptures, which he does not relish, and wishes to reject. It is a shield against all the arrows of divine truth, even as, on the other hand, a true faith in God's Word, and in the Lord Jesus Christ, as presented there, is a shield from the armory of heaven against all the fiery darts of the Wicked One.

They who deny a plenary inspiration of the Scriptures, and they whose theology accepts such denial, and proceeds upon it, cut themselves off from all power in the Word of God, from all ability to stand forth in His name, under His authority, proclaiming, *Thus saith the Lord*.

But the Saviour of the world, in His ministry, unquestionably affirms *a verbal inspiration*, stands upon every word that proceedeth out of the mouth of God. EVERY WORD, for, indeed, if not, then a new revelation would be needed, to teach us which were, and which were not the very words of God in this volume; for those that are not would surely be merely human, fallible, of no authority. But the Lord Jesus founded His kingdom on no such quicksands, nor ever sent His disciples to any such school of uncertain theology, but gave them the very words of God wherewith to grapple, and whereby to hold, a world lying in wickedness.

Nor did Satan himself take *any other ground*. He

accepted our Lord's appeal, and stood upon the same theory of such an inspiration of the Scriptures, as makes *all that is written in them the very Word of God*. That is true faith in God, and loyalty to Him, which is faith in God's Word, and abides by it, and acts accordingly. And it was by such use of God's Word, that our Lord put Satan to flight, and not by any array of angels or any exercise of supernatural power, but by doing what He knew to be the will of God, *as it was written;* by drinking the cup which the Father had given Him. Thus was cast out the great dragon, "that old serpent called the devil, and Satan, which deceiveth the whole world." Our blessed Lord might have launched at him a single thunderbolt, and transfixed him in that bottomless pit, from whence, by mysterious permission he had broken loose, and was now ranging up and down Judea, seeking whom he might devour. He might have set Michael the Archangel again upon him, to rebuke him, or to remand him, under chains of darkness to the judgment of the Great Day. But He simply smote him with *the sword of the Spirit, which is the Word of God*, and that was enough. He used no other argument, no other compulsion than that of *divine truth*, in the simplest, plainest announcement of the will of God. He gave no other reason but this, *that God says it*, and that settled the matter. Even so His disciples were to overcome the Accuser, the Diabolos of mankind, "by the blood of the Lamb, and by the word of their testimony"; loving not their lives unto the death.

It was an example for us all, for the ministry, for the churches, in the conflict against sin and Satan. We must throw ourselves on God's Word, and use it, and apply it, *not as the word of man, but as it is in truth, the very Word of God only.* We are not to be afraid of it, nor to play at blind-man's buff with it; (see II Cor. iv. 4), we are not to doubt it, we are not to withhold it, nor conceal it, we are neither to suffer its perversion, nor to thrust it as a sword into the scabbard, instead of into men's hearts and iniquities, but we are to draw it forth and smite with it on every side. Neither man's expediency nor permission is to be the rule, but only God's Word. *Thy Word have I hid in mine heart that I might not sin against Thee.* But again, "I have *not hid Thy righteousness* within my heart, I have *preached righteousness* in the great congregation. I have not refrained my lips, O Lord, Thou knowest. I have declared *Thy faithfulness and Thy salvation.* I have not concealed Thy loving kindness and Thy truth."—Ps. xl. 10.

No emergency could have happened, no mischievous contingency been brought about by Satan, to which our blessed Lord would not have instantly applied some pertinent and commanding passage or example. "For the Word of God is quick and powerful, and sharper than any two-edged sword," and illimitable and eternal in its search and application, "piercing even to the dividing asunder of soul and spirit, and of the joints and marrow, and is a discerner of the thoughts and intents of the heart." Our Lord needed no other library, no other weapon, no other education; neither needs any Christian, for that is all in all.

XXI.

THE CHARACTERISTICS AND LIMITATIONS OF INSPIRATION, AS THUS SETTLED BY OUR LORD — ITS DEFINITIONS FROM GENESIS TO THE APOCALYPSE, THE SAME—THE AMOUNT OF CHRIST'S TESTIMONY ON THE LOWEST COMPUTATION—CHRIST'S OWN VERACITY INVOLVED AS THE WITNESS FOR GOD—STEPS IN THE HISTORY OF THE TEMPTATION —THE FINAL DEMONSTRATION WROUGHT OUT BY IT.

If there be inspiration at all, it is in this volume called by Christ, THE SCRIPTURES; and the volume being of many ages, the inspiration is one and the same in all, and is proved by its own signs and seals. If a river runs under ground, but reappears after a great distance, you may demonstrate its identity, by its qualities, its fishes, the very mud that it carries and deposits; and if it disappears again for a season you may know it when it again rises to the light. It cannot be salt water in one place and fresh in another.

The volume must be one, known in all its parts by the presence of the same inspiration. "*Thy Word is true from the beginning, and every one of thy righteous judgments endureth forever.*" If the Redeemer of men says, "*In the volume of The Book it is written of Me,*" and we know the parts of that volume that were in it when the Redeemer referred to it, we know that all those parts were there by the same infallible inspiration.

By what language, in what terms, is this inspiration intimated, in the volume itself from which the Redeemer quoted? The following instances are drawn from the Old Testament, to which Christ always referred as the only divine authority given among men. No reliance can be placed upon language, if the words in which God conveys His own thoughts, and sets forth the law of an eternal salvation, are not inspired.

These testimonies are from Genesis and Deuteronomy down to Isaiah, Daniel, Malachi,—the whole collection of *the Scriptures* known in Christ's time as the Law, the Prophets, and the Psalms; no other inspired Scriptures existing in the world. Christ's integrity in quoting one authenticates all.

"He that made them at the beginning said." "God commanded, saying." "By every word that proceedeth out of the mouth of God shall man live." "Remember ye the law, which I commanded in Horeb." "Every Word of God is pure; He is a shield unto them that put their trust in Him." "Add thou not unto His words, lest He reprove thee, and thou be found a liar." "The Law of the Lord is perfect, converting the soul; the testimony of the Lord is sure, making wise the simple, the statutes of the Lord are right, rejoicing the heart; the commandment of the Lord is pure, enlightening the eyes." "The Words of the Lord are pure words as silver tried in a furnace of earth, purified seven times." "As for God, His way is perfect; the Word of the Lord is tried; He is a buckler to all those who trust in Him." "Ye shall not add unto the Word which I command you, neither shall ye diminish aught from it, that ye may keep the commandments of the Lord your God." "Whatsoever thing I command you, observe to do it; thou shalt not add thereto, nor diminish from it." "To the Law and to the testimony! If men speak not according to this Word, it is because there is no light in them." "My Spirit which is upon thee, and My words which I have put in thy mouth shall not depart out of thy mouth, nor out of the mouth of thy seed, nor out of the mouth of thy seed's seed, saith the Lord, from henceforth and forever."

Now the assurance of this testimony is in the words of the Lord Jesus, affirming nothing less than the authority of a verbal inspiration in the Old Testament Scriptures, as binding upon the Son of God Himself. Is the testimony honest? Is it true? Whatever latitude, under the pressure of things not yet by us understood, difficulties not explained, perhaps as yet inexplicable, we may be compelled to admit in our definitions, or in our speculations concerning the requisite characteristics of an infallible divine inspiration, *these affirmations in regard to the Hebrew Scriptures as the Word of God, are Christ's Words, and His character is staked upon them.* Are they honest, unexaggerated, to be received in the length and breadth of their fair meaning?

Let us see. On the lowest computation of infidelity, the testimony is that of a good man. The very scoffers at a divine revelation admit the goodness, the honesty, the unquestionable integrity, in the perfect character of Christ. He is an unimpeachable witness. They who reject every other part of divine revelation sometimes assure us that they receive without hesitation the words of Jesus as true. They admit that Christ was goodness incarnate, truth and love without mixture and without deception. But here is the testimony of such a Being, the personification and example of righteousness and goodness to the race; His testimony as to *His own rule of life and conduct*, as to the infallible perfection of that rule, and as to its supreme and unquestioned authority *over all mankind*. An unhesitating regard to it, and obedience of it, are presented as the principle of His own character, the inflexible determination of His conduct in all things; and He declares that what it is for Him it must be for all men, their sole and authoritative rule.

Now if this testimony is not true, those Scriptures are not true, and the Lord Jesus knew it; and we have this acknowledged trustworthy and good Being, the admitted personification and example of all goodness, basing His whole life upon a known lie; setting out in His public ministry of self-denying and suffering benevolence with the proclamation of an enormous falsehood as the foundation of it, and a compulsion in it, and endeavoring to impose the same falsehood upon the whole human race.

But this huge, vast swindle is inconsistent with the lowest supposition of any goodness or honesty whatever in the Being who, under such solemn circumstances, on such a stupendous theatre, publishes this testimony.

The Old Testament Scriptures must therefore be received as the perfect Word of God, or this witness, whose words are claimed above all other testimony on earth as being sincere and true, and whom all men acknowledge to be the most perfect example of purity and truth, is infinitely deceitful and wicked, the very Alpha and Omega of falsehood; imposing, under the guise and influence of assumed goodness the greatest of all possible forgeries, an uninspired, imperfect, human production, as the authoritative revelation of Jehovah for all creatures.

We are shut up to this dilemma. Either this book, these written revelations, to which God in Christ refers mankind, are the Words of God, and we are bound to receive and obey them as such, or Christ Jesus, the admitted personification and reality of truth and love, on whose testimony this fact of divine inspiration stands, is a false witness, a person of incontestable and immeasurable wickedness.

This wondrous Being, the light of life, the light of the world, the incarnation of love and mercy, who went about doing good, who could stand amidst malignant enemies, and say, with His life and character as transparent in their view as the air of their own landscape, "Which of you convinceth Me of sin?"—this Being, in the admiration and eulogy of whose moral loveliness and glory, with the transcendent beauty and grandeur of His life and death, the genius of unbelievers themselves has been exalted and employed, is the greatest of deceivers, and the light that was in Him was darkness, if the Old Testament Scriptures, to which He applied the comprehensive designation of "all that is written in Moses and the Prophets and the Psalms," were not the divinely inspired revelations of His Father.

Christ was predicted in the Scriptures in various ways as the Sun of Righteousness, the Light to lighten the Gentiles, and the glory of His people Israel. He was to be the teacher and interpreter of God's Word, and the exemplar, the divine model of obedience to it, and of all the divine perfections described in it. And when He came, He was such a Being, fulfilling all these promised characteristics in Himself, and manifesting the divine glory. A Being, whose words are as suns, mountains of light, words that are spiritual creators, chronometers, artesian wells, living principles for infallible guidance, charts in unknown stormy seas, safety lamps for laborers in mines and labyrinths of sin and of death. He could stand on the throne of God and say in His name, "Heaven and earth shall pass away, but My words shall not pass away." They shall shine, when the Pleiades and the North Star are extinguished. They shall light your way through death and eternity. "I am the Light of the world. He that followeth Me shall not walk in darkness, but shall have the light of life."

And all His arrangements and institutions on earth, all the forms in which He wielded infinite power, and crystallized infinite wisdom in organizations for man's good, were in the same spirit of the Father's all-loving will and Word, as *His* will. The Sabbath was made for man in love, and therefore He, the Son of man the Saviour, was Lord of it, in redeeming love; and hath all God's authority over it, to make it perpetually His own day of love and worship, to put into the heart of it His dying love, His sufferings, death, resurrection, to give to all mankind the light of life in it, as an inalienable heritage and inseparable fixture of life-giving truth; a Sabbath which should be the gift of God to the whole world, and the glory of the Word in preaching Christ crucified, for the chief of sinners; so to make it man's refuge and rest from toil and temptation, letting down by it the air of heaven over every man's homestead, in which the household plants may grow, and no man or state, or human authority shall take away its holy freedom, or drive their trains of traffic and amusement over it.

The Sabbath and the Saviour are alike from God for man, to make men partakers of God's holiness and happiness and glory; to save them from themselves, and from the despotism of Satan, and from the legions of sins, and temptations to unbounded irreligion and sensual indulgence, which, under the pretence of a progressive scientific socialism, are whirling society to perdition.

The Sabbath is Christ's own Day for heaven's gifts unto men, to fit men for heaven, by making them partakers and possessors of heaven's blessedness on earth. It is not an exaction, or a tax from God upon humanity, or a robbery, or imposition of spiritual bondage, but a jubilee of freedom for Satan's bond-slaves; a redemption of our time, our days, our weeks, for ourselves and our own mercies, because we are so depraved, so turned away from God, and in subjection to appetite and passion, that we are neither willing nor able to take care for ourselves of our divine interest and welfare.

XXII.

THE FINAL DEMONSTRATION OF THE CROSS, AND ITS PRACTICAL POWER—THE LIMITATIONS OF CHRIST'S OMNIPOTENCE BY HIS DIVINE NATURE—HIS WORK AS APPOINTED BY GOD'S WORD—THE BLESSEDNESS OF A PARTICIPATION IN HIS SUFFERINGS.

"I AM the Good Shepherd: the Good Shepherd giveth His life for the sheep. Therefore doth My Father love Me, because I lay down My life that I might take it again. This commandment have I received of My Father."—John x. 18.

And now for the last divine, unassailable proof of the eternal truth and life-giving power of these Scriptures, through the life and death of Jesus, for the new creation of our being in God's holiness! Even so, we hasten to the Cross;—through the storm of hell in the malice of men and devils, hurrying Jesus through mockeries, cruelties, jeers, blasphemies, tortures, to the last tragedy. And in all that highway of sacrifice and suffering, agony and endurance, the tempting work of Satan is terrific though unseen; and Christ Himself at every step is in the dreadful conflict treading the wine-press alone, and of the people none with Him. But He shields His own, though they reject and desert Him. How wonderfully, at the gleam of the sword of the Spirit in the blows of the conflict, the central, all-governing and absorbing truths of eternity and salvation flash forth as streams of fire within and around the soul.

And the intensest and most blessed significance of all, for us, the infinitely blessed opportunity of being made like Christ, possessors of His Spirit, sons and heirs of God with Him, and even partakers of His sufferings, and of His absolute inability to do anything or desire anything contrary to God's

Word and will! That is infinite perfection, that is eternal life, that the being filled with all the fulness of God. Glorify God is the rule of heaven, and of love, and of all good beings. Glorify, and enjoy self, save thyself, is the rule of death and hell, and of the carnal mind, at enmity against God.

"If thou be the Christ, the Anointed of God, the King of Israel, come down from the Cross, and SAVE THYSELF." The blasphemers by classes are set down in the gospels, scoffing and cursing. The people, and the rulers with them, derided Him, saying, He saved others, let Him SAVE HIMSELF, if He be Christ the chosen of God. The soldiers also mocked Him, If Thou be the King of the Jews, SAVE THYSELF. And one of the malefactors railed on Him, saying, If thou be the Christ, SAVE THYSELF AND US. The chief priests with the Scribes and elders said, He saved others; HIMSELF HE CANNOT SAVE. "If He be the King of Israel let Him now come down from the Cross, and we will believe Him. He trusted in God; let Him deliver Him now, if He will have Him; for He said, I am the Son of God." Thus were these accusations and taunts repeated at successive intervals, and shot forth by all classes, as fiery darts, railing upon railing, blasphemy upon blasphemy, against God and His anointed, even as predicted in the prophetic 2d Psalm.

It was like the roll of musketry from regiment after

regiment, battalion succeeding battalion, with the boom of fresh parks of artillery, stationed at all points in command of the field of battle!

And the central object of attack and conquest, a Cross, with a dying Man nailed upon it, between two thieves; but over the cross, over His own head, the reality, engraved of God, the truth, for the assertion and fidelity of which He was dying; the inscription, meant by the Jews as an accusation, but written by Pilate under divine constraint, the Messiah's Kingly Diadem of suffering and glory,—This is Jesus of Nazareth, the King of the Jews!

Would the blasphemies and taunts move Him, who had foreseen them all? How terrific had been the spectacle, how full of horror and darkness for the universe, had the Son of God stepped down from the Cross, and assumed the Crown, saving Himself from that death, which He came into the world to endure that He might save others!

Could the instigator of these blasphemies have imagined that they would succeed? There must have been some such supposition of a possibility, even as in the wilderness. If Thou be the Son of God, it is God's will that Thou shouldst save *Thyself*, and all men will adore Thee.

SAVE THYSELF! That is supreme, self-chosen law, for fallen humanity! That was the intended sting of all these darts; the venom of the poison of the Tempter was in them all in that suggestion, as at the first. When Satan put it into the heart of Judas to betray Christ, perhaps his success with the traitor was owing to that suggested hope of the devil, that Christ might yet be persuaded to draw back from death, might not suffer Himself to be given up to the will of His crucifiers, and thus, as Satan intended, He would demonstrate Himself a selfish impostor, by setting His own salvation before the promise and the will of God.

SAVE THYSELF! That was the suggestion and the hope conveyed by Peter's word at the beginning, and attempted violence at the close, which was but an imitation of the work of the Tempter in the wilderness, Save Thyself. Then said Jesus unto him, "Put up again thy sword into his place: for all they that take the sword shall perish with the sword. Thinkest thou that I cannot now pray to My Father, and He shall presently give Me more than twelve legions of angels? But how then shall the Scriptures be fulfilled, that thus it must be?"

And now comes the climax of all the proofs thus far of the sinlessness of Jesus, and His infinite spotless superiority to all mankind, in the actual annihilation of self at the will of God, even when He might, had He chosen, by prayer to God, have done otherwise. For when, by this answer to Peter, and this refusal of all help from heaven and earth, it was manifest that the Lord Jesus was really resolved to carry the Scriptures of the Prophets into a literal fulfilment of the Father's word and sword against Himself, *then all the disciples forsook Him, and fled.*

But Peter followed Him afar off, unto the high priest's palace, and went in, and sat with the servants, to see the end. It was as if he had said within himself, I will not, even yet, give up all hope; but if He does permit Himself to be condemned, I will deny *Him*, and will perform the first of all claims upon humankind, to save myself. And not till Jesus, from the midst of the mockings, and scourgings, and blindfoldings and blasphemies of His crucifiers, turned and looked upon Peter,—not till then, and under that look of compassionate anguish and reproach and forgiveness, did Peter realize what he had done, and how Christ's own prayer was saving him.

And yet the Lord Jesus could not save Himself. It was the law of redemption given by the Father, consented to by the Son, and made known by divine revelation, that without the shedding of blood, His own blood, and the tasting of death for every man through that propitiatory sacrifice, there could be no remission of sins. If Thou be the Christ, save Thyself and us! Thyself first, and every self-seeker shall forever be justified. Thyself first, and that will be the lesson for us, which our self first will gladly accept and keep: but not self last, not self-denial.

Thyself first, and us by Thy divine power, not Thy divine self-renunciation! Come down from the cross, and we will *believe Thee*, and Thou mayst *save us!* Come down from the cross! It is the cross that we deny; not Thee. Come down from the cross, and take the crown; we will put it upon Thee.

The devil that put it into the heart of Judas to betray Christ, and of Peter to deny Him, put it also into the heart of His crucifiers to make this proposition to Him. And at any time Christ could have put an end to all this agony, and changed the scene into triumph. While life lasted, He had the power to have avoided death, and to have put away from Himself, from His own soul, the cup which the Father had given Him, and which He drank openly, as on "the central gallows of the universe."

Himself He cannot save! It is the last seal of inspiration, of infinite truth, of divine love, a testimony of supernatural mystery and meaning and power, ministered even by Satan, and the soldiers, and the men that drove the nails, and the priests that had secured His dying, and the disciples who forsook Him and fled. In the very nature and essence of His all-conquering and suffering benevolence, Himself He cannot save! He was crucified through this weakness, but it was the strength of God, the cannot of omnipotence and infinite love. He cannot deny Himself. He cannot come down from the cross, for He made it for Himself, and bore our sins upon it. "Now is my soul troubled, and what shall I say? Father, save Me from this hour? But for this cause came I unto this hour. Father, glorify Thy name! Then came the voice from heaven, I have both glorified it, and will glorify it again." Trouble, even unto death may be the very place, the very time, the very experience unto which we have been appointed by the Father to do His work, to accomplish the glory of His divine love among men.

Himself He cannot save! It is only through His own death, that He is life and salvation to others; through suffering and death borne meekly, voluntarily, for a sinning, dying, lost world; only thus that He is the light and life of the world; because He will and must save others, by the sacrifice of Himself. What wonderful utterances of the very principle of the Atonement, as by the souls of murderous Caiaphases, inspired against their own purposes and selfish will, and made vocal by the infinite, constraining, prophesying Spirit, uttering Christ's meaning in their own counsels and words, their own selfishness and pride Christ's divine watchword, when they meant their own!

If Thou be THE CHRIST, THE KING OF THE JEWS, said His revilers, save Thyself. A most wonderful crystallization into two words of the principle of sin and human selfishness, brought face to face with the divine principle of suffering love.

The watch-word of the King of Israel, the Saviour of the Jews and of mankind, was this: "Sacrifice Thyself for others"; seek not Thine own, but others' good. The maxim that always *crucifies* Christ is this: *Save thyself.* The maxim that enthrones and honors Christ is this: Lose thyself for Christ's sake, and He will find thee, and thou shalt find thyself in Him. And therefore the inscription over the cross was left by Pilate, *just as he had written it,* in spite of every remonstrance. THIS IS JESUS OF NAZARETH, THE KING OF THE JEWS. This crucified One, Who could not save Himself, and so, in and by this very self-sacrifice, is their ETERNAL KING! This is He: And what I have written, I have written.

And so, the maxim of faith and self-despair—faith out of the bosom of self-despair, beholding Christ, is just this, Lord save me! I perish! Christ on the cross dying, is the power, both of demonstration and salvation; not Christ coming down from the cross where men's malignity and cruelty had nailed Him. But Christ on the cross, bearing our sins, and refusing to put aside this burden, refusing to save

Himself in order that He might save us! That is God's demonstration; that indeed is divine.

The discovery of every man's scientific experiments through life and the trial of life, and so far as he can do it, of death, in his own laboratory, is, I PERISH! The result of every man's own inquiries into the conservation, correlation, and conversion of forces, is just this: It is sin, that is alone conserved, correlated into misery, and converted into death. For sin, when it is finished, bringeth forth death, and nothing but faith in Christ dying for us that we may not die eternally, can stop it.

XXIII.

BEARING OF THE NARRATIVE OF THE RESURRECTION UPON THIS WHOLE ARGUMENT: FIRST, OF CERTAINTY; SECOND, VARIETY; THIRD, CONGRUITY; FOURTH, OF FORGIVENESS AND ASSURED SALVATION, AS IN PAUL'S TESTIMONY IN FIRST CORINTHIANS, FIFTEENTH CHAPTER.

In the narrative of the Resurrection there is the same great and noticeable law, IT IS WRITTEN, bearing all things onward to the mighty invisible predicted triumph; and we have the effect of this amazing event upon the mind, as the successive opening of its wondrous gates discloses the reality, before yet there is calmness and leisure to gather into one conception and belief the whole overwhelming glory; the meaning of the plan of prophecy fulfilled in such an ending. We have the hurry, the amazement, the dismay, the sudden joy, the sudden bursts of doubt and faith, despair and hope; returning disbelief as clouds after the rain, and tempests after the rainbow; the alternations of doubtfulness and certainty, sorrow and joy, tears and smiles, an April day of storm and sunshine; or a storm at sea with lightning at midnight like that upon the lake of Galilee, with Christ walking on the sea, and the terrified beholders of His Majesty themselves crying out for fear in the belief that they have seen a spirit. It is a succession of events, the meaning of which evidently as yet no one knows. It is not yet disclosed, it is not yet comprehended. And the brokenness of the narratives, the inextricable combinations, complications and confusions, as of images flitting with the suddenness of spirits among each other, and across each other's path, and apparently within each other's personal identity, and sometimes not even the presence recognized or remembered, of the very fellow-witness, or dear friend, or brother, who went with you and stood by you and shared your amazement at the overwhelming discovery; so that, if you were put upon the stand and cross-examined, you could not possibly account for it or make it comprehensible, how you should have seen what your companion did not, or how he should have seen and remembered what you did not, though both were equally sincere and earnest, with equal command of all the means of knowing the truth.

It is a most wonderful picture, so that it may almost be affirmed that nothing in the Resurrection is more supernatural, supposing that it did take place, than the contrivance or creation of this forgery of it, and of the conduct of those who saw it, supposing that it did not. It is a narrative that no impostor, nor forger, nor a hundred thousand experts at forgery, though each possessed as great a genius as Shakespeare's could ever have produced. For that lightning-like photograph of the Resurrection transactions is as the revelation of the midnight storm over a vast mysterious country of mountains and hamlets, suddenly disclosed in a flash of lightning shining from the east to the west; everything seen for one moment in startling distinctness, and then gone, and then again partially and momentarily visible, and then again gone in darkness!

Now it is a very remarkable feature of all this testimony, and this demonstration of overwhelming amazement, and yet incredulity, maintaining its hold over them so long, that not one of these witnesses pretends to have seen the Lord Jesus arise. They profess nothing more than just this, that they beheld Him, conversed with Him, ate and drank with Him, and received their commission from Him, in such continuance of demonstration, that when it was concluded by His ascension into heaven, out of their sight, left them no more room for doubt. They had certainly seen Him taken down from the cross, and laid in the grave. If now they should see Him living again, they were competent witnesses; for there is no conceivable jugglery of imposture, by which they could have been deluded. They could not be mistaken about Christ dying. That took place in view of all the world as spectators. But the Resurrection took place irrespective of men's speculations, observations, arguments, efforts; and what is the central evidence, as of the divine self-existence, it took place without witnesses. No created being saw the Resurrection, or God's or Christ's exercise of power in it; there is no description of it, though there is of the earthquake that preceded it, and of the angel from heaven rolling the stone from the door of the sepulchre, and sitting upon it, and saying, He is not here, He is risen!

It was the hiding of God's power; there was no more witness of it, or description, than of the Incarnation. When the Son of God became man, and when He rose from the dead, the mystery of power and glory is alike invisible, secret, divine. No man saw, or knew, or revealed it, as a witness. Only angels told, or were admitted to the honor of telling that Christ had risen, and they did not say that they saw Him rise. Angels were the first preachers of the Resurrection, as they had been of the Incarnation.

He is risen, He is not here, as He said. And go quickly, and tell His disciples that He is risen from the dead. Ye shall see Him in Galilee. Mary Magdalene saw Him first, but her testimony was not believed. And Christ Himself upbraided the eleven for their unbelief and hardness of heart, because they believed not those who had seen Him, after He had risen. The belief of mankind in all ages must necessarily rest upon the testimony of those who have seen; for all mankind could not possibly see for themselves. If, therefore, men required to see and know by demonstration of their own senses, or else would not believe, they must live and die unbelievers, and so dying were lost, even by inexorable necessity of their senses.

For to this very end Christ came, suffered, died, and rose again, that through faith in Him men might be saved from their sins; and if not thus saved, not believing, that they might be saved, then lost. If their testimony of Christ having risen was true, it would be proved true by the results, in a demonstration increasing from age to age, by the glory of the rising kingdom of the risen Lord; if not true, there could be no such results, nor even the possible embryo or beginning of them. But if true, and this transaction, completed and accomplished by God for the salvation of the soul, for the soul's deliverance from sin, and its redemption in the likeness of the risen Saviour, by the power of His own Spirit dwelling in the soul through faith; —then certainly a denial of all this, cutting off the possibility of faith, cuts off also the possibility of salvation.

And therefore, when God Himself presents truth for faith to accept and act upon, it is necessarily infallible; and yet, even while infallible, it necessarily leaves power in the soul to reject it, if it will; the power of free-agency, even of opinion; ability to stand up, even against God's own testimony, and deny it, if it will. Hence the fearful responsibility of men undertaking to deal with God's money, God's truth, to sweat it for the profit of their own business, by selling their own fictions in its place.

Now if this had not been absolute truth, if it had been a studied forgery, it never would have been submitted to mankind with such appearances of carelessness and falsehood. Every vacuum would have been supplied, every incongruity cemented or accounted for; and if it had been a story, the work of premeditated collusion, the four witnesses would have compared notes beforehand, and erased, as far as possible, every trace whether of ignorance or complicity. Therefore we would not change this account, with its apparent discrepancies, even were they tenfold what they are, for the most accurate, perfect, lawyer-like, or mathematically fitted history, that the art of man could execute, or the imagination conceive. The testimony to the truth of Christianity in the very incoherence of these recitals of the fundamental miracle of Christianity, is invaluable.

XXIV.

THE WALK TO EMMAUS, AND ITS KEY TO THE WHOLE SCRIPTURES.

The walk to Emmaus is as the fresh, reviving dawn, and cloudless sunrise after such a storm. It constitutes one of the most interesting and important portions of the whole New Testament, besides holding as in a separate safe the duplicate key to the interpretation of the whole of the Old. It presents Christ to us and to all the world as the sole divine authoritative Commentator on the Word of God, as given for men's salvation. It brings our blessed Lord delightfully near to us, under the most familiar and endearing characters, as our Teacher, Friend, Saviour. We love again and again to walk with these two disciples, to place ourselves in their circumstances, to go back to Judea on that evening of the Resurrection day, and to listen ourselves to the divine Being, expounding unto us in all the Scriptures the things concerning Himself.

We begin with the transactions of the morning. The Saviour had been laid in the grave by Joseph of Arimathea, laid there in his own new sepulchre, wherein never man had been laid; and the darkness of despair seemed to have closed over the prospect. The deed had been accomplished that darkened the earth and the heavens, and yet was the ministration of the light of an eternal salvation over both. The sacred body, during the silence of a whole Jewish Sabbath, reposed within the tomb. The morning of the first day of the week drew towards its dawn. The priests had triumphed, the few disciples trembled and wept. None knew the brightness of the glory that was forever to invest that day. They stole early to the sepulchre, under cover of the darkness, for fear of the Jews, some to perform the last sad offices of love, which the interposition of the Sabbath had prevented their accomplishing, some to see the place, and weep at it, where Nicodemus and Joseph had, on Friday night, laid all that was mortal of Him whom they loved; and some with a half acknowledged hope, they knew not what, connected with the third day after the crucifixion.

So they came unto the sepulchre at the rising of the sun. And they said among themselves, "Who shall roll us away the stone from the door of the sepulchre?" The stone was already rolled away, and they could enter in; but, wonder of wonders, their Lord was gone. The linen clothes were there, and heavenly watchers by an empty sepulchre. A vision of angels surprised them, declaring, "He is risen, He is not here, as He said." The occurrences were as yet too overwhelming for joy; full of trembling and amazement, they hurried to and fro, not knowing what to think. They made a careful examination, and repeated it; but only one of them, the beloved disciple, seems to have seen and believed, on the spot, before meeting Jesus; for as yet they knew not the Scriptures that He must rise from the dead. The words that were told them seemed as idle tales, which they believed not; and the empty sepulchre could not by itself convince them; for plainly, the body might have been removed from it without a resurrection; and such was the assertion of Mary Magdalene to Peter and John: "They have taken away the Lord out of the sepulchre, and we know not where they have laid Him." And so the disciples when they had ascertained the truth, that He was not there, went away again to their own home, leaving Mary at the door of the sepulchre weeping; all of them full of perplexity, wondering in themselves at that which had come to pass, and not knowing what to make of it.

As the disciples sought each their own habitation, the two from Emmaus sought theirs. Would they ever be gathered again in the glad living presence of Him whom they loved? One of them was Cleophas, the brother-in-law of the mother of our Lord. Probably his habitation was at that village, and his companion was some dear disciple, who was going with him to spend the night at his house, where they had often enjoyed, amidst their family circle, the company of our Lord Himself. They left the sepulchre and the city, anxious, sad, doubtful, and astonished. It was seven miles and a half from the city to the village, but they had enough to talk upon, if the walk had been a pilgrimage of seven days.

They talked together of all those things which had happened. How did they perplex themselves with oft-repeated examinations of the strange events which they had heard reported, and partly seen! They never could have believed, before the crucifixion, that the chief priests and their own countrymen would have carried their wickedness so far. They did indeed trust that it was Christ, who should have redeemed Israel, but not by suffering and death. And now they had lost Him forever and as to any possibility of His being still alive, even the vision of angels reported by Joanna and the wife of Cleophas might have been only some new wickedness of the priests themselves, some stratagem of their malice, some deception for a more annihilating disappointment.

So they communed and reasoned, in much darkness, and in great grief, agitation, and excitement of mind. Amidst it all, one thing is manifest, namely, their deep love to Christ; and this it was, in fact, that laid the foundation for the after correction of their mistakes in regard to Him.

"Their views indeed were indistinct and dim,
But yet successful, being aimed at Him."

The poet Cowper, who has given in these two lines so profound and blessed an utterance of the security of the soul that even in weakness and darkness, and from the midst of smoke and anguish—a bruised reed, a heap of smoking flax,—is seeking after Christ, has most beautifully drawn the picture of their feelings, and of their walk and conversation together.

> "It happened on a solemn eventide,
> Soon after He that was our Surety died,
> Two bosom friends, each pensively inclined,
> The scene of all their sorrows left behind,
> Sought their own village, busied as they went,
> In musings worthy of the great event.
>   They spake of Him they loved, of Him whose life,
> Though blameless, had incurred perpetual strife;
> Whose deeds had left, in spite of hostile arts,
> A deep memorial graven on their hearts;
> They thought Him, and they justly thought Him, One
> Sent to do more than He appeared to have done;
> To exalt a people, and to place them high
> Above all else, and wondered He should die."

That was it: they wondered He should die! They wondered, when they remembered that He had said, If any man keep My saying he shall never see death. They had wondered when they heard Moses and Elias speak of His decease at Jerusalem. They wondered when He had said, My Father loveth Me, because I lay down My life that I might take it again. They wondered when they heard Him say, I am the Good Shepherd, and the Good Shepherd layeth down His life for the sheep. And when He said, signifying what death He should die, I, if I be lifted up from the earth, will draw all men unto Me, they, with all the people, wondered, and answered Him, We have heard out of the law that Christ abideth forever. And how sayest Thou, The Son of man must be lifted up? Who is this Son of man? How can He die Himself, who giveth life to others? They wondered because they had heard Him say, I am the Resurrection and the Life. He that believeth in Me, though he were dead, yet shall he live; and whosoever liveth and believeth in Me, shall never die. They wondered, when Mary anointed His feet with spikenard, so that the house was filled with the odor of the ointment, and Jesus said, Against the day of My burying hath she kept this, for the poor always ye have with you, but Me ye have not always. They wondered the more, the longer He staid with them, and the more they beheld His glory, that ever He could be taken from them.

So indeed, it was not so much the want of faith, as it was the superabundance and misdirection of their faith, that affirmed for Him the impossibility of the cross, and the necessity of a self-existence in glory and happiness on earth, of which He would make them also, and all that followed Him and loved Him the beatified partakers. Every day that they staid with Him, and He with them, they were living more and more habitually in the blessedness of His existence, and desired no greater thing than to have

Him with them forever. A little longer, and they would have wished for no other heaven, there was such infinite attraction in His love, such communication of the bliss of heaven in His loving words, so that, ever since they knew Him they had prayed like the restored demoniac sitting peacefully at His feet clothed and in his right mind, that they might abide with Him forever, and He with them. It was their very love, and the fervor of belief in His power and glory, as the coming King of Israel, that made them wonder that He should ever die.

They had seen Him dealing with the powers of nature as a Being of supreme authority over them, commanding even the devils and they obeyed Him, dispensing the forces of life and dispersing the terrors of disease and death, as one might drop syllables from his tongue, or breathe away the frost-work of a winter's night from the windows. This was certainly the King of Israel. Lift up your heads O ye gates, and let the King of glory enter! Ye gates of nature and of life, unfold before Him, that He and all His train may occupy the kingdom of the Lord. Hosanna to the Son of David! For behold He cometh in the name of the Lord, Hosanna in the highest!

It was the inevitable outbreak of the concentration and observance of three years' miracles in power, and yet greater miracles in holiness and love. The wonder was that the hosannas had not broken out long before they did, making the mountains and the vales of all Judea one resounding hymn of praise, and adoration, and that the people could have been kept back from an uproar of the proclamation of their King.

But after all these miracles of grace and glory, who was He? Jesus of Nazareth, the Son of Joseph the carpenter, whose first lesson was that of accepted poverty, humiliation, self-denial, suffering, and simplicity and humility as a little child's. Oh how impossible, when we know what human nature is, under the curse of the habit of self-worship, and self-indulgence, from which Christ came to save us, that they should have understood this, until Jesus Himself had baptized them also with suffering.

With their minds and hearts full of the Old Testament glory, and of wonder, awe and ecstasy at Christ's manifestation of it in miraculous authority and power, and with the confidence that they were all beginning to exercise in Him, as the Christ, the Son of the Living God, it was next to impossible that they should take the suffering and death, which had not yet been demonstrated, and interpret and believe in their light, the august manifestations of glory and grandeur, through which even then they were passing.

They could not see nor understand the Cross,

through the bright cloud that overshadowed them; and though in their hearing Moses and Elias spake of His decease, which He should accomplish at Jerusalem, yet they heard it as dreamers do, when heavy with sleep; and they could only be filled with amazement, as they journeyed with Him towards the holy city, and observed with awe His supernatural brightness.

In the record of the Transfiguration, what wonderful reticence! What infinite dignity in the appearance and disappearance of Moses and Elias! What reverence and sacred awe in the whole transaction, so brief, so unsatisfactory to those who were craving for signs and wonders! "Who appeared in glory and spake of his decease, which He should accomplish at Jerusalem"; but not one word is given of their conversation. Had this been apocryphal, or a forgery to be imposed upon men's credulity, Moses and Elias would have been led into Rabbinical prattle, would have referred to their past existence, would have betrayed the vanity and talkativeness that clumsy forgers have always fallen into in their lies.

But not a word of their communion with Christ is detailed save only that they spake of His decease to be accomplished at Jerusalem. Thither the disciples knew that He was going, and as He Himself had taught them, *to be crucified*. And yet, not one word did they understand; and so entirely was the meaning hidden from them, that even on the mountain the desire of them all was expressed by Peter, in the prayer that they might be permitted then and there to build three tabernacles, one for the Lord, one for Moses, one for Elias. Not a word in behalf of Peter, James, and John! Self, itself, was swallowed up and transfigured in that petition.

They wondered that He should die, and the wonder would have been if they had not wondered. For what had the mighty God, the Father of eternity, the Prince of life, to do with death? They had heard out of the law that Christ, their Messiah, the Desire of nations, abideth forever; He that should come and set up Daniel's predicted everlasting kingdom with such dominion and glory that all people, nations and languages should serve Him; so that the saints of the Most High should take the kingdom and "possess the kingdom forever, even forever and ever."

They had heard that this wonderful Being should Himself eternally reign over them; and certainly He must so do, or these august predictions were lighter than vanity. For what could a dying man do with them, or by them, a man whose breath is in his nostrils? The first enemy that the predicted King of glory should overcome was death; otherwise, like common men, whom God turneth to destruction, and who none of them can keep alive their own soul, "His breath goeth forth, He returneth to His earth, in that very day His thoughts perish;" and what then becomes of His kingdom and His seed forever, and His throne which was to be as the days of heaven, and as the sun and the moon before God, established forever?

So, just in proportion to the greatness of their faith in God and in Christ, and in the word of God, as (with understandings yet darkened), they received it, in regard to Him, was their confidence that He should never die, but that He should live, as the Author and Giver of life, the Ancient of days, and should make all His chosen people Israel, good, wise, holy, happy, like Himself.

They had expected a temporal deliverer, and though that expectation had been much purified from its grossness by their long abode with Christ, yet all the instructions of our blessed Lord could not disabuse their minds of this expectation. They clung to it with such pertinacity and fondness, that it was as a blind to keep them from seeing anything in its true light.

The very miracles that proved Christ's divine power, every one of them confirmed their faith in the continuance of that power, through His divine personality and presence. And they themselves were to sit upon twelve thrones around the throne of His glory. And every one of them that had left houses or lands, parents, brethren, wives, children, for the kingdom of God's sake, were to receive manifold more in this present time, and in the world to come, life everlasting. Well, in order to all this, the Lord and Giver of all this must certainly remain with them, and Himself bestow it upon them. If not His gift, they did not desire it.

The record in Luke's Gospel, xviii. 31-34, is a passage presenting their state of mind a very short time previous to the crucifixion, on occasion of the announcement by Christ of the nearness of that coming tragedy. So completely were their views of the Messiah's kingdom limited to this side the grave, and to the continuance of His existence in this world, that even the scenes of the last three days of our Lord's life at Jerusalem, the exhibitions of infinite condescension and love which He made for their instruction in washing His disciples' feet, and the repeated assurances of what was certainly to happen had little or no effect in convincing them.

One would have thought that His sufferings in Gethsemane, His betrayal, His arraignment, would have been enough to dissipate their delusions; but no, not even the crucifixion itself could cure them. They returned again with His resurrection from the dead;

and even after the forty days still spent by Him on earth, and at the very last moment, just as He was to be received up into heaven, they proposed to Him the question, Lord wilt thou at this time restore again the kingdom to Israel? It was a national prepossession of patriotic and religious pride, and hope, and glory, more powerful, more intense, and unmanageable, because in its origin unquestionably divine, than any similar impulse that ever swayed, or could sway, either rulers or people.

XXV.

THE INEVITABLE RESULT OF THE CATASTROPHE—A DIVINE PRESENCE ALONE COULD HAVE PREVENTED UTTER DESPAIR—IT WAS LOVE TO CHRIST THAT ENLIGHTENED AND PRESERVED THEIR SOULS.

And now the contrast and the clashing, the shipwreck of their brightest hopes, was a ruin that seemed impossible for them to endure. Hopes that had been fostered as the personal inheritance of every mother and daughter and first-born son in Israel, for three thousand years? The mind is at a loss to conceive the extremity of despair and unbelief resulting from such an appalling conclusion as that of this vast tragedy. No wonder that they feared, as they entered into this cloud.

The deepest ignorance and darkness were the necessary result, at first, of all these cherished misconceptions. It was the profoundest mistake that ever any kingdom or nation on earth had been educated upon, and the character of a whole people trained in it from their infancy. It is difficult for us to imagine the amount of exalted faith which must have possessed the hearts and minds of such men as Simeon and Zechariah, and such women as Anna the prophetess, looking for redemption in Israel, and exclaiming, Lord now lettest Thou thy servant depart in peace, according to Thy word, for mine eyes have seen Thy salvation, which Thou hast prepared before the face of all nations, A light to lighten the Gentiles and the glory of Thy people Israel. How could this ever be accomplished through the death of Him in whose eternal life and kingdom they were to reign over the whole earth?

The whole fabric of their hopes had been annihilated, for Christ had died. And there was no possibility for the forgery of a new Christ to have been palmed upon them. The archangel Gabriel, had he come to them from the tomb could not have deceived them. After more than three years of loving communion with Him, and friendship and intimacy such as they had enjoyed, all the universe could not have supplied a counterpart for His place in their affections. For it was not as a mere temporal deliverer that they had loved Him. Our Lord had drawn them by the infinite loveliness of His character, with such a power of attachment, that no exhibition of grandeur in Himself, nor promises of greatness to them, could ever have excited or sustained.

But instead of glory, he had promised them humiliation; instead of riches, poverty; instead of ease, persecution; instead of self-enjoyment, tribulation; instead of honor in this world, disgrace and contempt; instead of a throne, the prison; instead of a crown, the cross. And yet they loved Him! Most remarkable phenomenon! They had been with Him by night and by day, and they could not help loving Him. They loved Him in spite of themselves, in spite of their own ambition, in spite of all His assurances of persecution and distress, in spite of all His rebukes of their spirit of worldliness, in spite of all His repeated denial and destruction of their temporal hopes and expectations; still they loved Him. They loved Him indeed, with a deeper love, the more He broke their hold on the plans and things of this world, the more He severed them from all that as men and as Jews they held dear. The more He chastened their spirits, and taught them His grand lesson of lowliness and self-denial, the more they loved Him. The nearer He brought them to Himself in spirit, the more entirely they loved Him and rested in Him, and found in His love the beginning of eternal life.

There is something infinitely beautiful and convincing in this exhibition of the power of our Lord's character. They had discovered in Him a Being, to know and to love whose personality, was the very peace of God, that passeth all understanding, was perfect rest and blessedness to the soul. No other such Lord of life, and Giver of conscious blessedness could ever be known or imagined in the world. For this reason they could not be imposed upon. The forger would have been detected the instant he appeared. And so, these loving, trusting, simple-minded, but keenly and morally discerning men, in whose hearts no place could be found but for Christ crucified, were chosen as the fittest first witnesses of His resurrection when they should have received its proof. They knew *whom* they had believed, and could no more be deceived by another, than Jesus Himself could have deceived *them*.

The disciples had this sustaining and inwardly convincing and discerning love, but they had not yet a corresponding faith, or but very little of it. And when Jesus died, their love itself seemed to have been changed into hopeless, unbelieving sorrow; grief without faith. They could not penetrate the future, could not understand our Lord's plan. Everything seemed broken up, interrupted, destroyed forever. Even our Lord's last discourses, as detailed with such simplicity, preciousness, and graciousness by John, seem to have failed of being appreciated, except that their unequalled tenderness could not but draw the disciples more closely still to Him; but yet they knew not what He meant. When He died, they were overwhelmed. An impassable gulf seemed to have opened at their feet, and they could not cross it, even in imagination; and when the bridge had been thrown over it, connecting the past, the present and the future in our Lord's resurrection, and taking up and renewing again the dissevered tissue of their fondest expectations, they could not at first believe their own eyes, much less understand the wonderful transaction. The bridge itself was too aerial, and shot up too suddenly into heaven, and was so terrifying in its loftiness, that they dared not trust themselves upon it. So they now pursued their lonely desolate pilgrimage, to Eternity, caring little, now that Jesus had gone from them, how soon their own life might be ended.

In the midst of their grief, as they thus communed and reasoned, in anguish uncontrollable, yet not unreasonable, a stranger overtook them. With tones of sympathy and love, He enquired the cause of their sorrowful and earnest conversation. "What manner of communications are these that ye have one to another, as ye walk, *and are sad?*" And then, in the simplicity of their astonishment that any person should think that any other subject than Jesus of Nazareth could occupy their attention, they took it for granted that He must be a stranger in Jerusalem, or He would not have dreamed of their talking about anything else; and so, with their hearts won by His benevolence, they poured out all their sorrows and doubts before Him.*

* In the "Revised Version," the simplicity and tenderness of this recital are greatly marred by the omission of the words *"and are sad,"* from verse seventeen. The inimitable beauty of the record is in the expression of Christ's own sympathizing notice of the dejection and distress of the pilgrims. While they communed and reasoned Jesus Himself drew near, *and went with them.* He did not stop them, but joined them walking, and as they walked, put the question, What are these, your conversations, as ye walk and are sad? The sadness of their communion was what He had observed and inquired about, as if He had said, Tell Me, for I would share in your sorrows.

The revisers have put it in such a shape, that the sadness seems to have been a sudden result of the stranger's question, What are you talking about as you walk? The revision reads: "And they stood still, looking sad." As if the interrogation of the newcomer had itself stopped and saddened them. This intrusion is not in the Greek text of any authoritative MS. The revisors give no reason for the alteration except a marginal reference to S. V. A. MSS, *"and they stood sad,"* but the revision gives it, *" And they stood still, looking sad."*

How were they astonished, when He broke forth, as master of the whole subject, O fools, and slow of heart to believe all that the prophets have spoken! Ought not Christ to suffer these things, and to enter into His glory? Should you not have known, with the slightest spiritual acquaintance with the tenor of the prophets, that the path of your Messiah's glory led through suffering and death? And then at once He opened to their minds such new views of truth, and poured such a flood of light over the prophetic Scriptures, as made the Bible seem to them a new revelation. With what sweet and gracious power and clearness did He lead them through its various eras and vast fields of thought, presenting explanation after explanation of its mysteries.

Then first did they begin to comprehend the reign of their Messiah, and the scheme of redemption. Well might their hearts burn within them, when an unknown Saviour was expounding unto them in all the Scriptures the things concerning Himself! That this exposition was the conquest of death and sin by the undeserved sufferings and death of the sinless and blameless Deliverer, through His own blood shed for the remission of sins, and that this exposition has ever since been proved the only source of the happiness of heaven among men, is itself the crowning demonstration before the opening of Eternity, that Christianity is divine.

Oh what a furrow of light did His path trace, over the sacred pages! What notes of soul-entrancing melody, what celestial regions of thought, what profound depths of meaning, as the Hand that made the Harp of sacred Prophecy swept across its strings! Every passage, every line, every word in the Scriptures, as He brought them to their remembrance, was spirit and life to their souls. As passage after passage rose up before them, the film passed from their moral vision, and everywhere they beheld the Lamb of God that taketh away the sin of the world!

XXVI.

POINTS OF VISION AND INTERPRETATION UNQUESTIONABLE—NECESSARY MINUTENESS OF THE SURVEY—THE WHOLE A DIVINE PREPARATION FOR PREACHING AND TEACHING CONCERNING CHRIST, THE WAY, THE TRUTH, THE LIFE—THE PROPYLÆUM OF CHRIST TO THE ACTS OF THE APOSTLES AND THE EPISTLES.

There were particular passes across which the unknown Stranger carried them in His course, where it seemed as if they could scarcely sustain the power of light He was flinging upon their souls. There were mounts of spiritual vision they had never climbed before, where it seemed as if they were caught up into the third heaven of glory. As He led them down from the very first prediction in the garden of Eden, through the history of Abraham, who had seen Christ's day so long before He came, the trial and issue of the Patriarch's faith, in the sacrifice of Isaac, was one of those summits of light. When he came to the death bed of Jacob, there was another. The blood of the slain lamb, sprinkled on the door posts in the Institution of the Passover, was another. The lifting up of the Brazen Serpent in the Wilderness was another. He revealed the meaning of the whole system of sacrifices and ceremonies; that ceaseless shedding of blood, without which there is no remission of sins. He revealed Himself as the Prophet promised by Moses in Deut. xviii. 15-20, the Prophet like unto Moses, with God's whole name and pardoning prerogative in Him.

As the lightning at midnight, as the *corona* after a total eclipse, shining from the east even unto the west, so were the gates of this Apocalypse of the coming of the Son of Man, to the vision of these disciples. It was as if a photograph of every mountain and valley, every river and forest, city, village and hamlet, all the heights and depths in the landscape of the world of divine revelation, had been suddenly engraved within their consciousness, never more to be obscured or forgotten.

The divine revelation of an atonement for sin and an all-compassionate mediatorship between God and man, came before the giving of the Law, and was indeed a necessity of forgiving mercy, contemporaneous with the very first act of disobedience. It was the corner-stone and the Sabbath-perfection, of all soul-saving theology, in adoring gratitude and praise. It created the walk of Enoch with God, and sustained the triumphant faith and patience of Job, and inspired through his afflictions those watchwords and fore-running beacons of an Eternal victory of faith out of the experience of Despair;—those songs of the dying Swan of Antediluvian theology and prophecy, "The Lord gave, the Lord hath taken away; and blessed be the name of the Lord."—"Though He slay me, yet will I trust in Him."—"For I know that my Redeemer liveth, and that He shall stand in the latter day upon the earth: and though after my skin worms destroy this body, yet in my flesh I shall see God."

The Redeemer of Enoch, Job, Moses, the Resurrection and the Life, stood now upon the earth, Himself God manifest in the flesh, God raising the dead, God in Christ, reconciling the world unto Himself.

These footprints of the primeval searchings after

God and discoveries of Him by penitential faith could not have been omitted from our Blessed Lord's survey of the witnesses of divine inspiration in all past ages. For the whole Book of Job is an anticipation of the coming of the Redeemer, and the Resurrection unto Life in Him. The preaching of Elihu, Job's youthful Consoler and friend, is the very mercy and compassionate discipline of the Gospel of Christ, revealing unto men His righteousness, in their forgiveness and salvation.

And when our Lord entered on the Book of Psalms, what surprising revelations! The 2nd Psalm was the foreshadowed universal throne of the Messiah, and the proclamation of it by the Father: the 16th, Christ's dominion over the grave, entering the prison of its gloom for us, and for us rising again: the 110th, His supreme Lordship and Priesthood, after the order of Melchizedek. The 22nd opened with our Lord's own dying exclamation, My God! My God! Why hast Thou forsaken me! The 69th described as in prophetic history, the very circumstances of His sufferings.

And all this minuteness of prediction, so often objected against by critics after the fashion of Porphyry, as being incredible,—this divine characteristic of inspiration, was maintained as such by our Lord from the beginning, both in history and prophecy.

So that, on the one hand, as His own Interpreter, He showed to the disciples the glory of Christ in Isaiah as the glory of Jehovah, when the great Prophet saw His glory and spake of Him; and on the other, His humiliation and His dying blood, as the propitiation for the sins of the whole world: and both were demonstrated with a microscopic and telescopic power and clearness, equally impossible ever to have been forged or imagined.

Indeed, the whole earth had been seeded with prophecies and preparations of His coming, as demonstrated in the epistle to the Hebrews. They were held as divine germs for development in the bosom of empires, as well as in the Jewish institutes, even till the subsoil plough of God's mighty providences should bring them forth to light and demonstration. All the grand disciplinary methods of God's government among the nations, the stupendous eras of history, the ideal and eternal truths that alone could lay the foundations of a holy society, the tides of thought and feeling, convincing, instructing, new-creating:

> "The vast successive thoughts,
> That all the nations sway,
> As billows o'er the deep,
> In thunder rolled away."

And then, the night-visions of Daniel, the setting of

the judgment, and the opening of the Books before the Ancient of days, and the coming of One like the Son of Man with the clouds of Heaven, and the dominion given Him, the glory and kingdom, that all people, nations, and languages should serve Him: His dominion an everlasting kingdom which shall not pass away, and His kingdom even that of the Saints of the Most High, who shall take and possess the kingdom forever, even forever and ever.

But in comparison with this sublime description of the High and Holy One inhabiting Eternity, how inevitable for our Blessed Lord to dwell upon the depths of His own humiliation and sufferings for the sins of the whole world. So then especially in correcting the prejudices and guiding the minds of His future preachers, our Lord would fasten their attention upon the fifty-third chapter of Isaiah: "Who hath believed our report, and to whom hath the arm of the Lord been revealed?" Oh wonderful portraiture by the Spirit of Christ so many ages beforehand, when it testified the sufferings of Christ, and the glory that should follow.

"Despised and rejected of men, the Man of sorrows, and acquainted with grief. Surely He hath borne our griefs, and carried our sorrows: yet we did esteem Him stricken, smitten of God and afflicted. But He was wounded for our transgressions, He was bruised for our iniquities; the chastisement of our peace was upon Him, and with His stripes we are healed. All we like sheep have gone astray; we have turned every one to his own way, and the Lord hath laid on Him the iniquity of us all. ·He is brought as a lamb to the slaughter, He was cut off out of the land of the living; for the transgression of my people was He stricken. And He made His grave with the wicked, and with the rich in His death. When thou shalt make His soul an offering for sin, He shall see His seed, He shall prolong His days, and the pleasure of the Lord shall prosper in His hand. He shall see of the travail of His soul and be satisfied; by His knowledge shall my righteous servant justify many, for He shall bear their iniquities. Therefore He shall divide the spoil with the strong, because He hath poured out His soul unto death, and He was numbered with the transgressors; and He bare the sin of many, and made intercession for the transgressors."

Wonderful, minute, demonstrative, unanswerable history beforehand, of the infinite whole mystery of the Incarnation! And now the whole divine process so impossible in the view of an unbelieving rationalism, is completed by the sight and sensible appearance and indwelling of the despised, crucified, buried, risen, Almighty Redeemer, forever interceding at the right hand of the Majesty on high.

As He prayed for Peter before His death, and for His betrayers and murderers in dying, even so, of old, the prayers of Intercession for the pardon of the guilty, the fore-gleams of a divine Mediatorship, as in the prototypical examples of Moses and David and Samuel, and of Solomon in the dedication of the Temple with its Mercy-seat, and of Noah, Daniel and Job, had been a divinely characteristic and most merciful feature of salvation, even before the publication of the Decalogue, with the Sabbath of a believing worship centralized in it. With this were bound up, and wreathed around it, in circles of forgiving mercy, all the allusions to God's never-failing riches of long-suffering love in the gift of His only Son to die for sinners. All these perpetual magnetisms of the Holy Spirit in the Word of God, drawing us to Himself, and in the methods of His discipline, were noted in their connections.

The prayer of the soul forsaken of God in the 22nd Psalm, was followed by "The Lord is my Shepherd, I shall not want," in the pastoral 23rd; and the 102nd was codiciled by the 103rd; and the 69th supplemented by the 71st and 72nd. And all these particulars in the Covenant of forgiveness, the word of God's mercy which He commanded to a thousand generations, and confirmed the same for an everlasting covenant, ordered in all things and sure, were postulated for belief, till God manifested in the flesh should appear, the gracious Testator and Executor of the Whole in One.

"Comfort ye, comfort ye My people SAITH YOUR GOD. Say unto the cities of Judah, BEHOLD YOUR GOD! And the glory of the Lord shall be revealed, and all flesh shall see it together. He shall feed His flock like a Shepherd: He shall gather the lambs with His arm, and carry them in His bosom, and gently lead those that are with young. THY GOD SHALL DO THIS. He giveth power to the faint, and to them that have no might He increaseth strength. They that wait upon the Lord shall renew their strength. They shall mount up on wings as eagles. They shall run and not be weary, they shall walk and not faint."

There was nothing in all these amazing delineations of the mercy of an Almighty Saviour that Christ did not make to pass before vision of those favored disciples, admitted to look through the telescope of an instructed faith at these Messianic Nebulæ of His forgiving love. The baptism with the Holy Ghost and with fire was in all these revelations. It was the fire of divine love, and all the dear affectionate attractive pictures of the Shepherd of Israel and His tender watchfulness over the lambs of His flock, leading them in green pastures and by still waters, till the travail of His soul should be satisfied, when all the families of mankind should be gathered in one fold, under One Shepherd, were illuminated forever.

In the 23rd chapter of Jeremiah, as they followed the transparent explanations of their Divine Instructor, they beheld, growing, "the Righteous Branch of David, the King that should reign and prosper, and execute judgment and justice in the earth. In His days Judah shall be saved, and this is the name whereby He shall be called, THE LORD OUR RIGHTEOUSNESS." And in Jer. xxxi., God's covenant with the whole house of Israel, writing His law in their hearts, forgiving their iniquity and remembering their sin no more; also the same in chapter xxxiii. 8–26. Nothing could be more comprehensive and explicit, nothing more divinely glorious.

Then again, Ezekiel xxxiv. 23, "And I will set up one Shepherd over them, and he shall feed them, and I the Lord will be their God. And I will raise up for them a plant of renown. Thus shall they know that I, the Lord their God, am with them, and they, the house of Israel, are My people, saith the Lord. And ye, My flock, the flock of My pasture, men, and I your God, saith the Lord." Then Ezekiel xxxvi. 25, 26: "Then will I sprinkle clean water upon you, and ye shall be clean; from all your filthiness and from all your idols will I cleanse you. A new heart also will I give you, and a new spirit will I put within you and ye shall be My people, and I will be your God."

Then the great resurrection chapter, xxxvii. 13, 14: "Ye shall know that I am the Lord, when I shall have opened your graves, O My people, and brought you up out of your graves, and put My Spirit in you, and ye shall live; one fold, one Shepherd. My covenant of peace shall be with them: it shall be an everlasting covenant with them. My tabernacle also shall be with them; yea, I will be their God, and they shall be My people. And the nations shall know that I the Lord do sanctify Israel, when My sanctuary shall be in the midst of them for evermore."

The angel of the covenant was there; and in all the afflictions of His people, He was afflicted, and the angel of His presence saved them; in His love and in His pity He redeemed them; and He bare them and carried them all the days of old; Thou O Lord, our Father, our Redeemer, Thy name from everlasting. There is no more doubt as to the trains of exposition by our Lord, and the method of His tracing the course of His own life and divine nature as the Redeemer of mankind, than there can be as to the texts which He chose from the prophets Isaiah and Micah for His first and His latest sermons. No doubt He took those amazed disciples to the mountains of Midian to behold in the vision of Balaam the Star out of Jacob and the Sceptre out of Israel, and to hear and understand, as never before, the question, "Who can count the dust of Jacob, and the number of the fourth part of Israel? Let me die the death of the righteous, and let my last end be like His."

And Isaiah's vision, in the year that King Uzziah died! Who but Christ, in the way to Emmaus, could have revealed to those sorrowing disciples, that it was the Lord Jesus Himself, whose goings forth were from everlasting, that sent the prophet on His mission of mercy, having first taken away his iniquity and purged his sin. He that took for His first sermon on earth that divinely compassionate passage, "The Spirit of the Lord God is upon me, to bind up the broken-hearted, to proclaim liberty to the captives, and the opening of the prison to them that are bound; that they might be called Trees of Righteousness, the planting of the Lord, that He might be glorified." "These things said Esaias, when he saw His glory and spake of Him." Christ Himself and no other Being was the expositor to these disciples of His own Autobiography from eternity.

But this exposition itself was only as an index or table of contents, according to which the disciples now, looking back and remembering all the words of our Lord, could gather up and connect the whole train of events and teachings with the conclusion. Let any man read the 8th, 9th, 10th, 11th, and 12th chapters of John's Gospel, and consider the terribleness of our Lord's denunciations against the unbelieving Jews, whom He styled murderers and liars, like their father the devil, and compare and contrast those dreadful accusations with the assurance they all thought they had, by the very covenant of circumcision, of their being the children of Abraham; and he will cease to be astonished either at the wrath of our Lord's enemies, or the uninterrupted blindness of his friends.

It is not much to be wondered at, that after all these discourses, and the declaration of our Lord, *before Abraham was, I am*, the Jews took up stones again to stone Him. The wonder rather is that for three years or more, our Lord could have continued such sermons, with incessant and accumulating proofs of His divine Messiahship; and that the rulers of the Jewish Hierarchy, seeing and knowing that their power, and the very continued existence of the temple and the nation, were imperilled by such truth and such miracles, should not sooner have put Him to death.

But how then could the Scriptures have been fulfilled? How could the education and discipline of His disciples have been completed, and the foundations of His Church settled, in divine suffering and love, in the apostleship of witnesses and expounders of His doctrines and His death?

A premature explosion by the passions of His enemies was restrained, as by divine safety-valves, until the whole people of Judea should become so imbued with the knowledge of His character, His words and His miracles, that immediately after His resurrection, they should believe by thousands, and would bear out and justify the bold and fiery sermons of Peter and John, and the arraignment of the High Priest and the rulers, as having been themselves the murderers of the Messiah, and thus the unintentional instruments of God's own fulfilment of all those things which He had before showed by the mouth of all His holy prophets, that Christ should suffer.

Then again in Hosea and Micah, Joel and Jonah, Zechariah and Malachi, and the historic as well as the prophetic Hebrew Books, He traced the outlines of His own predestined humiliations and sufferings, death and glory, the cross and the crown, the inheritance of Him, and for Him, whose coming was to be "the Desire of Nations." "Rejoice greatly, O daughter of Zion; shout, O daughter of Jerusalem! Behold, thy King cometh unto thee: He is just and having salvation: lowly and riding upon an ass, and a colt, the foal of an ass." He showed them the thirty pieces of silver, the price at which He was valued, when betrayed. He showed them how they should look on Him whom they had pierced, and how the Spirit of grace and supplications should be poured upon them; and every family and tribe be blest with that penitential and believing baptism, till the prayers of David the son of Jesse, should be ended.

And thus he passed down through the minor prophets, to the last great predictions of His coming, and the Messenger to prepare His way, and the purification of the sons of Levi, and the coming of Elijah the prophet, that the heart of the fathers might be turned again to the children, and of the children to the fathers. How divinely clear, how ravishingly bright, did everything appear beneath His teachings! In truth, the abundance of the revelations was such, that our Lord must have communicated, along with them, an apportioned power of comprehension, a supernatural illumination of their intellects. It was just such as on the evening of the same day He bestowed upon all the disciples, when He opened their understandings to understand the Scriptures. The veil was removed, the darkness swept away, and everywhere they beheld the Saviour's glory, and the Word speaking of Him. Everywhere, in all their preaching ever afterwards they knew that they had the mind of Christ.

XXVII.

POWER OF THE GREAT PERSONAL REVELATION AFTER THIS SURVEY—THE DIVINE PREPARATION FOR IT, THE ETERNAL ASSURANCE AND BLESSEDNESS OF IT—THE INFINITE PRIVILEGE AND HAPPINESS OF THE MINISTRY OF SUFFERING LOVE.

In the midst of such conversation, they drew near to their abode. It does not appear that they had any suspicion who this wonderful Stranger really was, though He was making their hearts burn within them every step of the way by His exposition of the Word of God. His theme was the dearest of all themes, and they loved Him for the interest He took in it, as well as the wonderful knowledge He possessed of it, and the divine instruction and consolation He communicated to their minds.

He made as though He would have gone further, but how could they let Him go? They held him as Jacob did of old, when He said, Let me go, for the day breaketh; and he said, I will not let Thee go, except Thou bless me. Now He said, Let Me go, for the day declineth; but they said, Abide with us, for it is towards evening, and the day is far spent.

Towards evening! Ah! it was the morn of an eternal sunrise, the beginning of a day of glory never to end. With affectionate urgency they constrained Him, till He entered their peaceful abode, to which indeed He was no stranger. With joyful hospitality they made ready their evening meal, and sat down to partake of it, still talking of Him, of whom now they began to have such new, such glorious and soul-ravishing views.

Singular enough it was, that while their inward sight had been irradiated to behold their Lord in the Scriptures, so that now they knew Him better than ever before, their outward vision had been so holden, as not to recognize Him, though He had walked several miles with them, and was even now sitting with them in personal bodily presence at meat. Perhaps our Lord chose this deeply interesting mode of communicating with them, because, in such a conversation He could gain their more undivided and meditative attention to the truth.

It was the truth, and not the person of the Stranger, that was overcoming them, commanding them, possessing them; striking in their hearts, and chiming, like the bells of the Holy City, like voices out of the throne, as the sound of many waters; words that were as flames, as burning coals, as electric rainbows, as the living creatures in Ezekiel's vision, running and returning as the appearance of a flash of lightning. Through and through their hearts, down into the thoughts of their souls, deeper than consciousness had ever sounded, and awakening thoughts of which they could not have deemed themselves capable, and feelings that they never knew before, went these words of this calm but sympathizing Stranger, taking their whole attention; words quick and powerful, and sharper than any two-edged sword, and yet sweeter than honey, and the droppings of the honey-comb, and more refreshing and softly penetrating than the dews of summer nights on the borders of the Lake of Galilee.

The words that they heard sank all the deeper for their previous deep sadness; and indeed, in order that the truth might thus quietly and stealthily gain attention and possession, it was as necessary that the melancholy meditative mood, in which they set out from Jerusalem, and were sadly communing when Jesus met them, should be preserved, as for a plentiful dew fall it is necessary that the wind go down, and the night be calm and cloudless. Any whirlwind of emotion or amazement, as at the supposed appearance of a ghost, or a supernatural being, would be a fatal disturbance. If at first setting out, Christ had revealed Himself to them, and afterwards attempted to instruct them, they would have been in such a fever of surprise, agitation, and joy, that a calm listening would have been impossible. But our

Lord graciously and sweetly prepared their minds for the disclosure.

And now they were counting upon a continued evening of just such holy conversation, and would have closed it with the reading of the Scriptures and family worship by their sacred guest, when suddenly, as He takes the bread, and looks up to heaven, they behold Him, just as He sat with the twelve disciples four days ago at the institution of the Last Supper, when He spake those solemn words, "This is My body, broken for you." Yes! it is He! the same form, the same holy countenance, the same heavenly gesture! He took bread, and blessed, and brake, and gave to them. It is He! And they knew Him, and He vanished out of their sight. No more doubt, no more darkness now! They have seen the risen Saviour, and away they fly, the same hour, to Jerusalem, to tell the glad tidings to their fellow disciples. Did not our hearts burn within us, while He talked with us by the way, and while He opened to us the Scriptures? How is it that we did not know Him before, that we did not remember that never man spake like this Man?

Happy beings, happy disciples! Thenceforward, the joy of the Lord was their strength, and they were transfigured by it from gloom to glory, even as they had been prepared for it, by the grace of

God, through their first discipline and development of love to Christ, and afterwards their hearts being wrung with grief and anguish for His sake. "For unto you it is given, in the behalf of Christ, not only to believe on Him, but also to suffer for His sake."

This privilege of suffering for Christ was manifestly regarded as the highest of all the blessings of the Christian life; and this was the greatest demonstration that human beings could be capable of making for their divine Redeemer; this confession of Him before men and angels, the world, the universe, friends and enemies, at the cost of the sacrifice of everything in this life that men could hold dear. The revelation was that of infinite divine truth, demonstrated through divine love, as the ground-work, purpose and method of all truth.

Dear and blessed, loving and suffering disciples! As their commission was in many cases, that of a living martyrdom for Christ, so the crown of their glory in His blessed service was to be the brightest that ever could be worn by mortals. They were to sit on twelve thrones, judging the twelve tribes of Israel. To them was to be given the glory of turning many to righteousness by the blood of the Lamb and the word of their testimony; and they were to shine above the brightness of the firmament forever and ever.

How wonderful to see that the whole evidence of our faith is passed, for its perfection, through the medium both of human and divine suffering. "For it became Him, for whom are all things, and by whom are all things, in bringing many sons unto glory, to make the Captain of their salvation perfect through sufferings." And so with His own ministers, and spiritual soldiers, so that the whole evidence of divine inspiration from Genesis to Revelation passes through the anguish of prophets and apostles; passes through agonized and bleeding hearts, and through the wrath of men and nations made to praise God, and through demoniac natures subdued by redeeming grace, and brought to sit at the feet of Jesus, the author and finisher of faith. Nothing is left to mere theory or conjecture, but all is divinely experimental.

And so we learn by heart the truths for our life, without which we know nothing but death;—we learn and know them in and for ourselves, just only in proportion as we learn them from God in Christ, and employ and teach them in His love for God and our fellow creatures. Thus God benevolently makes all regenerated men fellow workers with the Redeemer in working out their own salvation, through the power that worketh in them to will and to do; learning and understanding, by believing, loving, acting. Doubtless all the apostles learned for themselves as much as they taught others, by writing their own epistles; for they wrote, possessed by the Spirit, and raised above self, out of the fulness and self-forgetfulness of divine love; as for example the Epistles of Paul, Peter, and John, an outpouring of truths profound beyond all possibility of the human mind to have discovered; but written out, in order that men dead in trespasses and sins may come to life; written out of their own hearts' blood, with compassion and weeping and joy, that all the disciples might, young and old, be presented before God faultless in Christ; and might even in this world rejoice and be made steadfast in Him, and know what is the hope of His calling, and what the riches of the glory of His inheritance in the saints.

XXVIII.

GOD'S METHOD OF DEMONSTRATION, PERSONAL, EXPERIMENTAL, AND CONSONANT WITH OUR NATURE—GOD'S ETERNAL NATURE BEING LOVE, THERE IS NO OTHER POSSIBLE WAY OF KNOWING HIM, THAN THAT OF LOVING HIM—THAT LOVE KNOWN ONLY IN CHRIST, AND IN THE SCRIPTURES CONCERNING HIM.

"For God hath shined in our hearts, to give the light of the knowledge of the glory of God in the face of Jesus Christ." Hath shined in our hearts, and so, by the very laws of human nature, hath made the hearts thus illumined and filled with glory and power, the attractive magnets to all other hearts, by the indwelling and example of such power. "I beseech thee," said Moses, "show me Thy glory," when this revelation was beginning among men. If Thou hast appointed me to speak of Thee and for Thee, show me Thy glory, that I may speak irresistibly, convincingly, attractively, all that which I have seen, and may testify that which I have known. And such was the watch-word of Paul's power, "I know WHOM I have believed, and that HE LOVED ME, AND GAVE HIMSELF FOR ME."

God's method of demonstration is thus always that of love. How coincident with our nature, how appropriate to the foundations of belief, and to the ring-bolts wrought in our intellectual and moral constitution, on which the truth might lay hold, to draw us up to God!

This may be seen, it had been already seen, even when Christ came, in the influence exerted by Plato's writings concerning Socrates. We believe that there was such a personage as Socrates once teaching in the world, attracting disciples, and molding their characters on his own, more by the discourses give in Plato's dialogues, and by the sympathy and love there manifested, than by any other demonstration. No man could ever be persuaded that this account was a mere fiction. Let such a fabulist as Strauss try his wit upon it. It is quite impossible that such a myth could have been invented, or could have grown by natural selection or evolution.

And so the gospels hold mankind by an irresistible demonstration, the power of which will be felt and acknowledged as long as the world stands, renewed as long as the gospels are published. And they are the Word of God that liveth and abideth forever.

So we are held to .God, brought back to God from our ignorance and disobedience, *relegated* by this true divine *religion* of the personality of God in Christ Jesus; to be made *like Him*, by seeing and knowing *Him as He is*, and not by silent worship of the Unknown and Unknowable. "But as He who hath called you is holy, so be ye holy, in all manner of conversation, because IT IS WRITTEN, *Be ye holy, for I am holy.* And if ye call on the Father (and such return unto Him and true worship of Him, and renewal of the soul in His likeness, is not possible but by prayer and faith, which is the soul's true calling on God), pass the time of your sojourning here in fear; *forasmuch as ye know* that ye were not redeemed with corruptible things, as silver and gold, from your vain conversation received by tradition from your fathers, but with the *precious blood of Christ*, as of a Lamb without blemish and without spot. Who verily was foreordained before the foundation of the world, but was manifest in these last times for you, *who by Him do believe in God, that raised Him up from the dead and gave Him glory;* that your faith and hope might be in God. Seeing ye have purified your souls in obeying the truth through the Spirit unto unfeigned love of the brethren, see that ye love one another with a pure heart fervently; being born again, not of corruptible seed, but of incorruptible, by the Word of God that liveth and abideth forever. And this is the Word which by the Gospel is preached unto you." And the beginning and the end are LOVE.

And so, "God was manifest in the flesh," and in all the most intimate conjunctures between our souls and bodies, being so manifested, is known as the object of a reasonable faith, disclosed to us by and through the structure and workings of our own personal existence; sympathizing with us, and in this compassionate and loving humiliation of the divine nature on earth, under the vesture of our humanity, justified in the Spirit, seen of angels, preached unto the Gentiles, believed on in the World, received up into glory. Faith, sight, sense, reasoning, experience, all appealed to, all satisfied and fulfilled in the knowledge of Christ, that we might be filled with all the fulness of God.

Now then, full in the face of the arrogant pronouncement of philosophers that God cannot be manifested, but is forever unknown and unknowable, there shoots forth as the lightning the sentence that GOD WAS MANIFEST IN THE FLESH, AND DWELT AMONG US, AND WE BEHELD HIS GLORY. "For the life was manifested, and we have seen it, and bear witness, and show unto you that eternal life, which was with the Father, and was manifested unto us;" manifested in the flesh, *in order* to be justified in the Spirit, *in order* to be seen of angels, ("and when He bringeth in the first-born into the world He saith, Let all the angels of God worship Him"), *in order* to be preached unto the Gentiles, *in order* to be believed on in the world, and then, when received up into glory, to be the "Head over all things to the church, which is His body, the fulness of Him that filleth all in all."

Him that filleth all in all! And so He who was the Word made flesh, the Word in this incarnate divine personality, must expound the prophecies in those inspired documents that had foreshadowed His coming, in order that men, when He came fór their salvation, might believe;—He must expound to His witnesses, as the appointed teachers of mankind,

"IN ALL THE SCRIPTURES, THE THINGS CONCERNING HIMSELF."

In this designation or proposition we have therefore arrived at the great centre of thought, significance, and argument; the great hinge and standpoint of all divine revelation; its whole object and importance. THE THINGS CONCERNING HIMSELF. This is our central sun; here the light shines and hither the whole universe of truth and being gravitates. How mighty is this sentence, as comprehending all the appointed pathway of the Scriptures of God, the purpose of God in them, their infinite worth and infallible certainty; all that needed to be known for the accomplishment of God's designs for human salvation. THE THINGS CONCERNING HIMSELF. It is like the great sentence, IT IS WRITTEN, with which, in the opening of His ministry, Christ confronted and confounded Satan in the wilderness. And here, at the close of His ministry, in committing its continuance and completion to the hands of His disciples, THE THINGS CONCERNING HIMSELF.

For this was their stewardship with divine truth, their wholesale commission business on earth, *Christ and Him crucified*. This was what made the Scriptures interesting. This was what gave them their power. The importance of the Old Testament as well as of the New consists in its revelation of Jesus Christ. Noth-

ing else in it was made the subject of exposition by
our Blessed Lord to the two favored disciples. External things were all passed by, the traditions of the
elders, and the learned rubbish of the synagogues,
cabbala, and mysteries, philosophy and speculation.
Beginning at Moses and all the prophets He expounded unto them *in all the Scriptures the things concerning Himself.*

XXIX.

NATURE OF THE SWEEP OF THIS PROPOSITION —
CHRIST ESTABLISHED IT WHILE HIMSELF ON
EARTH, SO THAT THERE SHOULD BE NO DIS-
PUTING OF IT, NO ATTEMPTS AT THE BREAKING
OF THE WILL, NO CASE IN CHANCERY, NO COUN-
CILS—THE WHOLE VOLUME, AND ITS DOCUMENTS,
GOD'S VOUCHERS, AND HIS ALONE.

Now there are these two considerations,—first, the
clean sweep of this proposition, its thoroughness, de-
cisiveness,—*all the Scriptures;* second, Christ did this
Himself, *while He was yet on earth,* and would not leave
it to an after inspiration, not even to the mission of
the Comforter, who was to convince the world in His
stead, when He should have gone to the Father,
and no more be seen or heard speaking among men.
There was a divine order and sequence; a logic of eter-

nal truth pursued by Him, who was the Way, the Truth, and the Life; *Moses and the prophets first*, and *all the Scriptures*, in their light, as God's light.

But what are all the Scriptures? Is there certainty or uncertainty here? Is this the infallibility of God informing His creatures, or the fallibility of men compounded into the pretence of infallible history, by the medium of successive infallible councils? Nay, we have here the God incarnate, testifying to the Word of God, the Creator, Revealer, and Covenant Keeper, and Redeemer of mankind. It is not man but God, who assures us what be the very words of God, on which we are permitted and commanded to build our faith in the promised Saviour of guilty lost men.

The Lord Jesus Christ had made His will before His death, in regard to His own kingdom, as the kingdom of His Father; and now He was Himself its sole Interpreter and Executor, after rising from the dead, and before ascending to His Father. What that will, as the will of His Father, was, He had made absolutely sure for all generations; and now the probating of it, and the administration, He made equally clear and explicit. The Scriptures of that will were known as the Oracles of God committed to the Jews alone as the keepers of them for mankind. There were no other oracles ever delivered from God to man; "And whatsoever things were written before the coming of Christ were written for our learning, that we through patience and comfort of the Scriptures might have hope."

Could there have been any doubt as to that "*whatsoever*," the very first thing the Divine Messenger from God, the Messenger of the covenant of life and peace from Him, must do, would be to clear it up. The solution of it would be the very first exercise of God's truth and goodness. If ever the promised Messiah came to do the will of God, it was not only to be expected, but infinitely certain, that this exposition and proof of that will would be made as sure as the covenant itself forever settled in heaven. This must have been one of the things that the Saviour would do in the world and for the world, before He left the world to return to His Father. When He prayed God for His disciples, "Sanctify them by Thy truth," and directed them to study *that truth*, for their sanctification, He would not leave them ignorant or uncertain *what really was that truth to which He referred them as the very Word of God.* This is our security; and this would be enough, if we had no other, or none marginal or additional; but we have. There is at the same time a wondrous combination and harmony of witnesses human and divine, inspired, and also uninspired, but ordinarily or humanly historical; along with a chain of events and providences, bearing upon themselves God's seals, for our deliverance from doubts, that otherwise here at the very foundation of our faith might trouble us.

We have the Word of God, the only divine revelation then upon earth, as by testimony of Christ, then already *written, in a volume;* then so absolutely known, so received and relied upon, that he could reason from it as an undisputed, sure, acknowledged quantity. *We have this volume*, as translated from the Hebrew into the Greek, some centuries before Christ came Himself to appeal to it as "*the volume of the Book written of Him.*" We have the evidence and the date of such translation in the works of journalists, philosophers and historians, such as Philo and Josephus; historians as credible as any on whose books or records the world of believers in human history ever built their faith in the existence of Alexander the Great, or the Commentaries of Julius Cæsar.

It was this known volume of writings, to which Christ referred and appealed, and which He charged the Jews with disobeying, and in some cases nullifying by their own added traditions, setting the precepts of men in place of the commandments of God; and He attributed all their calamities to that, and all their peril; but never charged them with not possessing or not confessing, or not carefully preserving from mutilation those records, or not knowing, and being conscious of, their importance and authority as divine.

But the Jews did never receive these Scriptures as divine, merely or mainly because certain historians acknowledged them as such, or testified of them that they were such; but those historians testified that these very writings were the books that at the time of the coming of Christ had been translated into the Greek tongue, at Alexandria, and were in habitual use for reference as of divine authority, in all the synagogues; "where," said Luke, "Moses hath in every city those who read them every Sabbath day." When the Hebrew tongue was passing out of existence as a vernacular language, which however was not till the volume of the Old Testament inspiration was closed, God put the inspired records in the ark of the Greek tongue for transmission; that tongue made immortal by the genius of Homer and Plato, and carried through the world by the conquests of Alexander; that tongue, in which Christ Himself was to make His own communications to mankind. The genius of the Hebrew passed into the Greek, carrying into its more modern and universal dialect the baptism of the old divine inspiration; the Greek being as it were thus clothed upon, that its mortality might be swallowed up of life.

Now we are entitled to ask, Can there be anything

more sufficiently and satisfactorily demonstrated than this? And what unbeliever can ever find fault with God, if judged according to this evidence? We have the very same Scriptures that Christ declared to be the Word of God. They were a perfectly well known and indisputable quantity and quality; the very books, and none others, of that divine revelation, out of which Christ's mind, from childhood to manhood, grew and was nourished, in the completest fulfilment of the condition of a perfect life, that by every word that proceedeth out of the mouth of God shall man live. The very Scriptures, and the books of Scripture, in regard to which, at the age of twelve years, He conferred with the doctors of the law in the temple at Jerusalem, both hearing them, and asking them questions; and out of which, through all His ministry, He had been teaching the people. He knew what these books were; and His hearers knew the same; but now they knew by a distinct personal affirmation and enumeration from Christ Himself. There was no uncertainty, there could be none. There was not one book, vouched for by Christ, about which there was the least doubt, that it was the Word of God.

All the things in that Volume of the Book, covered and governed by the words of Christ to the tempter in the wilderness, IT IS WRITTEN, were as known certainties of divine revelation, as the axioms of geometry, or the quantities and laws of astronomical science. And *the Scriptures as they had them*, and as Christ referred to them, and expounded them, we have them also, and know them; the very same Scriptures, as truly, as indisputably, as the planets that shone upon the Judean landscape were the planets that now shine upon our globe. The books that Christ referred to, and expounded and taught, were the infallible Word of God.

XXX.

SUFFICIENCY OF OUR EVIDENCE—NO ANCHORAGE FOR ETERNITY IN UNCERTAINTIES—GOD'S MERCY NOT HIDDEN IN OBSCURITIES, BUT HE SETS HIS BOW IN THE CLOUDS—THE PROVERBS OF THIS WORLD, PROPHECIES OF THE NEXT—QUESTIONS AND CONCLUSIONS OF EXPERIMENTALISTS.

Here then we have a positive double anchorage for our faith, from which we cannot be dislodged. Moses and the Prophets, where Christ began, are a part of the Scriptures of God. There is no room for doubt as to that position. That one thing is settled, *Moses and all the Prophets*. But in the forty-fourth verse, it is, *Moses and the Prophets and the Psalms*. These all are Scriptures of God, infallible, and which must all be fulfilled, because they are God's Word. Here is a second position where our anchorage holds, Moses and the Prophets and the Psalms.

Now we just as certainly know what writings, what books, were comprehended and referred to by our Lord Jesus Christ under this designation, as when the poems of Homer are named, we know that the books referred to are those of the Iliad and Odyssey. We know what those books were to which Jesus Christ referred, as being the books of the Word of God, about as certainly as we know that Jesus Christ existed. And those Jews, to whom Christ was expounding those Scriptures, knew as well as He did what they were, what precisely was the Hebrew Canon of books, which they preserved with such inviolable carefulness and security, and to which Jesus Christ referred as being beyond doubt the Word of God, and to which He anchored the minds of His disciples, as the immutable foundations of truth, provided by the God that cannot lie, for the gift of life eternal to men dead in trespasses and sins.

Moreover, He stood now as a Being bearing witness from the other world. He had gone into His eternal glory and returned. He had entered the grave, and risen from it. He had entered heaven, and carried with Him the soul of the penitent thief, from the Cross into Paradise. He had returned among the disciples with the declaration, All power is given unto

Me in heaven and on earth. And He it was who on earth expounded these Scriptures, leaving no possibility of any uncertainty as to their identity or divineness.

Now this is a perfectly conclusive and triumphant argument. It has all the guards and logical requisites of the completest reasoning, from the *à priori* demonstration to that of experience. Nevertheless, scientists that do not of themselves know all things, must begin their knowledges by taking some things for assured as taught them by authority, and so, they too must be justified by faith. Can we possibly make an argument, can God Himself address one to the human reason, that shall stand in the place of faith, that shall compel, as sight compels, by demonstration to the senses, so that there shall be no room for doubt? He that cometh to God must believe that He is, must come without seeing Him, and cannot possibly know Him, but by so coming, and must believe in His attributes just as He Himself has revealed them, and in the consequences of disobedience as He has made them known.

But sufficient evidence is given to all for the beginning of action, for coming to God in prayer; and then comes the witness of experience by the Spirit of God, promised in answer to prayer. But that witness is impossible, without action by faith upon the preliminary evidence. The Word of God is infallible. It is contained in the Scriptures. But the things of God there revealed by the Holy Spirit knoweth no man but by the Spirit of God. And we cannot construct an argument to the reason, that shall stand in the place of the Spirit, and of an eternal experience, and do the work which the Spirit alone can do. Just as we cannot construct an argument from nature, or a demonstration from the works of God, and the methods of discovered law in those works, that shall reveal God to the senses, and so supersede the necessity of faith, compelling men to see and acknowledge God; not the forces of nature merely, but the God who produces them.

Always, even to the end, men may be unbelievers if they will. And there is what is called a sea-push of skepticism in our day, a whirl, a black knot, in the surf, the tide, extremely powerful and dangerous. There is an undertow that sets out from the beach, after a high tide of faith; a reaction as of cold ague after fever, a return of the pendulum to the opposite extreme. It is an undertow that bathers have to watch against, for it is so strong, that even those who have gone in to help others out have been carried beyond their depth, and lost their footing and their life. Any one of the gospels is a life-preserver in the wildest sea that ever raged, the worst storm that ever came down on Galilee. If Christ be there, you are safe. But if you will not admit Him into your ship, but treat Him as an impostor, and His life as a romantic fiction, there is no help for you. There is no help for poor human nature, if Christ be not the Way, the Truth, the Life.

XXXI.
"THEY DON'T COME BACK TO TELL"—COLERIDGE AND JOHN FOSTER—PAUL AND JOHN.

A great thinker upon the mysteries of our being, and an experimentalist, almost to the last degree, of the consequences of character in our sins, (Coleridge, the philosopher and poet), was wont to say, *Quantum sumus, scimus;* we *know* just as much as we *are.* Our consciousness, our experience, under the inward teachings and witness of the Spirit, are the exponent of all our real self-knowledge. And our self-knowledge of all that we have become and *are*, if we find ourselves living without God and without Christ in this world, and so laying the foundations of an eternal character for the next world, is a convincing demonstration of all that we *shall be*, if we carry these habits of living beyond the article of dying. "I am the Resurrection and the Life," belongs only to those who now, in the time of God's offered mercy, *confess Christ before men.* Otherwise, the rejection of Him, and its consequences, abide upon the soul forever.

But, exclaimed John Foster, profoundly musing on the mysteries of death, the state of the lost, and the veil impenetrable, behind which all results are hidden, except in the Gospel of Christ, " *They don't come back to tell!* They don't come back to tell!" Why should they? If they did, it could only be to point to the Cross, and say, "There is all that we know about it. And you on earth know that, by the word of God. We know that we suffer, and that justly, receiving the due reward of our deeds. But as to the Eternity of it, we know *that* only by the Cross. The sufferings and dying of the Son of God are the Logarithms of the Eternal World. There is no hope for us out of Him, none for you if you reject Him, and die in your sins. There remaineth no more sacrifice, forever."

Hence the importance of an exceeding faithfulness even unto death, in Christ's witnesses, both in word and doctrine. For who, otherwise, is sufficient for these things? " Hold *fast,*" said Paul to Timothy, " the form of *sound words,* which thou hast heard of me, *in faith and love,* which is in Christ Jesus. Continue thou in the things which thou hast learned, and hast been assured of, knowing of whom thou hast learned them; and that from a child thou hast known the Holy Scriptures, which are able to make thee wise unto salvation, through faith which is in Christ Jesus."

And John's testimony! "Who is he that overcometh the world, but he that believeth that Jesus is the Son of God," and taketh into his heart all that is comprehended in that article of faith, and in Paul's again, II Cor. v. 14, 15, "Because, we thus judge, that if one died for all, then were all dead; and that he died, in order that they who live should no more live unto themselves, but unto Him, who died for them and rose again." Knowing therefore the terror of the Lord, before whom all are to stand in judgment for all things done in the body, *we persuade men.*

There is no other persuasion for Eternity, neither any hope held out for those who choose to die, not in Christ, but in their own sins, having neither sought nor found his forgiving grace and mercy. Death in sin, and the wages of sin, are the end; and who can arraign God's benevolence in it, seeing that He hath made it as clearly known as His own nature in Christ?

Now assuredly the infinite importance of all these communications from God in Christ, as to our Eternal Destiny, lies in their everlasting and infallible certainty. It is absolutely certain that God would not leave us in doubt. All our own happiness, and the possibility of communicating it to others, reside in the use of our opportunities with God's certainties, not obscurities, *to-day*. For the whole Eternity of men, as to character and its results, depends on the confession or rejection of the name and claims of Christ, *before men, while it is called to-day*. The tides in every man's affairs of life, the seizures of favorable instants at the forward top, the crest of the wave just where it is bending, the faiths, purposes, resolutions, not sicklied o'er with doubt, nor palsied by delays—these are the things that make us, or their wanton wastes that mar us forever.

Go into a foundry, whether of iron, or brass, or gold, for the building of monuments of moral character and glory; or watch the determination of success or failure, in the process of converting iron into steel; the necessity of the measurement and seizing of a single second for the decision, or the whole experiment is ruined. These are analogies, apocalyptic as the lightning upon our work and destiny for Eternity.

Mark the proverbs of society, and observe how they are the principles of endless success or irretrievable disaster and ruin. To-day, if ye will hear His voice, harden not your hearts. Agree with thine adversary, quickly. Walk in the light, while the light is with you, and in you, and upon you. Walk in love, while the offered Spirit of Love, and of Power, and of a sound mind, disposes and enables you. Keep thy heart all the way, with all diligence, all watchfulness; take the water-power at the wheel, and the will at the stroke of the walking-beam, for the dynamite of the heart is in it to the last point; the irresistible, all-conquering force of the whole machinery thrown through its blow, in body, soul, and spirit, a unit in the explosion, hurling the man, through all the energy of a life-time, into Eternity.

Now it is not wonderful that a thoughtful mind and awakened conscience, such as John Foster, should have demanded that the truth of an Eternal Retribution, if true, should be thundered as with the sound of many waters, and reiterated, as with the blast of the Archangel's Trumpet, from generation to generation, and from Genesis to the Apocalypse. For this demand God Himself has fully met in the Incarnation and Death of His own Son. This is the explosion of the artillery of all God's Providences and Scriptures. It is the very concentration, and ever-acting pressure of infinite certainty from Eternity upon the finite mind. What less is that transaction, as to the understanding of the whole government of God, and of all the divine attributes, and all the destinies of man, than the forerunning lightnings and thunders revealing an Eternal Judgment? What less than the thunder of Eternity is the peal of the tragedy of the death of Christ, reverberated from the childhood to the death of all generations, in its testimony against sin, out of love to the soul of the sinner? It is the lesson of all our hearing, the light of all our seeing. And there can be neither charity, nor liberality, nor benevolence, nor largeness of mind, in concealing or adulterating any of these truths, or throwing the shadow of a doubt upon them, or teaching mankind to rely upon the obscurities of divine revelation as more merciful than its certainties.

XXXII.

THE COURSE OF NATURE—THE LANGUAGE AND THE LAWS OF FAITH—THE EXPERIMENT OF TIME, THE INVITATION AND THE ACCEPTANCE OF DIVINE GRACE, THE DEATH OF DEATH AND HELL'S DESTRUCTION THROUGH CHRIST, AND THE BEGINNING OF THE LIFE ETERNAL.

The course of nature is a promulgation of law: the consequences, if nature be violated, are a promulgation of penalty. The power of foresight and opportunity of provision against evils otherwise certain and inevitable is an element and arrangement of probation, in which there is offered a salvation from future evils, a safeguard against the wrath to come. The necessity of obeying nature is really a demonstration of the necessity of obeying God and our spiritual destiny.

And in natures merely animal and mechanical, God, to prevent evil, has set this law of instinct as a mainspring, answering the place and purpose of reason in intelligent creatures. Instinct winds up their watches as a mechanical intelligence, and works for them inevitably a future salvation. It is involuntary. But reason acts upon information, and is voluntary. Reason receives and obeys warnings, and is responsible accordingly. Instinct obeys a mechanical necessity. Instinct is the working out of a character preordained and conformed to nature. Reason is for the formation and exercise of a voluntary character according to God's own teachings. The devil in the beginning did not say, *There is no God*, but, "He is *not a true God*, you cannot trust Him. He conceals from you what you ought to know, and tells you what is not true, what cannot be proved, and requires you to act accordingly. Yea hath He said, In the day that thou eatest thou shalt surely die? But I tell you that God doth know that ye shall become as gods knowing good and evil. That demonstration is what He withholds from you. But you must have that, or else do not believe what He tells you. You can trust Him no further than you can see Him."

Now that is the language of men towards a known villain; and that is the way in which unbelief treats God. And that is John's logical definition of unbelief, HATH MADE GOD A LIAR.

In requiring the demonstration of sense, and pretending to base your denial of the Word of God on that necessity, you treat God as a liar, and cut yourself off from all possibility of communion with Him. He cannot give you demonstration and save you; for in the first place to put you into the eternal fires, and so convince you, would be your ruin. But even *that* would not be demonstration; for as to the *eternity* of any thing, whether happiness or misery, a demonstration would require that you live *through that eternity,* that you experience that eternity, and measure it yourself, which no created being can do.

And therefore the very angels have to take God's Word for it. Christ's dying is the demonstration for them, as for us, of the worth of the soul and the reality of eternal death for those who are not made partakers of His life; the only *demonstration* that even angels can have, or beings of any kind in any world.

Even the rich man tormented in hell might have answered Abraham, when he told him there was a great gulf eternally fixed between him and Heaven, How do you know? You have never gone half way through eternity. You know not what may be in the future; you must have demonstration. I know as much as you do. You have to take all things on the Word of God. You have a creed as God teaches it. But I believe nothing but what I see and know by demonstration. I believe only my own senses, myself.

And Abraham might have answered, "Well, you have your reward. Believe on. Your senses are true, and what they tell you, and what you are in them, is your experience; and because you would not be affected by higher spiritual testimony, even God's testimony, *these flames* are your experience. But what God is, you could not know, nor what God would do, except by what God told you would come upon you. And the impossibility of dwelling with God, or being happy in Him, unless you believe and love and obey Him, you now find out, alas, too late, forever."

Now if a man say, There is no need of all this terrible haste and clamor, this ringing of alarm bells and thundering of fire-engines, this repetition of the terrific theological watchwords of Retribution. It cannot be that this is our only chance; there must be an ophthalmic hospital in the world to which we are going, and a quarantine there, where men may be healed. The answer to this is found in Christ's own declaration, that if we, the guilty and the lost, whom He came to seek and to save, by saving us from our sins, refuse to accept of His mercy, to avail ourselves of His healing ministrations, now, while they are offered, to-day while it is the accepted time and the day of salvation, it will be too late when Time is ended and Eternity begun. "If ye believe not in Me, (Christ's mercy forewarns us), ye shall die in your sins. While ye have light believe in the light that ye may be *children of the light.* He that believeth not in Me, and abideth not in Me, he is as a withered branch that is to be cut off from the tree, and carried away to be burned."

Besides, if a man say I will not believe until I see, until I know by my own sense and knowledge, that it is the last chance, and that if I do not believe I am certainly and irremediably doomed and lost forever; it is perfectly plain that such a man never can be saved by believing in Christ, never can know the power of faith, nor its vitality; for all the faith that such a person ever will exercise, or ever can, is not in God nor in Christ, but in his own senses, and in the testimony of hell-fire; a kind of faith that even if it could be supposed to save the soul, would evidently do it by dishonoring and disobeying God as long as possible.

The question for the soul through eternity is just

this, Can you trust God? Do you take Him at His Word, or do you suspect Him of some deceit or exaggeration, and are you resolved to wait upon your own experience as your only infallible teacher?

If the latter, then you are the worshipper of your own senses, and you are forming and fostering that carnal mind, which is enmity against God. You can truly worship God only by faith, seeing He has thought fit to address you in His Word, and to warn you what is best for you.

A man should therefore say, If I am ever to exercise any virtue by faith, now is the time. Now will I trust in God and obey Him. I will not go into the eternal world a mean, suspicious, self-worshipping and self-indulging brute of the senses. But I will come to God in Christ, and so, through His infinitely merciful grace, I shall be made worthy of Him, worthy to be accepted by Him. I will awake, at His voice, from the dead, and go into Eternity A LIVING SOUL IN HIM, through His most precious blood. Not a despairing leper into a hospital, nor a blind man to be operated upon, nor an abortion of sin to be treated with the surgery of hell; but I will go, complete in Christ, an heir of God by faith in Christ, and a joint heir with Him, made meet to be a partaker of the inheritance of saints in light, in His image; dear unto God, to be presented in Christ before His throne in His likeness, without spot, or wrinkle, or any such thing.

O wonderful prophecy of the Eternal fulness of Christ's dying love! And the riches of the glory of HIS INHERITANCE in the Saints! And the infinite reward of the confession of His Name by sinful men on earth! "We shall be like Him, for we shall see Him as He is. Whom, *having not seen, ye love;* in whom, though now ye see Him not, yet, believing, ye rejoice, with joy unspeakable and full of glory. When Christ, who is our life, shall appear, then shall ye also appear with Him in glory."

The spirit and the Bride say, Come! And let him that heareth say, Come! And let him that is athirst, Come! And whosoever will, let him take the water of life, freely.

The offer and the possibilities now, in Christ Jesus the love, the mercy, the forgiving and sanctifying grace; its available methods, directions, and certainties, now, for all souls; are God's infinitely compassionate and perfect TIME-PIECE FOR MAN'S ETERNITY.

XXXIII.

THE REVELATION OF SIN AND ITS CONSEQUENCES CONSIDERED AS A CENTRAL PROOF OF THE PLENARY VERBAL INSPIRATION OF THE SCRIPTURES.

Both the consequences of unbelief, and the rewards of faith, demonstrate the necessity of a plenary verbal inspiration in any revelation of the attributes of God and the sinfulness of man, for the soul's instruction in the way of life. Sometimes these principles are concentrated as in a mountain of fire for all ages, as in the great central seventeenth chapter of Jeremiah, verses 5, 7, 9, 10. "Thus saith the Lord, Cursed be the man that trusteth in man, and maketh flesh his arm, and whose heart departeth from the Lord. Blessed is the man that trusteth in the Lord, and whose hope the Lord is. The heart is deceitful above all things, and desperately wicked: who can know it? I the Lord search the heart, I try the reins, even to give every man according to his ways, and according to the fruit of his doings."

Here we have the divine eternal laws of justice and judgment, beginning with the heart. And in these words God hath set for us these tremendous postulates of faith, in regard to sin and eternity, for universal human knowledge and experience, heathen as well as Christian, through all ages.

As to the heart, which is what concerns us for eternity, its condition by sin is a cardinal doctrine of truth in moral science, in government, in religion, in theology; an incontrovertible postulate in all our dealings one with another and with God. God's description of it, and statement of the consequences, are at the same time the demonstration of sin, hell, redemption, grace, and heaven. There can be no exaggeration, for it is God's own Word; and throughout the Scriptures, from Genesis to Revelation, deep answers unto deep at the noise of these terrific waterspouts. Yet above all such terrors the rainbow of God's mercy is brighter than the lightnings of justice. And through the whole, and in all men's experience, as in water face answereth to face, so, in this mirror of man's sinful nature, given by God's compassion for man's guidance, the heart of man answers to man, as when God saw that the wickedness of man was great in the earth, and that every imagination of the thoughts of his heart is only evil continually.

"Every way of a man is right in his own eyes; but the Lord pondereth the hearts." And if thou sayest, Behold, we knew it not;—was it not thine own self-blindness that veiled thy consciousness, and hid from thee the eye of God? "Doth not He that pondereth the heart consider it? And He that keepeth thy soul, doth not He know it? And shall He not render to every man according to his work? And shall not the Judge of all the earth do right? Or is God unrighteous that taketh vengeance? God forbid! For then how shall God judge the world? For God requireth that which is past, and will bring every work into judgment, with every secret thing, whether it be good or evil."—Prov. v. 21, and xxi. 2, and xxiv. 12, and Eccl. iii. 14, 15, with Rom. iii. 5.

These concentrated questions and answers are as the charge of an army of God's hosts, with bayonets of electric fire. Antediluvians that rebelled, and patriarchal theologians that walked with God; representatives of human nature, and witnesses for the divine attributes; Enoch, Noah, Abraham, Job, Joseph, Moses, Samuel, David, Isaiah, Hosea, Jeremiah, Ezekiel, Daniel, Peter, Paul, John, lift up one and the same voice of warning in these vast and mighty utterances; the testimonies of man's experience, and God's merciful interpositions accordingly; for the good of the universe, out of mercy to the universe forever.

Such is the testimony, repeated in the Book of Ecclesiastes (ix. 3), that God hath not only set Eternity (both the idea and its warning) in the heart of the sons of men, but that, notwithstanding this, the heart of all generations is fully set in them to do evil; so that madness is in their heart, while they live; and in this quality and character they go to the judgment.

All this evidence, from Genesis to Malachi, is the infallible instruction and warning of infinite, incarnate TRUTH AND LOVE. The love itself demands and creates the infallible verbal certainty. For God's administration is in all mercy and wisdom, especially in its heart-probing severity. He begins with the heart, at the fountain; and thence onward the whole history of mankind is one of vast, instructive, heart-searching and demonstrative experiments: laying open the carnal heart and mind at enmity against God. Experiments, of like vastness of ages, races, and nations; and all the illustrations are of man's depravity, even under all the divine incarnate lights of forbearance, mercy, warning, instruction, and holiness; in the midst of Abrahamic, Mosaic, prophetic, Messianic promises, inviting, forgiving, through a Saviour to come.

The consequences of sin, in retributive justice and self-misery, from Sodom and Gomorrah, down to the whole seven hells of Canaan are revealed; with miracles all the while flaming through the world, the reports of which, and the awful reverberated glory of their judgments, went through all kingdoms; yet

God's Timepiece for Man's Eternity. 257

all the while the human heart unreclaimed, mad upon its idols, desperately wicked. ' And because of all this, precedents of law and grace in a divine revelation always accumulating, and instructions how to deal with the heart, and confessions and prayers written out for our use, full of contrition and faith in God's mercy, and disclosing the experiences of penitent and trustful souls in the way of redemption; a divinely prepared liturgy, inspired by the Holy Spirit for the whole world of sinners, acknowledging the plague of their own hearts, and imploring God's mercy.

And then comes the Redeemer, God Incarnate, GOD MANIFEST IN THE FLESH, and the history of the Crucifixion, and the way in which men have treated God's own ascended Son, and God's whole inspired Word; and the bold denial of both, after ages of the knowledge of Him, who is the Way, the Truth, and the Life, yesterday, to-day, and forever!

God, in all His Word from the beginning, reveals sin as against Himself and against man, in itself and in its consequences, for time and eternity. All His statutes and judgments are infinite in mercy *on account of sin*, and for the *discovery* of sin, and *sense of guilt*, and disclosure of new-creating grace; all His dealings and revelations benevolent, wise, heart-searching, for the eternal saving of men from sin and self and Satan. History, description, the human race in individuals, societies, ages, empires, and God's own legislation for man; in all things searching and illuminating the heart in its wickedness, and demonstrating the impossibility of peace or happiness or good government, except the heart be renewed by divine grace. And so the rejection of God's Word, and of its infallible *word-inspiration*, and the denial of the cardinal truth of man's entire depravity, and of the need of God's methods of grace in Christ, are the destruction of all good, and of all hope of bringing men to repentance.

XXXIV.

INFALLIBLE INSPIRATION OF ALL THE WORDS OF GOD'S LAW-BOOK DEMONSTRATED BY THE NATURE OF ITS TRUTHS; AND BY THE SAVIOUR'S WORDS; AND BY THE CONSEQUENCES OF IDLE WORDS.

And now we come to the links of a *demonstration of the necessary Plenary Verbal Inspiration of every part of the Law-Book of God's government*, with all His own illustrative precedents set down for man's guidance to Eternal Life; by faith in Him, and in His Word, *who is the Author and Finisher of Faith*.

All possible conceivable securities are in this Chronometer and Chart for a safe voyage to Eternity; nothing is wanting for its absolute perfection. If we may trust in God as our Creator, we may also, to the uttermost, in His provisions for us as our Redeemer.

Consider now the immensity and multitude of the truths made known to us in the Hebrew Scriptures, and in the Gospels, Acts, Epistles and Apocalypse. The creation and fall of man and its consequences; the incarnation, death, resurrection and ascension of the Son of God; His unsearchable equality and personal identity with the Father, in all the attributes of God made known to us, or conceivable by us; the succession and multitude of predictions fulfilled in His life and death; the dependence of the destinies of all mankind on His words; His revelations of futurity, immortality, and the judgment to come;—and all these truths, and the knowledge of them, the very truths by which the righteous Judge of all mankind will order the retributions of Eternity. In His infinite righteousness and mercy He can do nothing less.

Does the human reason admit the possibility of a revelation of such truths, without a Plenary Verbal Inspiration of them, *so that by the words* in which they are conveyed, the Judge of all the earth may be justified? Could such truths have been left, as uncertain glimmerings or marsh-lights, or spangles of gold, to be discovered and assayed by human ingenuity from mountains of mere quartz and pyrites? Judgments, statutes, principles, precedents and precepts of righteousness, by which a universe of intelligent immortal beings are to be judged, left to be doubtfully discerned, amidst volumes of forgeries and lies, demonstrated to have been such from the beginning! And so left at the mercy of unscrupulous judges of fact and law, that unprincipled lawyers may keep infinite estates in chancery by technicalities for their own profit from generation to generation! If there be a God revealing Himself to mankind for their good, this is impossible.

And now we carry these surveys back to the qualities, purposes, extent, application and eternity of God's Revelation, as defined in Deut. xxix. 29 (see page 7, ch. 2), and lay them alongside the methods of God's providence, and the histories of His successive revelations to mankind, and the disclosures of human depravity and guilt, and consequent self-caused ignorance, blindness, and darkness; and we ask, *Could anything less than a plenary verbal accuracy be required* of a benevolent and just Creator and Governor, in the volume of attributes and laws by which the subjects of His government are to be rewarded according to their works?

There can be but one answer, and that is given by

Christ. "The words that I speak unto you, they are Spirit and they are Life. There is One that judgeth you; and My words are not Mine, but the Father's that sent Me. All things that the Father hath are Mine. And if any man hear My words and believe not, I judge him not; for I came not to judge the world, but to save the world. He that rejecteth Me, and receiveth not My words, hath One that judgeth him. The Word that I have spoken, the same shall judge him in the last day. For I have not spoken of myself; but the Father which sent Me, He gave Me a commandment, what I should say and what I should speak. And I know that His commandment is life everlasting; whatsoever I speak therefore, even as the Father said unto Me, so I speak."

These are the last words of Christ to the whole world before His death. "I am come a Light into the world, that whosoever believeth on Me should not abide in darkness." It is impossible that anything less than a divine verbal infallibility can be proposed or understood in these communications of Christ for the salvation of mankind.

Our Lord Jesus assumes *as His own* the Divine Attributes of Omniscience and Supreme Deity, by which *He will Himself judge the world*, when He says, (Rev. ii. 23,) "I am He that searcheth the reins and hearts: and I will give unto every one of you according to your works." And in Matt. xii. 34–37, as well as Luke vi. 45–47, "I say unto you that *every idle word that men shall speak*, they shall give account thereof in the Day of Judgment. For by thy words thou shalt be justified, and by thy words thou shalt be condemned." Every word is a work; and word and work, thought and habit, out of the same heart. Every idle word therefore an infallible revelation of character.

Is this a righteous judgment? Heedless words, recklessly scattered by men or angels, may be as fire-brands, arrows, and death, in their lighting on unguarded souls, and rankling as fiery darts of Satan. With what measure ye mete, the consequences as well as the contents, shall be measured to you again. Every idle word! Beyond question, in the face of Eternity, this judgment is righteous. And the same righteous law applies to God Himself, and to God's heart, and to Jesus Christ, God manifest in the flesh, as to all mankind. If God, or the Son of God, could be imagined ever to have spoken or inspired any careless, exaggerated, uncertain or idle words, or ever circulated a fallible word or law, instruction or precept, as infallible truth, and binding upon men as God's Word, that cannot lie, He would Himself be judged by the same rule, and the same law of consequences.

Only this is to be considered, that the consequences of careless words, or false uncertain words or propositions, would be as much vaster and more terrible in God and in Christ, the God incarnate, than in man, as the character of God is infinitely more important than man's character, and the universe of God greater than a man's birth-place, and the government of God than a man's government, and the thoughts and words of God as high above those of man, as heaven is above earth, and unsearchable and germinating and creative as the infinitude of Eternity.

Now out of this unquestionable demonstration by the Lord Jesus, there arises a proof incontrovertible of the infallible divine inspiration of the whole Scriptures; their plenary verbal inspiration; so that every word is divine truth, and no careless words possible, from Moses in the Pentateuch down to John in the Apocalypse.

For we must inevitably apply the rule of consequences, *by which we are to be judged*, to God's own rule, *by which He is to be justified;* to God's Law of Love proclaimed by Moses and again by Christ, by which Law, as given by Moses, the whole universe is quickened, balanced, governed, and beatified forever. Where is that Law first enunciated? In the Old Testament, in the books of Moses! Where and whence did Jesus quote it, and apply it, to all mankind, and for all Eternity? From Moses, and in Deuteronomy, and to the whole universe of God.

Now take Mark xii. 28-34, with the preceding paragraph beginning, "Moses wrote unto us," and concluding, "Have ye not read in the Book of Moses," and compare Luke x. 25-28, What is WRITTEN IN THE LAW, as to the way of Eternal Life? How readest thou? And he, the lawyer, answering, said, "THOU SHALT LOVE the Lord thy God, with all thy heart, soul, strength, and mind; and THY NEIGHBOR AS THYSELF." The words quoted as written in the Law were from Deut. and Leviticus, and comprehended in the phrase "written in the Law," THE WHOLE SCRIPTURES, from which the Pharisees, Scribes, Sadducees, and all Judea, as well as Christ and His Apostles, reasoned alike, as from the whole and sole body of divine truth, all from God, and all unquestionable and infallible.

The whole of Christ's integrity, for us and for all mankind, rests upon the words and authority of that quotation, and upon the truth of Christ's testimony, *that it was given from God to Moses and written by him.*

The two quotations recorded in Mark and Luke are a combination of Deut. vi. 5, and Lev. xix. 18; and both these books are presented and appealed to under the same title and description of *the Law* and the *Scriptures*. The lawyer who put the question, "What shall I do to inherit eternal life?" was answered by Christ, *What is written in the Law? How readest thou?* And the lawyer immediately put Leviticus and Deuteronomy together in his answer. And Jesus said, *Thou hast answered right.*

Part of the first commandment was in Deuteronomy; the other part in Leviticus;—and no question, either with the Jews, the lawyer, or the Saviour, that both books were the same inspiration from God, and both written by Moses.

And then again in Mark, the same reasoning of Christ followed a quotation by Him from the Book of Exodus, on immortality; so that we have Exodus, Leviticus, and Deuteronomy, all here affirmed by the Lord Jesus and the Jews, and their scribes and lawyers, as being THE SCRIPTURES OF GOD, and the LAW OF GOD, and the WRITING OF MOSES, separately and together.

And the great subjects that prove them are the highest attributes of God, as revealed and worded by Himself, for all mankind. But the criticism of the destructives, or what is absurdly called "The Higher Literary Criticism," tears these books and texts asunder, and affirms that only half of what our Lord quotes as the first commandment was ever given by Moses at all; and the rest never revealed

by God, or even proposed as God's law to the
Jews, till near a thousand years later, and then
wrought out as a forgery, to bring about a political
revolution!!

XXXV.

THE LAW OF THE SABBATH, WITH OUR LORD'S DOMINION OVER IT, AND THE GOSPEL TO THE POOR, DEMONSTRATE A VERBAL INSPIRATION—THE FIRST SERMON IN NAZARETH.

The Sabbath is a concentration of the two first
commandments, in the Decalogue, as set forth by
our Lord, (Mark xii. 29-31), "The Lord our God
is ONE LORD; and thou shalt love the Lord thy God
with all thy heart;—and thy neighbor as thyself."
And from the history and laws of the Sabbath, and
their intricate and minute connections with the whole
work of human salvation, we derive a comprehensive
proof of the verbal inspiration of the Scriptures. This
is illustrated in the universality of the Sabbath Covenants of promise, as referred to in Isaiah, chapters
55, 56, 58, compared with Eph. ii. 12, 13, and iv.
4-16, and Phil. ii. 9-11, and Rom. xiv. 9;—covenants
embracing all mankind, Gentiles as well as Jews,
once afar off, but now made nigh by the blood of

Christ, and brought into blissful unity with God, in Him of whom the whole family in heaven and earth is named.

God's law of love lays hold upon men's hearts, and is the only legislation that does this. All other is a mere external *vice;* holding its subjects as for the biting of a file. God's law never deals with symptoms merely, but is the work of Him who judges the hearts of all mankind. All its knots are knee-timbers, growths of its loving life; thou shalt not covet, lie, steal, murder, or commit adultery, growing out of this, *Thou shalt love* thy neighbor as thyself. The not doing this becomes enmity against both God and man.

All the laws of God, whether as to omission or commission, are gifts of His mercy, that we may, by obedience and use, be made like unto Himself, partakers of the divine nature. So, the formula of everything that comes from God is just this, of generosity, and loving care for our good, for Time and Eternity, physical and spiritual.

The Decalogue with all its ramifications, passes *through the Sabbath*, fastening the whole of man's spiritual existence to it, in the provision that six days of labor shall supply man's daily bread for seven days; consecrating the seventh, as a heaven on earth, in its blessed uses and enjoyments, in the worship and love of God. All the successive laws run through this, as through a pulley, and are grappled in the divine organization of human society. For by this foreordained gift and grace of the Sabbath as Christ's day, co-eval with the Eternity of His own holiness and glory, and purpose of human salvation, "the creature itself should be delivered from the bondage of corruption into the glorious liberty of the children of God."

And so the Law of the Sabbath, with all its purposes and appropriations by our blessed Lord, in His incarnation, sufferings, crucifixion, resurrection, ascension, and the gifts of the Holy Ghost attendant on His Word, becomes the law of gravitation in the spiritual universe; upholding all things by the Word of His power, the government being upon His shoulder, even forever.

The Sabbath of God, at the first Creation, is that of Christ for the New Creation. And for this purpose, and in all the divine laws, precepts and promises connected as a spiral of causes within it, the Sabbath is like a *ganglion*** of nerves and will-power, running from the brain and spinal cord in our bodies; conveying the impulses and noting the paths of obedi-

---

* "A mass of nervous matter, forming a centre, from which nervous fibres radiate." Dunglison. In the Hebrew, "*a holiness-day*, a Sabbath of rest to the Lord."—Ex. xxxv. 2.

ence in all directions. Is. lviii. 13, and lix. 21. These arrangements in the human frame, so fearfully and wonderfully made, are forth-shadowings of the sacred verbal minuteness and accuracy of the Divine Words (Spirit and Words, Is. lix. 21), in the creation of the Scriptures and their institutions, by the infallible inspiration of Divine Love. The Sabbath in Christ, and Christ in it, its Lord and Life, are our central illustration and proof of the methods of God's mercy, from the Creation of mankind to the Day of **Judgment.**

How comprehensive and instructive are the graphic accounts concerning it, in God's early, intense, and jealous discipline of the Hebrews in the wilderness, and His carefulness and grace in giving them the reason and the rule of its particulars. Compare Ex. xvi. 29, and the parallel passages. "See! for that He giveth thee the Sabbath, therefore He giveth you, on the sixth day, the bread of two days! Let no man go out of his place on the seventh day." And Ex. xxxv. 3, "Ye shall kindle no fire throughout your habitations." The supposed severity was the fulness of divine compassion and mercy, with a double miracle, perpetual to secure it.

Because, from the Creation of the world He hath given thee the Sabbath; the miracle of thine own rest, as founded in His, prophesied, qualified, and patterned after His; therefore He giveth thee leisure and relief from temporal and bodily wants and anxieties, by the supply of these last beforehand! Thy daily bread and thy spiritual are thus mutually sanctified, in that one good and perfect gift from the Father of lights, who hath engrafted in it and in us, the word of truth, which is able to save our souls, the perfect law of life and liberty in Christ.

Thy daily bread and thy spiritual, acting and interacting in all things for man's good, for body and soul, this world and the next, time and Eternity! A double portion of thy daily bread, over and above all that thou wouldst need in thy six days, is foreordained and provided, for the blessed uses of the seventh, as thy day of rest, in accordance with and enjoyment of God's own rest; in prayer and praise, and the study of His word, without distraction. Thou shalt have no need of kindling a fire of thine own, in any of thy habitations; for the Lord God is thy sun and shield, and thy God thy glory. Ex. xxxv. 2, 3. Is. lx. 2.

Miracle to secure miracle; time, to secure Eternity; the second miracle for daily wants, to increase your faith and gratitude for the first and greatest; in order that ye may at all events not fail to secure *that*, for your spiritual, everlasting life and blessedness.

Ex. xxiii. 25. God does this to all generations, in an organic law of human society, for all the races and families of mankind; enabling them, on their six working days, to provide for the seventh, "that thou mayest rest on that day, *and thy poor and thy stranger with thee.*" Ex. xxiii. 12; Deut. v. 14, 15, 1 Kings, viii. 41–43.

In all this we behold God visible, God manifest in the flesh even before the incarnation of Him who said, "The poor ye have always with you; Me ye have not always;" love them for my sake, and that ye may love me forever. It is my Sabbath service and missionary law. "THY POOR AND THY STRANGER WITH THEE. IT IS MORE BLESSED TO GIVE THAN TO RECEIVE." See Ps. lxxii. 4, 5, 8, 13, 17; Is. xlii. 5–7, and xlix. 8–11, and li. 16, and ch. lv. and lvi. 6, 7; with Acts xxi. 35, Mark xiv. 7, 8, Deut. xv. 11. And so Christ is magnified, and ever shall be, in the whole body of Divine Revelation and in all its institutes, and in all the members of His body, whether by life or by death. For He is "Head over all things to the Church, which is His body, the fulness of Him that filleth all in all."

The deniers of the Divine integrity and authority of the Mosaic Statutes,—more superhuman, more supernatural, than the architecture of the heavens, —are shipwrecked on the records of these unacknowledged Sabbath truths, as foolhardy navigators against sunken rocks.

For the infinite benevolence of this Sabbath Law, promulgated at the creation, established among the Hebrews, connected and co-everlasting with the duty and blessedness of the stated worship of God by the whole world through all ages, is demonstrated, even by scientific sagacity, and search, in the correlations of the human body with its earthly dwelling-place; and more yet, the older the world grows, by sanitary, social, industrial, economical, commercial, historical and spiritual experience. It is the only stay and interruption of human selfishness and worldliness, avarice, ungodliness, and oppressive cruelty, divinely set in the very Almanac of weeks and days, months and years, and seven-fold jubilees; the tides of an angel-watched Bethesda of mercy, as regular as day and night, sunrise and sunset, amidst the incessant toil and misery of sinful men.

If ever there was or could be a supernatural divine demonstration of infallible inspiration, it is this. It is God always, but never man, that promulgates and supports this law; and by a perpetual providence, sends the Sabbath, wherever the Gospel of Christ is proclaimed, with its law of truth, liberty and mercy, indiscriminate, universal, for the security and universality of divine grace, for all nations, through all time, in Christ, THE RESURRECTION AND THE LIFE!

"*Thy poor and thy stranger with thee.*" "The stranger that cometh out of a far country;—do thou, O Lord, according to all that the stranger calleth upon Thee for, THAT ALL THE PEOPLE OF THE EARTH *may know Thy name to fear Thee, as do Thy people.*" All shall possess and enjoy the freedom of thy Sabbath, and its purposes and powers of worship and of prayer. 1 Kings, viii. 43; 2 Kings, xix. 19; Ps. cii. 18.

And then if thou say, What can we do with such immigrations from all nations, and how protect ourselves, supplying them? God Himself shall give *them* the same Sabbath-miracle of all-sufficing manna, as for thee; and their keeping of the Sabbath through thy faithfulness shall be the security both of their prosperity and thine.

In the Lordship of the Sabbath the government of God should be upon the shoulders of God's Messiah, and of His kingdom there should be no end; nor of the supremacy of the Jews over all nations, if they themselves would but keep the Sabbath as God had given it. The keeping of the Sabbath, with its law of freedom and of love, was to be the chariot and covenant of dominion for the Jews, over all nations, and by it they should ride upon the high places of the earth; for the mouth of the Lord had spoken it; thy Redeemer, the Holy One of Israel; THE GOD OF THE WHOLE EARTH SHALL HE BE CALLED.

See the clauses of this covenant drawn out from the fifty-second to the sixty-second chapters of Isaiah, inclusive; and compare these with the ninth and the forty-second. The glory of the Sabbath, and the proofs of a Divine Redeemer in its universal sacredness and dominion, were to be the security of truth and love and liberty to all mankind forever, through His incarnation, sufferings, crucifixion, resurrection, and the interceding, atoning efficacy of His own blood, as our High Priest eternal in the heavens.

The Sabbath, and the Temple services, and the Prayer of Solomon, and the "House of Prayer for all nations," were all typical, prophetic, Messianic; all preparations, by grace and providence, by institutions and securities in them, for the way and coming of the Lord, and for the emergencies of His redeeming ministry and mercy. So, when the Lord of the Sabbath came to His temple and His people, it being for Him, and His gospel uses of salvation, that that "*hallowed*" day was given, and secured from God for all nations, He took possession of it, authoritatively, openly, publicly, as the Divine Lord of it, for the poor and needy. "TO THE POOR THE GOSPEL IS PREACHED;" and the Sabbath by the Lord is guaranteed to them in such preaching, as His divine institution for their good. And this compound and indivisible universal miracle was to John and to the Jews, and to all mankind, the undeniable demonstration of the presence of the Saviour of all.

"In every nation, *without respect of persons*, (see Peter's parenthesis in Acts x. 36), He is Lord of all." This is the divine seal. And now we come to the opening of that seal, at the very beginning of our Lord's ministry, in Nazareth, where he had been brought up. Then and there, known of all, He took for the text of His very first sermon, in the Jewish synagogue, Isaiah's sweet and beautiful silver-trumpeted notes, and said, reading from the book of the prophet Esaias, delivered unto Him, publicly, in the synagogue of Nazareth, on the Sabbath day, opening that book, and finding the place where it was written,—"The Spirit of the Lord is upon Me, because He hath anointed Me to preach the gospel to the poor; He hath sent Me to heal the broken-hearted, to preach deliverance to the captives, and recovering of sight to the blind; to set at liberty them that are bruised, to preach the acceptable year of the Lord." "And He closed the book, and gave it again to the minister, and sat down. And the eyes of all them that were in the synagogue were fastened on Him. And He began to say unto them, *This day is this scripture fulfilled in your ears.*"

It was the laying of the Corner-stone as predicted in the 118th Psalm, refused by the builders.

All the combining prophecies and providences of God, for the Jews and for mankind, were brought to a culmination in this whole illuminating passage of Scripture. The moral and material, the heavenly and earthly, the natural and supernatural, the historical-human, and the fore-ordained, and now fulfilled, superhuman and divine; the testimony of God and man together, known, admitted, indisputable.

THIS DAY, THIS SCRIPTURE! The Lord's Day, the Lord's death, the Lord's resurrection, the Lord's Gospel, the Lord's Scripture of salvation for all mankind! The Sabbath for man; for his physical and mental constitution for Eternity, for man as he is, to make him better; for man self-deranged, depraved, and dead in trespasses and sins, to raise him up to holiness and life eternal, quickened and new created in Christ Jesus, the resurrection and the life.

The Lord's Day, for proclaiming to all nations through all time, the Lord's death, its infinite significance, its necessity for the soul's deliverance from the bondage and the guilt of sin, the terror of death eternal; its saving power, its constraining omnipotence of grateful love and holy motive, and divine confession, and communion of saints. YE DO SHOW FORTH THE LORD'S DEATH, TILL HE COME; all the soul-convincing and converting and sanctifying truths connected with that death, and the Scriptures that rendered it necessary for eternal life to man the sinner, through the grace of the Son of God, the Saviour. The day of infinite glory, on earth and in heaven; in which were set all the laws and means of death to sin and life to God; the whole reckoning and reasoning of souls, dead indeed unto sin, but alive unto God through Jesus Christ our Lord, forever and ever?

XXXVI.

THE QUALIFICATIONS OF THE NAZARENES AS THE HIGHEST LITERARY CRITICS.

If ever a set of critics or textual experts were prepared and eager to detect a word of falsehood, a statement not unquestionably accurate, an alleged authority having the least doubt, or capable of suspicion, it was these guardians in Judea of the Hebrew oracles. And they were the same books, the same chapters and verses, the same minutely scrutinized, established and appointed portions *in all the synagogues in the land*. There was not a rabbi or scribe or lawyer with the key of knowledge anywhere from Memphis to Babylon, from Alexandria to

Jerusalem, but knew where the roll of Isaiah's indisputable prophecies began and ended; not one elder of a synagogue but could and would have detected it instantly if Christ had mistaken or misplaced book or text, or misquoted one of the sacred books, or misnamed its author; much more had He interpolated a single sentence, and still more, had He forged a whole chapter, and applied it to Himself as the writing of God, that had been in existence as a prophecy more than eight hundred years, and was now in His person appropriated and fulfilled.

But of all tribunals to which Christ might proclaim the divine Word, the synagogue of these Nazarenes would be the keenest to detect and the sharpest and most eager to expose and punish a misstatement. They had a sectarian and blind-hearted prepossession and jealousy, so despotic, fanatical, and irresistible in behalf of the Jewish national traditions, and interpretations of a proud worldly dominion, by which the letter and Spirit of the Word of God had been covered up, as by *palimpsests* of human authority, that nothing could have lulled their suspicions, or quieted their rage, at the discovery of an infidel disobedience.

It was as when the lava of Vesuvius had overwhelmed and buried the cities and fields of Pompeii and Herculaneum, incinerating the literature, and erasing all the title-deeds and bounds of possession, and by process of ages creating a new soil and vegetation. So that, if the old inhabitants and owners had risen from their ashes, and laid claim to the land, they would have been put to death as invaders and robbers. Even so, and with a ferocity of patriotic rage, would these people of Nazareth defend their faith against the pretensions of Christ, as the forgery of a traitor and blasphemer, worthy of death. These traditionary smugglers and Thugs of Palestine kept possession of their den and its fortunes, in the name of the Most High. They had a Tarpeian Hill for Lynch law, by the mob of enraged Traditionists.

There are learned men and modern critics to-day maintaining that such extreme prepossession and confidence on the human side of evidence by tradition, are the best possible qualifications for judging the assertions and proofs of the supernatural and divine. These Nazarenes were so perfect and just in this method of criticism, that they swept everything before it; put it in the place of trial, judge and jury. "We have a law,—our Scriptures, and for their interpretation, our traditions;—and by that law He ought to die, because He makes Himself the Son of God and our lawgiver, and the Sabbath, and the Temple and its worship, His. And this He says to us, who know His father and mother and brethren from their infancy."

It was so plain a case, that they could not wait for the slow procedures of justice by witnesses, but their righteous indignation could be satisfied only with the swiftness and certainty of a violent mob-murder. This pretender had set Himself on the highest pinnacle of the Temple of Jehovah, and they would cast Him down instantly in the act of such blasphemy. What need had they of any witnesses? The prophets, and especially the prophecies of Isaiah, which He had perverted, were enough. The whole world knew what those were, and every Hebrew of the nation was ready to die for them, if need be; how much more to punish with the highest penalty of the law so daring a blasphemy of their sacredness!

And now we note, as powerfully illuminating and confirming *the testimony of all the references to Isaiah in the four Gospels, and in the Acts, and in Peter's and Paul's Epistles*, the singular minuteness of the record of the conflict of these Nazarenes against Christ,—the particulars, microscopically photographed as to the proof, the items and the reception of our Lord's first sermon; the calm and serene truthfulness and deliberation with which He is said to have taken every step, spoken every word, and with the most intense watchfulness of all the assembly.

Let us recapitulate the points; for there is no other recital more remarkable for verification.

First, He came to Nazareth; (2), He had been brought up there; (3), He went into the synagogue on the Sabbath day, as His custom was; (4), He stood up to read; (5), the book of Isaiah the Prophet was delivered to Him; (6), He opened that book; (7), He found the place where what He would read was written; (8), He closed the book; (9), He gave it again to the minister; (10), He sat down; (11), the eyes of all in the synagogue were fastened on Him; (12), He began by saying, This day is *this Scripture* fulfilled in your ears; (13), all bare Him witness and wondered.

There was a divine purpose in this minute, life-enacting, vivid, reproducing tracery of words, characters, witnesses, actors, scenery, the synagogue, the Sabbath, the book, the passage, the result.

Nothing in the Gospel of Mark, or any other Gospel, presents so minute and microscopic a tracery; so full of life and reality, and sketched as if a reporter for the Sanhedrim had set it down, as material for the trial and conviction of the criminal. For such was Christ instantly adjudged and condemned to be, by the tenor of His own discourse; as was afterwards His first martyr, Stephen, when Saul also, with the same fanaticism, was consenting unto his death.

That last point, ALL BARE HIM WITNESS. There was no surprise as if an unknown or interpolated chapter or passage had assailed their ears, no suspicion, no uneasiness, but unmingled gratification and assent at the gracious words of the well-known prophet, and of Jesus in reading them, with such divine and loving emphasis and intonations. The fulfillment of them was what they rejoiced in, until He came to the announcement that *they belonged not to the Jews only, but to all mankind; and not for their temporal or national aggrandizement*, but for the salvation of the soul; for the poor, the broken-hearted, the bruised of sin and Satan.

Had He proposed to them to take up arms for Him, as the King of Glory, and to follow Him to victory for the dominion of the Jews over the whole earth, they would have done it; would have acknowledged Him as the Messiah. But otherwise, when they came to understand what He meant, the asserted fulfillment of that great prediction of Isaiah in Himself, and for Himself, the son of the carpenter, as the Son of God, was a blasphemy that changed their satisfaction instantly into the hatred and the fire of hell.

Seeing all this, we no longer wonder at Nathanael's question, Can any good thing come out of Nazareth? But it was God's infinite, providential wisdom, that by these very Nazarenes, who had known Christ from His childhood, the testimony of the prophet Isaiah, *on which Christ rested all His claims*, should be confirmed beyond question, as that of the very Scriptures of God, the undisputed oracles of God, committed to the Jews for safe-keeping, from the beginning.

The same argument applies with equally crushing force to the accusations brought against the books of Moses quoted by our Lord, and against the whole Pentateuch, as a mass of documents, interpolated from beginning to end, and not only never written by Moses, but never known by the Hebrews themselves till near a thousand years after the age of his existence.

And yet there are Christian teachers at this day so liberal, and proud of such charity for sceptical writers, that they aver that the rejection of Moses as inspired may be consistent with a truly sincere and religious belief and character. But they fail to ask or to answer *as to the kind of character that such belief makes Christ Himself to have possessed, and as to the crime of imposing such a forgery upon the world, as the very foundation of the Word of God.*

For the Pentateuch, from Genesis to Deuteronomy, is just that foundation, and verbally inspired of God by Moses, as assured to us by Christ; without whom, and whose Deity as the Son of God, there is no proof of truth or inspiration in any part of the Scriptures, from Genesis to the Apocalypse.

Now mark the strength of this demonstration, as against the criticism of modern Destructives affirming that the prophesies of Isaiah quoted by Christ, and evidenced by the Synagogue of the Nazarenes, and the belief of the whole nation, were an imposture; the forgery of some anonymous villain assuming Isaiah's name and authority. If these critics had been there in Nazareth, thus blaspheming the Hebrew Scriptures, they would themselves have been hurried to the brow of the mountain and flung down headlong. The Isaiah that Christ quoted was the Isaiah of the only Hebrew Bible, that ever Greeks or Jews or Samaritans knew or believed; the only Scriptures that ever God gave to the people in Hebrew; the very books of Scripture translated for the whole world in Greek, some two hundred years before the Son of God came.

This being the case, if Christ *had* forged a single passage, *that* would have been the crime, for which they would have put Him to death. If he did *not* forge the passage, but the whole people accepted it as Isaiah's by inspiration of God, then these critics stand pilloried as in the stocks; and instead of being treated as Christian scholars and believers, are worthy only of the scorn of all Christendom. For under pretence of accurate and unprejudiced investigation and "scholarship," such as never before was known in the world, and a jealousy for truth, superior to that of the World's Saviour, and a sublime intuitive discernment of falsehood such as He never possessed, they put forth in behalf of all mankind, on their own assertion, without one particle of fact, or truth, or history, or even tradition, *an accusation against the very Isaiah as a liar, whom Christ appealed to and quoted as the Prophet appointed and inspired of God to prepare for His coming;* and consequently a charge against Christ Himself, of being base enough and blasphemous enough to allege *that particular passage of those lies, which He must have known to have been forged,* in proof of His own mission and authority from heaven, as the Son of God and Redeemer of mankind!

There they stand,—these "Higher Literary Critics," these rational detectives of the modern age,—confronting Christ, with "Books of Origins," traditions, conjectures, and chronological eras of their own devising, and lives of the Saviour of the world and His apostles, written to order, accordingly; denying, at the outset, the supernatural, infallible inspiration of the Scriptures, as impossible.

What is to be said of the multitude of modern commentaries, exegetical essays, and volumes of "the progressive theology of the future," written on these principles, and not unfrequently commended by professors of Biblical Exposition for the education of students for the Christian ministry? For such writers (even the most learned and genial of them) are worse than the peddlers of plague-stricken garments from the purlieus of rag-markets in Oriental Bazaars. If their postulates are believed by themselves, they are deliberately, "as learned experts," expending the whole energy and subtlety of their faculties and life on the exposition and circulation of the productions of liars and forgers, as being the foremost treasures of the human intellect, and worthy to command the services of the greatest scholars in the world, in bringing out the exact meaning of their lies, for the satisfaction of all generations.*

* Dr. John Pye Smith, eminent alike for his piety, learning, and candor, quotes, in the second volume of his "Scripture Testimony to the Messiah," p. 289, John Fred. Rohr's Letters on Rationalism, published in 1813, as an example of the way in which not only the Old but the New Testament might with little trouble, and very plausibly, be stripped of everything supernatural; and even the doctrine of a future state, under any conception of it, be got rid of. And he adds, "These are the principles which have been for several years promulgated in the theses, lectures, annotations, and still more elaborate works, of some of the men *who hold forth themselves, and compliment each other, as the enlightened and liberal* SCRIPTURE CRITICS *of Germany.*"

"Yet unwittingly," (says Dr. F. W. Upham, in his recently published volume of "'THOUGHTS ON THE HOLY GOSPELS," by the author of "The Wise Men, and who they were,") "and against their will, they are of some little use. For where the

XXXVII.

A PLENARY VERBAL INSPIRATION, NECESSARY TO SUSTAIN AND JUSTIFY THE APPEAL OF CHRIST TO THE OLD TESTAMENT AND MOSES.

Whatever of divine revelation there is any proof of in this world is comprehended in the Old and New Testaments, and embraces the Old as the whole possibility of the New, and the New as the whole and sole demonstration of the Old, in and through THE DIVINE PERSONALITY OF JESUS CHRIST. The ap-

sceptic's finger points in scorn, *there the treasure is concealed.* As these sorcerers go up and down, peering about, muttering their curses, and weaving their spells in the holy land, the divining rods in their unhallowed hands bend downwards, where, beneath the surface, are hidden veins of water and seeds of gold."

The names and writings of Semler, Paulus, De Wette, Strauss, Baur, Ewald, Kuenen, Keim, Renan, Colenso, Smith of Scotland, Davidson, and others, have become familiar in England and America. "In the meantime," says Dr. Pye Smith, "the caution administered by the early Christian writers may prove to be the wisest and best, namely; let those who regard the Lord Jesus Christ as a figurative Saviour, a figurative Lawgiver, King, and Judge, beware, lest, in the day of their extremity; *they find only a figurative salvation!*"

pearance and utterances of such a Being in the world demonstrate all things in the Scriptures to which He appeals. The divine characteristics seen and known in Him explain and fulfil all things. There is no marvel or miracle to be compared in self-demonstration of reality and glory with Him, the divine centre, to which all orbs of intelligence gravitate. All the miracles of the Bible are but as commas or semi-colons, in the Volume of which He is the sum and sun, the personal indwelling fulness of the Godhead bodily.

There is no more possibility of a preconception or forgery of His appearance or knowledge of its meaning, than there could have been that an ape should have created the sun in our solar system, or begotten a Newton to understand it. God alone could foreordain, God only could predict, and only God, in the fulness of time, could make manifest the glory, recording it in words.

The assurance of a verbal inspiration was given to Moses at the outset of his mission. "I will be with thy mouth."—Ex. iii. 13-18, and iv. 12. And when it seemed to him impossible to speak for God, being not eloquent, but slow of speech, a laggard with his tongue, God comforts his infirmity and consequent self-distrust, by giving him Aaron to share the responsibility, "Is not Aaron the Levite thy brother? I know that he can speak well." And it is added, with what an exquisite touch of nature in the recital, "Behold he cometh forth to meet thee, and when he seeth thee, he will be glad in his heart."—Ex. iv. 14.

And then it is added, "Thou shalt speak unto him, and put words in his mouth: and I will be with thy mouth, and with his mouth, and will teach you what ye shall do. And he shall be thy spokesman unto the people: he shall be to thee instead of a mouth, and thou shalt be to him instead of God." Ex. iv. 10–16.

What a graphic description, thus early in the ages, of the nature of divine inspiration, for the communication of the purposes of divine love and mercy to mankind!

"Who hath made man's mouth? or who maketh the dumb, or the deaf, or the seeing, or the blind? have not I, the Lord? Now therefore, go, and I will be with thy mouth, and teach thee what thou shalt do."—Ex. iv. 10–16. God Himself would inspire the words of Moses, and direct his actions; mouth and hands were God's, if Moses would wholly trust in Him.

Could there possibly be a more satisfactory and instructive delineation, a light to guide our steps, from Moses to Christ, and from Genesis to the Apocalypse. But if such a plenary and minute inspiration was deemed necessary in God's dealings with the Egyptians, and with His own people, to bring them forth from their bondage to a rejoicing freedom and confidence in God, how much more in all God's messages for the redemption of all mankind from sin and everlasting misery! How much more where the change of a single word might make all the difference between spiritual life and death!

In Habakkuk ii. 2–4, "The Lord said, WRITE THE VISION, and make it plain, that he may run that readeth it. *The just shall live by His faith;*" and as in 1 Kings, viii. 24, and 2 Sam. xxiii. 2, 3, concerning David; and Deut. xviii. 18, concerning Christ; "*I will put my words in His mouth;*" so in the eighteenth and nineteenth chapters of Leviticus, (both chapters beginning with the words "And the Lord spake unto Moses"), the statutes named are sealed with these words, "*I am the Lord your God,*" twenty-two times in twenty-three verses; the whole closing with this divine rule: "Therefore shall ye observe all my statutes and all my judgments, and do them: I am the Lord, your God." The instances of minute particulars with this formula of asseveration, *I the Lord*, are so reiterated, that the seals of inspiration glitter and blaze with every movement of the texts, as the stones in the Urim and Thummim supernaturally burning on the breastplate of judgment worn by the Jewish high priest.

From the Pentateuch down to Malachi these characteristics of unity and inspiration are indisputable, inseparable, positively declared, and illustrated and proved by the history, as clearly and irresistibly as the history by the contents of the prophecies, and the conflicts between God's holiness and mercy and man's depravity and despair. The argument is so powerful, so conclusive, that it can be met only by conjecture and assertion, as a road cut through mountains by dynamite; or the method of the Brahmin trampling under foot the instrument that convinced his reason against his will.

The prophecies of Jeremiah and Ezekiel are as impregnable in these evidences as the books of Moses and of the Minor prophets, and are sealed with the same seals. "Whatsoever I command thee, thou shalt speak. I have put My words in thy mouth. Speak unto all the cities of Judah, kings, princes, priests and people, all that I command thee. Behold, I will make My words in thy mouth fire. WRITE ALL THE WORDS that I have *spoken* unto thee in a book, and READ THE WORDS OF THE LORD in the ears of the people."—And to Ezekiel, "ALL MY WORDS that I shall speak unto thee receive in thine heart and hear with thine ears, and tell the people, THUS SAITH THE LORD, whether they will hear or whether they will forbear."

The twenty-third chapter of Jeremiah is such an intensely vivid and wrathful comparison and contrast between true and false prophets and teachers, "between the prophets whom God hath inspired, and to whom God hath spoken, and those that speak a vision of their own heart, and not out of the mouth of the Lord;" it is a description so terrible and convincing as to the crime of denying or forging or falsely interpreting the words of a divine revelation, that it might stand as an indictment of God against the volumes of the rationalism and higher criticism of our day; "the prophets of the deceit of their own hearts, by their dreams which they tell every man to his neighbors; the prophets that steal my words, saith the Lord, and put their own in the place of them, and prophesy false dreams and tell them, and cause my people to err by their lies and their lightness."

"I have not sent these prophets, yet they ran: I have not spoken to them, yet they prophesied. But *if they had stood in my counsel*, and had caused my people *to hear my words*, then they should have *turned them from their evil way*, and from the evil of their doings. The prophet that hath a dream, let him tell a dream; and he that hath my word, let him speak my word faithfully. What is the chaff to the wheat? saith the Lord."—Jer. xxiii. 21, 22, 28.

In the records of the historians, and in the books of the prophets, we have the same co-ordinate and successive historic demonstrations, growing out of and returning upon the root-ramifications of the divine inspiration, with a system of nerves, arteries, veins, muscles, intercalated, articulated, synchronized, mutually dependent and sustaining, in a manner so intricate, and yet so plain, so indisputable, that the most exquisite and skilful anatomists of the human frame can not find in man more irresistible proofs of unity, interdependence, assimilation, and growth, from infancy to manhood. So that in fact you could no more take away the proof of divine inspiration, and leave any living truth, than you could cut out from a living man, his spine and the fibres running from it, and leave life or activity in the corpse, that falls prone instantly and returns to dust. The death and worthlessness that ensue upon the completed work of these destructives and dislocators are demonstrations at once of the preceding life and preciousness, and of the actual crime of murder; just as the *corpus delicti* and the arsenic found in the body, are proofs of the means and malice of the murderer.

Their arguments drawn from the strata of human lying and depravity in all literature, against the divine origin and inspiration of Genesis, Deuteronomy, and John's Gospel, their pretences of the discovery and detection of forgeries, falsehoods, interpolations, are as if a hewer of stones or a blind-drain-builder should grope in the sewers of St. Peter's Cathedral, to prove that Michael Angelo never was the architect.

The argument is, in effect, merely that of Hume; all men are proved by all human experience to be liars; therefore, God's words, since they must be conveyed through human beings, and in human language to mankind, are only man's lies. All historical investigation and analogy especially as to reported divine "Origins," necessitates this conclusion. But the blasphemy of this logic is presented by John in the terrific declaration, "He that believeth not God HATH MADE HIM A LIAR; because he believeth not *the record that God gave of His Son.*"—I John v. 10. Where was that record? For answer, take only Christ's own words, undisputed, to the Jews. "Search the Scriptures; for they are they that testify of Me."—John v. 39. Did this appeal comprehend the writings of Moses? "There is one that accuseth you, even Moses, IN WHOM YE TRUST. For had ye believed Moses, ye would have believed Me: FOR HE WROTE OF ME. But if ye believe not HIS WRITINGS how shall ye believe MY WORDS?"—John v. 45-47. Moses and Christ, AND THEIR WORDS, stand together as God's witnesses and God's words, for the judgment of the Great Day. John xii. 48.

Everywhere the testimony of Christ to the authority, authenticity, and perfect truth and credibility of Moses, with all his recitals, is the same. And if there had been a possibility in Christ's day, of undermining the authority of Moses, of charging him with imposture, or any other prophet or writer with the false personation of Moses, speaking lies under Moses' mask, it would have been done. And this would have destroyed the influence and authority of Christ at the outset, and forever.

XXXVIII.

THE LAMB THE LIGHT THEREOF AND GOD THE GLORY—REFERENCES TO REASON AND CONSCIENCE IN THE SIGHT OF GOD—HUMILITY BEFORE GOD THE ONLY SECURITY OF REASON IN THE EXAMINATION OF GOD'S WORD—GOD'S WORD THE TEACHER; REASON THE LEARNER—THE PRAYER OF BACON—THE EXPERIENCE OF COLERIDGE.

The life and death of the Lord Jesus, as the Lamb of God that taketh away the sin of the world, are the Alpha and Omega of all that has any evidence whatever of being God's truth; for there is no moral truth on earth, no explanation of earth's darkness but commences there. It is the source and hopeful spring of all truth, purity, disinterestedness, love, submission to God's will, self-knowledge, discovery of the evil of sin, regeneration out of it into the lost likeness of God, the attainment of holiness and heaven.

So that there is no possibility of any faith in God, any belief in God's goodness, any deliverance from sin, any relief from the pressure of eternal demoniac mystery and evil, bearing the world down to despair, if we do not accept of Christ as God's Interpreter of God's Word and of Christ's endorsement and explanation of the book of Genesis, as the beginning of God's revelation of divine truth and mercy to mankind.

Here then we see plainly the law of a valid, just, and truthful examination and cross-examination of the Scriptures, and of the witnesses in regard to them, and of the mysteries contained in them. Christ is our Divine Interpreter, who only can make them plain. And as He gives them to us, so He stands with us before their transparencies, their scrolls of light, their fathomless perspectives, and directs our sight, our points of vision, that the Holy Spirit may take from them the things of Christ and show them to our souls. He repeats His rule of interpretation, for our teaching of them to others, by having them passed through our own experience. "Not handling the Word of God

deceitfully, but by manifestation of the truth commending ourselves *to every man's conscience in the sight of God.*"
For it is impossible to appeal to conscience as a safe judge in any thing moral, except under submission to God's Word. Conscience is worthless, just so far as the Reason is warped or darkened by sin, as it inevitably is, in a selfish creature. But all sinful creatures are selfish, and all the faculties of the soul partake of that demoralization and darkness, Reason itself being under the same bias, and therefore incapable of a perfectly disinterested and infallible judgment in regard to the divine revelation of law and its sequences for man through eternity. It is neither a judge of God's law written on the heart, nor of God's law revealed in the Scriptures; much less can it decide concerning the last by its ignorance and misconceptions concerning the first. Man having fallen, God alone can teach him what he has fallen from, and what is right and true divinely and forever.

Hence the dangerous tendency of such an affirmation as has been made in a *Symposium* in the *North American Review* concerning the authority of inspiration, "that no law even from God can have any moral force unless it requires *such perfection as man exacts from himself.*" Were we to suppose that God should command any thing of man which *either in kind or degree* man does not *impose upon himself*, His command would have no binding force. A conflict would at once arise between the personal influence or behest of the Creator, and the moral law which the creature finds written on his own heart. In such a conflict the creature, like Antigone is bound to obey the law of goodness, which he dares not offend, however much he may tremble before the wrath of the Sovereign who has power to kill and make alive."

Who but the Creator can tell a fallen creature what that law was and is, or can interpret infallibly its requisitions, and show the creature how he has departed from it and perverted it, putting evil for good and good for evil? His own reason, perverted, exacts from himself as perfection that which in the sight of God and by the judgment of His Word is not only imperfection, but crime. "Immortal man," said Dr. McLeod in India, "is seldom so degraded as not to seek some apparently good reason, and in the holy name of religion too, for doing the worst things. Thus the Thug strangles his victim, as he prays to the goddess of murder; and the member of hereditary bands of robbers consecrates his services to the goddess of rapine."* The same writer once said, "There are men who no more grasp the truth which they *seem* to hold, than a sparrow grasps the message passing through the electric wire on which it perches." They do not grasp it as the truth of God, or an inspiration in it, but an intuition of man's own discovery. These speculative critics resemble the sparrows on the telegraph wire. They are saying one to another, We are the judges; there is no inspiration unless it finds us coinciding with it, and the ultimate judge is our reason.

Was Adam's reason, after he had fallen, the same infallible ultimate judge of a divine revelation, or of the truth, and meaning and intent of God's Word, as before? Could he any longer recognize or judge God's Word, but by submission with a penitent believing heart and mind *accepting* what it might please God to reveal, and obeying God on trust? Man had ceased to be the judge, and coming down from the judgment seat must take his place at the bar as criminal, and must receive his sentence, and the mercy of a reprieve on God's grounds, not his own reasoning. Conceive his saying, I am the ultimate judge—my own reason and conscience. There is no authority higher. Conceive of his asking God, What are you going to do with the heathen? Until you let me understand that, I can not receive what is written as being divine. And if I am to leave the

* "Memoirs of Norman McLeod," p. 420.

heathen in God's hands without a revelation, and they are safe then and so, why am I not as safe, seeing that my reason can not accept a revelation that teaches an endless retribution nor one that avers that man as an immortal being can ever be lost by sin.

A Bible for learners, reconstructed on such principles even out of the Scriptures, with the reason of fallen men as the SUPREME JUDGE, could possess nothing in it of authority, or sovereignty, or certainty, from God the Saviour, for man the sinner. The right philosophy of reason itself is that which investigates *its condition since the fall;* and that can be known only by God's *own history of the fall and its consequences,* in the perversion of man's whole nature. Hence the French philosopher Condillac ("Origin of Human Knowledge," Part I, Sec. 1), made the declaration as a principle of right metaphysical logic, that "*the state of the soul in the ignorance and concupiscence produced by the fall is the only one that can properly be the object of philosophy,* because it is the *only one made known to us by experience.*" The Word of God appeals to *that experience,* shows its universality, and discloses the only redemption from it, by the new creation of the soul in Christ. Rousseau himself said, "The right of the gospel is always unquestionable and reliable, and consistent with itself. Reason teaches us that we ought to obey its precepts, but it also teaches us *that it is above reason.*"

Has the Reason of man been affected by the fall of man, and does it partake intellectually of his degraded condition morally? If this be admitted, then what can be plainer than the conclusion that the Scriptures are God's infallible Rule for our Reason, but our Reason can not be the infallible judge of God's Scriptures, God's thoughts. Hence the truth of the critical maxim of Lord Bacon, applied to the interpretation of Scripture, accompanied with the corresponding views of the profoundest scholars and holiest men of the seventeenth century, such as Lightfoot, Usher, and Howe.

"We are delivered up to the Scriptures *whereto ye were delivered,*" says Lightfoot commenting on Romans vi. 17, "as *they* are to be *our masters,* and *not we theirs.* As another apostle's expression is (James i. 23, 24, and iv. 11), 'We are to be *doers* of the Law and *not judges;* to be the students of the Scriptures, doers of the Scriptures, *not their judges.*' " *

---

* See Lightfoot's sermons on the "Reasons for keeping God's Law," and on the "First Resurrection," and on the "Difficulties of Scripture," and on "The Sabbath hallowed." *Works,* vol. vii. London, 1822. See also Lightfoot's argument on the

The prayer of Lord Bacon, for guidance through all his inquisitions in natural science, his adventures, suppositions and experiments, for improvement in

source of Luke's Gospel, *by direct inspiration of the Holy Spirit,* shown in his use of the Greek word, ἄνωθεν, *from above.* "Harmony of the New Testament," vol. iii. compared with the notes upon Luke, i. 2, 3, vol. xii.: *having had perfect understanding of all things,* not from men, or their narratives, or tradition, but *from heaven itself,* not from enquiry of others, but *by divine inspiration from the beginning.* So ἄνωθεν, *from above,* signifies οὐρανόθεν, *from heaven,* in John iii. 3, 31, and xix. 11, and James i. 17; iii. 17, etc. Compare also Lightfoot's defence of the Doxology, in Matt. vi. 13, and Lightfoot on Acts i. 2, "whether Luke does not, by the word" ἄνωθεν, declare that he understood all these things from heaven, and "*from above.*" "We have taken it as meaning *beyond all controversy,* that he was divinely inspired, and the Spirit from above governed his pen, while he was writing those things." Vol. viii. p. 354. Compare the declaration of Lord Bacon that the divine Scriptures are not to be interpreted as other volumes, but by guidance of the Spirit that made them divine and infallible, for a continuous, ever-adapted, and increasing fulfilment. "For they bespeak the nature of their Author, one day as a thousand years, and a thousand years as one day: and though the plenitude and summit of their accomplishment may be for the most part destined to some particular age, or even given moment of time, yet have they in the meantime, certain grades and stages of fulfilment, through different ages of the world." *Advancement of Science.*

natural knowledge, was the highest exercise of a truly scientific reason. It was, strictly speaking, a more scientific process of inquiry, than the silent worship of the unknown and unknowable, suggested by Prof. Huxley as the highest exercise of a religious spirit. Lord Bacon prayed "that *human* things might not prejudice such as are *divine;* neither that from the unlocking of the gates of sense, and the kindling of a greater natural light, any thing may arise of incredulity or intellectual night towards divine mysteries; but rather that, by our minds thoroughly purged and cleansed from fancy and vanity, and yet *subject and perfectly given up to the divine oracles, there may be given unto faith the things that are faith's.*"

Coleridge, in the account of his own education and early inwrought principles of thought ("Biographia Literaria") speaks of the "stirring and working presentiment that all the products of the MERE REFLECTIVE FACULTY partook of DEATH, and were but as the rattling twigs and sprays in winter, into which a sap was yet to be propelled from some root to which he had not penetrated, if they were to afford his soul either food or shelter." This was a vivid and startling discovery. How true to Paul's and Luther's experience! THAT ROOT WAS CHRIST. And the Spirit in the heart is Christ's interpreter, both of the Word of God, and of the life in it, and of the Heaven in the likeness of Christ, promised by it. This is the experimental demonstration so powerful and comforting to faith beforehand. Dr. South preached a sermon in Oxford in 1699, under this title, drawn from Matt. vi. 21, NO MAN EVER WENT TO HEAVEN, WHOSE HEART WAS NOT THERE BEFORE. Add to this, *no man's heart ever there, but only by the new birth in Christ*, and we have the central demonstration of Christianity.

Experience trusted in, without faith in God, without reliance on His grace, and on the guidance of His Word, makes us never any higher or better than men always have been by nature. Science by itself alone, with all its culture, at its utmost capacity and reach, can give us only a crystallization of selfishness. Genius may shine like a diamond, but it is only carbon, and when all things subject to fire are burned up, it must go the way of common earth. Now if any man trust in scientific experience to make the world or himself better, or if he boast the riches of such experience as a wealth of transfiguration for mankind, he will find himself and his generation in the predicament of the miner in California, reported to have broken open one of the *geodes* in the mountain, and drank from it the water of crystallization to quench his thirst, who immediately himself became a solid fossil. So mankind, though scientifically and to the last degree of perfection, crystallized, will be nothing better without faith, than walking fossils. Men cast anchor out of the stern, without Paul's spiritual science, and wish in vain for the day, not knowing what to do with it even when it comes, but drifting stern foremost.

Unmoored from Christ, and His infallible interpretation, we find the distinguishing truths of the redemptive and regenerating theology, which, sitting at his feet, we have gathered from the Old and New Testaments, gliding insensibly out of recognition, becoming more and more indefinite and distant, reduced, both in themselves and the original books, sources, and persons, from which and from whom, according to the discovered divine plan, we have received them,—reduced from certainties to uncertainties, from divine doctrines to human opinions, from granite to gravel, from truth with distinct angles, to smooth round pebbles, from divine inspiration to human intuition, and from one only true religion to many, equally acceptable to God, if the worshipper of them is only sincere. From a recognized, revealed, divine Sovereignty of moral government growing out of the eternal elements of God's nature, we are brought down to the sovereignty of human judgment, the verdict of a jury of human consciences and opinions as to what is right and wrong, not as that verdict might have been rendered by perfect beings, by angels or other creatures, in the image and love of God, but, as rendered by the moral sentiments of creatures confessedly in rebellion against God, and with darkened consciences.

These "cataracts of truth" in Christ for our eternal life "blow their trumpets" from the very throne of God.* They are not fog-bells, nor lighthouses whose flame may be hidden or extinguished by the ocean in a tempest. But we have an unction from the Holy One, and know all things; because, he that will do His will shall know of the doctrine, whether it be of God. There is our absolute test of certainty, personal, universal, such as no science can present. And of all sciences religion is the most absolutely and profoundly experimental, the most disciplinary; being a comprehensive working and discipline of the whole of man's nature, with examination and self-verification of all the facts. It is the true Health-Lift exercise, by which a man raises himself from death, and knows that he is raised only in, and by, and for Christ; but having that unction from the Holy One, knows by experience, all that he does know, and not by reliance on other men's experiments.

* Wordsworth's "Ode on the Intimations of Immortality in early Childhood." The Ode itself brings to mind the poet's exquisite sonnet on King's College Chapel:—

"That branching roof,
Self-poised, and scooped into ten thousand cells,
Where light and shade repose, where music dwells,
Lingering and wandering on as loth to die;
Like thoughts whose very sweetness yieldeth proof
That they were born for IMMORTALITY."

XXXIX.

ARGUMENTS OF ULLMAN, THOLUCK, LUTHER, AND BENGEL, ON THE USE AND PROVINCE OF REASON, AND THE NECESSITY OF A VERBAL INSPIRATION— IN WHAT SENSE IS THE BIBLE BREATHED FORTH FROM GOD?

"Faith in Jesus, and in His instructions," says Ullman, in concluding his profound treatise on the SINLESS CHARACTER OF JESUS, "is a kind of faith which is not blind and does not sacrifice the reason of man. In no way can that which we believe *on the authority of Jesus* contravene the laws of our own intellect. On the contrary, we feel ourselves *bound to receive his doctrines*, under the assurance that they are the outflowings of the DIVINE REASON, from which have proceeded not only these truths, *but also the nature, the laws, and the necessities* of our own *narrow*, but yet *divinely-related* intellect. We feel assured that there is a *pre-established harmony* between revelation and the human soul; and we are convinced that there will be discovered, at the last, a most exact *agreement* between the truths revealed by the Divine Reason, and the laws that regulate the human."

" Human reason," says Prof. Tholuck, quoting from Luther, "flits and flutters about the letter of the

Divine Word until it has got it to rights *for itself;* that is, in other words, until it has regulated the sundial *by the clock* in its own chamber. But if it is the Spirit of God, who alone teaches to understand the Word of God, then mere working on the letter cannot do this; on the contrary, one must protect himself from the haughty illusions of human reason, by learning rightly to distinguish between the human and divine."

Now how to do this, Tholuck shows in his remarks on the importance of regarding the Analogy of Faith, the whole Plan of the Author and Finisher of Faith. "As what a human author means in a single passage of his book is perceptible only from his meaning in the whole book, and as the importance of a single member of the human body can be known only so far as we endeavor earnestly to understand it from the structure of the whole frame; so also what the Holy Scripture means in any one passage only then is seen, when the reader compares the individual part with the whole, and so interprets. Luther used to say of his own translation, the good understanding was more to him than the disputatious letter." These remarks of Tholuck are to be found in his "Hours of Christian Devotion," on II Tim. iii. 16.

From a child, says Paul to Timothy, thou hast known the holy Scriptures; all Scripture given by inspiration of God, and profitable, that the man of God may be perfect. He could not be perfect for the ministry of God's Word by any Scripture not divinely inspired and infallible. And of such Scripture he could learn the meaning and application only by the mind of Christ, through the Holy Spirit, showing it to the soul, that the things thus learned, freely given of God, might be proclaimed not in the words that man's wisdom teacheth, but which the Holy Ghost teacheth, "Not walking in craftiness, nor handling the Word of God deceitfully, but by manifestation of the truth commending ourselves to every man's CONSCIENCE IN THE SIGHT OF GOD."

It is said that the ordinary barometers in the market are not to be relied upon by farmers, for several reasons, but especially because they so easily get out of order to a certain degree imperceptible; that is by admission of the air to such an extent, that the sensitiveness and delicacy of the instrument for detecting changes of temperature are lost. Now this is just the condition of the common marketable conscience, unless it be kept sealed up for God, hermetically sealed, as it were, under his Word and Spirit. If there is any leakage, any compromise, if the air of the world is admitted, the atmosphere of expediency, self-interest, reputation, convenience, wealth-worship, public sentiment, popular opinion, custom, human law, *to act upon* the spiritual barometer, instead of being *tested by it,* then it plays false, it is no more to be relied upon.

Conscience sealed up for God, under His Word and Spirit, and only thus, can be a true judge. The world and its maxims must not be admitted to work *upon* the conscience, or to get *within* it, for it is only a CONSCIENCE TOWARDS GOD that can be trustworthy, by his own Spirit, not the spirit of the world, nor of the natural man, but by the mind of Christ judging all things for us, and we receiving all judgment, all opinion, *from* the word, by the Spirit.

In the preface to his exposition of the Apocalypse in 1740, the illustrious Bengel says, "If somewhat of the truth has fallen to my lot, I found it in the common way or highroad to heaven, by searching the Word of God with simplicity." And he adds, "God hath taught me, *from my youth upward, to have a view to him only;* and in the meantime, I have undergone so many and so various judgments of men, that as to matters of conscience 'tis all one to me, whether God *and man,* or God *alone,* approve of my doings."

Bengel describes the grounds of his conviction of the verbal inspiration of the Scriptures in a suggestive note on I Peter i. 10-12, "Of which salvation the prophets have inquired and searched diligently," etc.

Bengel says, "We know that the Old Testament

Fathers could not and did not exercise their faith and expectation of the Messiah in such a manner as to exclude all conjectures about the time when He should come. We know this from the text in I Peter i. 11." And here he points out the inference deducible from Peter's words, relating to a question of great importance. "To the Prophets, who prophesied of the grace of God towards the Christians, it was revealed that these blessings did not belong to their own times, but to a then future time. But what the time was, which was signified by the Spirit of Christ in them testifying beforehand of the sufferings of Christ and the glory that should follow, was not revealed to them, else they needed not to have searched for it."

Now, adds Bengel, "where could they search but in *the very words of the prophecies* delivered by themselves *from the Spirit of Christ* in them testifying concerning the sufferings of Christ and the after glory? But *if these words were of their own choosing*, to express the ideas or notions they were inspired with,—it was in vain to search for any notions implied in or deducible from them, *other than what they themselves intended to convey by them, and which consequently were revealed, because well known to them.* They knew therefore that the words they spoke or wrote, *had a more extensive meaning than they themselves yet apprehended*, and implied things yet unknown to them, and likely to be found out by searching. Therefore, *the words* were not theirs, but *those of the Spirit of Christ in them testifying*, concerning the sufferings of Christ and what was to come afterwards. That is to say, THE VERY WORDS, IN WHICH THE INSPIRED WRITERS SPOKE OR WROTE THEIR REVELATIONS, WERE DIVINELY INSPIRED."

"Receive then," says Bengel, "the truth as the Truth, and conjectures as conjectures."

The Spirit of Christ in the Prophets *testified beforehand, before Christ's coming*. But where are those scriptures to be found, thus minutely testifying? It constitutes a demonstration of the antique integrity and truth of the whole book of Isaiah and of the Hebrew Canon, such as cannot be confuted. The whole book, known and quoted so abundantly by our Lord and His apostles was identical with that which we know under the same name.

See the argument of Alexander on Isaiah against the vaunted treatment and arrangement of its contents by the German critics, Ewald and others, as "the latest achievement of the *higher criticism*." "We need look for no invention beyond this," says Dr. Alexander, "unless it be that of *reading the book backwards*, or shuffling the chapters like a pack of cards."

Corresponding with these views are those so powerfully set forth by Prof. Eleazar T. Fitch, D.D., of

New Haven, in the "Bibliotheca Sacra," 1855, on "The True Doctrine of Divine Inspiration." The historical as well as critical argument is presented with cogent clearness and eloquence.

"If therefore," says he, "you inquire in what sense the Bible is breathed forth from God, the true answer is, the whole Book was prepared, by His direction, for the redemption through Christ, planned in His eternal wisdom; by men to whom He gave direct revelations and the wisdom and knowledge necessary to guide them in their writings; consequently the whole Book has endorsed upon it His name and authority. While all other books are *books of men*, this is *the Book of God*. While others are *liable to err* respecting truth or duty, *this is infallible*. While others are *subject* to our conscientious *judgments*, even in the decisions they pronounce, this book, *as the eternal rule of judgment, binds the conscience;* and our only inquiry is, What are its decisions?" "*The book contains, in every title, precisely that, which, in God's eternal plan He foreordained should compose the book; from which none can take anything, or to which add anything, without invading His right and prerogative* to be heard *just as he speaks in His Word.*"

XL.

DEMONSTRATION FROM THE CLOSE OF LUKE'S GOSPEL. THE HIGHEST CONSISTENT WITH FAITH—THE CERTAINTY OF THE OLD TESTAMENT CANON—PHILO AND JOSEPHUS AS WITNESSES — CHRIST'S VERIFICATION BOTH OF THE BOOKS, AND THEIR INFALLIBLE INSPIRATION — IN THE TEMPTATION, FIVE POINTS SETTLED IN REGARD TO DIVINE REVELATION.

The three last chapters of the Gospel according to Luke (the twenty-fourth being the consummation of all that precedes) appear as a rainbow bridge between two Eternities of Divine Truth, with Christ enthroned in the centre as the Keystone and Supporter, the Author, Builder, Interpreter of all. All mankind who would go safely into the invisible world must pass by faith in Him. Nor is there any chapter of divine revelation from Genesis to the Apocalypse more exquisitely pathetic, comforting and demonstrative than this, given by His Spirit, containing the record of the walk to Emmaus. It is a combination of all the sublimest truths both of the Old and New Testaments, from the first chapter of Genesis to the second and seventy-second Psalms, and from the fifty-third of Isaiah to the first of John, and the last of the Apocalypse. It is quite inexplicable how any reader of the whole book can doubt its divineness.

It may be challenged as an example of the wisdom and benevolence of God providing for His intelligent creatures absolute demonstration, as far as the constitution of the human mind would permit, and still leave room for a child's faith in the Heavenly Father's love, without which faith there could be no possibility of any reasoning creature being a child of God, or fit for the worship of God in the kingdom of heaven. It may be said of the demonstration of Christianity contained in these gospels, that the divine nature of the Saviour would not permit it to be less, while the constitution of the human mind for belief in the invisible God and Father would not permit it to be more.*

* Compare Sir Robert Boyle's "Considerations on the Style of the Holy Scriptures"; also on the "Reconcilableness of Reason and Religion"; also John Foster's Essays, Letter VI., on "A Man's writing Memoirs of himself," and Letter III., on "Decision of Character." Also his work on the "Evils of Popular Ignorance." "The withdrawment of the grand truth in question from a man's faith, that is, eternity, an invisible world, and a judgment to come, the whole of revealed truth, would necessarily break up the moral government over his conscience." Foster's argument demolishes the fabric of Secularism. It is a demonstration of the necessity of an education in the religion of faith in Christ, as the only protection of the State from moral disintegration.

Now if any one yet ask, "How can I be sure? There are those that say, This is no history, but only one-sided opinion; a mere sect of dreamers, imposing false statements on the world. There is no verification of all this, outside the little pale of the gospels. What proof is there that the holy canon of the Jews from Moses down to Christ was the very canon that Christ gave to His disciples and that we receive from Him?" The answer presents a fair and satisfactory demonstration by correlations and correspondence of admitted history, and witnesses confessed by the whole historic world, and watermarks extending over ages, and vouchers inextricably interwoven and attached. We have the Greek translation of the Hebrew Scriptures called the Septuagint, just after the conquests of Alexander the Great, demonstrating what were and had been the holy books of the whole Jewish people, in successive ages from Moses to Malachi. At the time when Christ came we have two great admitted historic philosophers and interpreters of Hebrew sacred literature, Philo and Josephus; and a vast population, of whose knowledges and beliefs they are the admitted unquestionable, credible exponents.

The references to these witnesses, if not their original works, are at command of every reader of the English tongue; so that no student need complain of any want of the means of verification. A brief but thorough and satisfactory confirmation of the canon of the Old Testament Scriptures as Christ quoted them is found in Eichhorn's "Historic Investigation of the Canon of the Old Testament," translated and published in New York as early as 1829, by Rev. Dr. Schroeder. The result is this, in Eichhorn's language, that "History attests that after the Babylonian Captivity, and indeed soon after the new establishment of the Hebrew State in Palestine, THE CANON WAS FULLY SETTLED, AND AT THAT TIME COMPRISED ALL THOSE BOOKS WHICH WE NOW FIND IN IT."

Whether the opinions of such men as Philo and Josephus or their interpretations of what is contained in the books be true or false; pure, or mingled with conceits, traditions, fables, philosophies outside, is of no moment whatever as to the question what were the veritable historical and prophetic books which they and the Jewish State, Nation, people, long before Christ came, received and transmitted as the Word of God, an inspired, sacred, infallible literature. They and their followers and readers constitute a body of witnesses, a collection of proofs, as credible in every respect as Julius Cæsar, Cicero, Tacitus, and their believers and the readers of their books; a testimony that never has been rejected by the toughest of sceptics, but received from age to age as historical, for two thousand years. That is one side of the equation of evidence, unquestioned.

Now on the other, we have the life and words of Christ recorded in the gospels, and the subsequent teaching of His apostles, and the growth and history of Christianity, and its work upon the world for two thousand years, referred to and springing from the Old Testament Scriptures, the old Hebrew Bible. And all the words of Christ refer back to those Scriptures as his divine authority, and for Life Eternal, preaching the love of God, and man's redemption, *ever from those Scriptures as God's infallible Word.* Can we conceive of Christ Himself as ever entertaining a doubt as to their authenticity, genuineness, infallibility? Can we imagine the possibility of Christ's appealing to God's Word, and yet admitting that in its reasoning, or its words, it might be broken, might *not* be God's Word? Could it be inspired by the Spirit of God, and yet *the words not so inspired*, as to convey infallibly the thoughts of God, the intended meaning of that inspiration?

There is no such intimation; but, applying them to Himself, as to all mankind, He always appealed to them as binding on every conscience, settled forever in heaven, and beyond question. There is no instance of His ever arguing that point of infallibility, or meeting any man on the ground that it could be debatable. An infallible inspiration, and God's Volume in which it was contained in words, were the ruling divine PREPOSSESSION of His soul.

There is thus settled, in the very first sentence in the ministry of Christ on earth, first, the fact that there is such a revelation; second, that Satan knew it, and acknowledged it, as well as the Son of God; third, that it was not of limited or local application or authority, as for the Jews only, but equally and completely for all mankind; fourth, that it was as binding on the Son of God, AT WHATEVER COST TO HIMSELF in the way of obedience, *as on any other man*, and that the very possibility of blessedness, and indeed of any thing except enmity against God, lay in such trust, obedience, and love; and fifth, that this revelation was and is so known, so determinate, so separate from and superior to all human writings, that the words IT IS WRITTEN, when issued as the final obligation for man's conduct and opinions, are instantly understood as referring to that revealed volume and settling the matter.

These five things do certainly comprehend, in the volume of which they can be affirmed, A PLENARY INSPIRATION, sufficient in fulness and infallibility for all the conceivable purposes for which a revelation from God is necessary for mankind. Absolute truth in such a revelation follows as its inevitable characteristic; and consequently a *verbal* inspiration just so far as *that* is essential to the plenary conveyance of absolute truth. Here then we have the meaning and fulfilment of that declaration in the Psalms (Ps. cxxxviii. 2), "Thou hast magnified Thy Word above all Thy name."

It stands in the place of God, and Christ invokes its verdict and authority as if it were God. There is not the shadow of a doubt about it. There is no more uncertainty in regard to it than there is in regard to God's own existence and attributes. The first manifestation of the grace of God in Christ, after His own baptism with the Spirit of God, is this unconditional exaltation of the written Word of God as the supreme arbiter of human duty, and this instant and perfect submission of all the interests and emergencies of life and death to its authority. This is the foundation and material of the ministry of Jesus Christ Himself, IT IS WRITTEN.

There is no abstraction, no uncertainty as to the enshrinement of this light, any more than there was to the old pilgrims and astronomers under God's heavens, when He took them forth at midnight, and appealed to the stars as His witnesses, His vouchers. Was there any uncertainty about Orion or Pleiades, or any of those glorious constellations beheld by

Abraham or Job, or any question as to God being the Creator of them? Or do we have any doubt that we see the same stars that they saw, and know them to be the same? And now we know through Christ just as unerringly the books of God's Word, as we do the planets of which His Word speaks, and which we behold now in the heavens. We know that they are the very same books that Jesus read, and obeyed, and appealed to, and walked and taught in their light. We know moreover as infallibly that none but God could make them, as we do that none but He could make the starry heavens. What we call the internal evidence of these Scriptures which Christ knew, and to which Christ refers us, is as great, commanding, and perfect, as the evidence of design, and of the being and providence of the Creator in these heavens, under which Christ was born and lived, and which He studied and loved as the works of His Father. None but God could have written one of the least of those letters of light, those all ruling planetary sentences; and equally, none but God could have written the book of Genesis, or Exodus, or Leviticus, or Numbers, or Deuteronomy, or bound them together in their divine unity;—or Miriam's song, or the prayer of Moses in the 90th Psalm, or Christ's reign and worship in the 2d Psalm, or the 19th, or the 40th, or the 72d, or the 103d, or the fifty-third chapter of Isaiah, or the Gospel of John, or the Epistle to the Hebrews.

Such is the immeasurable reach and power of this argument. The Lord Jesus Christ is confessedly the central personage and reality of divine revelation, the Author and Finisher of faith. To Him all truth converges, and around Him, as the central Sun, all light, all orbs of light, gravitate, and on Him they depend. To Him all the testimonies of God travel, and from Him all their rays are reflected back, as the renewed and repromulgated testimony of God; God being His own interpreter in Christ, and not permitting divine revelation to depend on any other than a divine witness. From the cross, uplifted as the Lamb of God, the Redeemer, in death bestowing pardon, and salvation, He flings the Eternal Light backward and forward. And then, in the morning and evening of the Resurrection He appears and travels with His disciples through the whole Old Testament; bidding them search it as for their life, because it testifies of Him in His sufferings, death and glory; assuring them that in it, it is not man, but God that testifies, and expounding unto them in all the Scriptures the things concerning Himself.

And thus, from the same central position, as the Way, the Truth, the Life, He creates and establishes the *method, the certainty, the matter and argument of the*

New Testament Scriptures, Himself their life, their convincing, sanctifying, new-creating radiance and power, in the record of His own life, sufferings, miracles, death, resurrection, ascension; in the Gospels, Acts, Epistles; Himself, His blood, His Spirit, His love, the fountain of all their inspiration, the vital element of their life-giving light. From Genesis to the Apocalypse He shines, the Alpha and Omega, the beginning and the end, the first and the last, the end of the law for righteousness, the manifestation of the divine attributes and glory, the object, consummation and proof of all divine revelation. From Eternity to Eternity it is the new song, ever old and ever new, of Moses and the Lamb. Great and marvellous are Thy works, Lord God Almighty! just and true Thy ways, Thou King of saints! Blessing and honor and glory and power, be unto Him that sitteth upon the throne, AND UNTO THE LAMB, FOREVER AND EVER.

XLI.

ARGUMENT FROM THE IMPORTANCE OF PARTICLES—JUSTIFICATION BY GOD'S WORDS—PAUL'S ARGUMENT OF THE RESURRECTION.

The discussions between profoundly learned men concerning the place and meaning of particles and articles in a dead language are full of instruction. If the view of a strictly verbal inspiration has been carried to an extreme, introducing difficulties that really do not exist, the denial of it, and the supposition that an infallible revelation could be conveyed without words, by the inbreathed thought merely, without the forms of speech necessary for its complete and accurate presentation, leaves the accuracy of the message open to a denial that may be fatal to its power, at the mercy of the merely human and uninspired utterance. There must have been, we are ready to say, a choice of words by the Divine Spirit, for the divinely inspired writer, a guardianship securing the utterance of the truth that God chooses to convey; an inspiration sufficiently plenary and verbal to make the message a thing to be received as the Thessalonian believers were praised for receiving it, *not* as the word of men, but *as it is in truth the Word of God*, which effectually worketh, *not in word only*, but in power and in the Holy Ghost, and in much assurance.—I Thess. i. 5, and ii. 13. The original utterance may be misinterpreted, may have suffered alteration in being transmitted, or translated, but as it came from God, it must have been infallible. And God in Christ, to reconcile the world unto Himself, and draw men by divine truth, must have been infallible in His own quotations from His own Scriptures. And so with Christ's inspired disciples. It was at His own pleasure to vary the language in quoting from Himself, but always without error, without contradiction; always in accordance with the fulness and accuracy of His own known meaning.

We have said, *as it came from God*. In this conviction, which was a just postulate, by God's own announcements, the Jews of old, *neglecting the Spirit*, which *giveth* life, and cleaving to the letter, which *conveyeth* it, went to such an extreme of superstition as worshippers of the letter, without the Spirit, that it was no longer the Divine Word, living in them, but, as in the worship of the brazen serpent, instead of the Saviour typified, they became idolaters. But they might well be worshippers even unto martyrdom, not without reason, not without a divine providence and intuition directing them, in belief and defence of the Word, as *letter and Spirit* in one, as in Is. lix. 21. So alone were they justified in their jealousy and scrutiny and painful accuracy as keepers of the oracles of God, because the words of their Scriptures in those oracles, were God's words. So only are we justified in the stress we are accustomed to lay upon the words of every passage which we contend for as inspired. The exact meaning of it could only be conveyed to us in exact words, perfectly truthful, without error; that is, such words in our own human language, as were sufficient for God's purposes of infallible saving truth, in the conveyance of His own thoughts.

Do we think in language, or does the language also, by divine commission, think in and for us? There is certainly a process in the mind, for and by which the language is minted, as there is melted gold before its pieces are coined and weighed and stamped. For exact thought, exact words; for loose thought, careless words may answer; but for divine thought, and eternal destinies and responsibilities, and with such a canon of eternal judgment as this, "By thy words thou shalt be justified, and by thy words condemned," God's words also must be *His* justification, as having been inspired by His Spirit, for our infallible guidance.

Now the argument from all these trains for the necessity of a divine infallible inspiration is as complete and perfect as that for the existence of God from the proofs of benevolent design in nature. Is God our Father? Would He then leave us without instruction? Would He leave us in the power of falsehood?

The answer is to be found in the examination of what He *has left us*, which, if it be not from God, there is no proof of a good God at all upon the earth. All such proof concentrates in Christ, the Author and Finisher of Faith; Christ, without whose coming and manifestation as the Light and Life of men there could be no such thing as trust in God, the affectionate obedient trust of the child in the Father, but only the relationship of distrust, remorse for the past and dread of that which is to come. But Christ living, dying, rising, hath brought life and immortality to light; life in the eternal presence and likeness of God; life in participation of the divine nature, through God's own promise of a new creating spirit in the soul of each believing man, according to God's Word.

This is Paul's own argument in regard to the resurrection. He proves that Christ rose the third day, *according to the Scriptures;* but if Christ be not risen, the Scriptures are false, and so our faith in God is vain, impossible. But, the Scriptures being inspired of God, Christ is risen, that inspiration being infallible. God's infallibility, absolute in His Word, is the foundation of all divine truth. Higher than this inspiration need not, can not, go; lower than this, it can not be from God, can not be God's testimony, but is worthless. This may be called reasoning in a circle; but it is God's circle, reasoning from Himself to Himself; beyond which there is no standpoint for intelligence, either of angels or of men.

It must come to this, an infallible inspiration, or none at all. Revelation is worthless, if not written; if written, dependent on the words; impossible to be written, except by inspiration from the Revealer, guiding the writer. In this case, the words must obey and follow the thoughts, not the thoughts the words. The thoughts inspired of God are creators of the words, in order that the words may be creators of the thoughts that God intended to convey, in other minds, the truths necessary for the object of revelation. Inspired truths, involving eternal consequences, can not be communicated infallibly, without inspired words. But if no eternal consequences, then not necessary to be revealed, and no divine inspiration requisite.

But Christ's appeal to all mankind, and in behalf of all mankind, because of immortality, and its eternal consequences correspondent with character before God, was, beyond all denial, to a known unquestionable record in sentences and words from

God, and for man's eternal good. A definite, divine revelation in writing, for the just guidance of the human conscience; a spiritual revelation connecting every soul with God the Creator and Judge; a Light of Life, over against tradition, naturalism, evolution, the imagination, thoughts, philosophy, and written intelligence and science of man. It is God's written word, authoritative, decisive, supreme, the last absolute tribunal. It may be traced back by human investigation, till it is lost from sight in the unsearchable source of all things, the Creative Fountain of all knowledge and force in the Old Testament; and then in the New, the boundless mystery of godliness in the Word made flesh; the first verse of John's Gospel answering to the first verse of Genesis, " In the beginning was THE WORD, and the Word was with God, and THE WORD WAS GOD." On earth incarnate, and in heaven enthroned, God over all, blessed forever, the Almighty Saviour of the never dying soul!

XLII.

THE NECESSITY OF A VERBAL INSPIRATION PROVED BY THE ADVOCATES OF EVOLUTION—IF IN THE MATERIAL, MUCH MORE IN THE SPIRITUAL UNIVERSE.—AN IMMUTABLE CERTAINTY THE ONE ESSENTIAL ELEMENT.

The possibility of infinite consequences resting on a single word, in the expression of thought, as on a single muscle or nerve and its position in the human frame, is presented in the reasoning even of Prof. Huxley so distinctly, that his scientific illustration may be taken as a very impressive argument of the necessity of a strict particular verbal inspiration for the guidance and welfare of men's souls, *if any inspiration is admitted at all.* Prof. Huxley's Philosophy of Evolution from a practical eternity without a personal God and Saviour does not admit it, nor any personal providential intervention in our affairs. But his argument from natural necessity in the physical universe which he maintains, applies with incomparably greater force to the spiritual which he rejects. Even if mind and matter were both merely forms of a natural evolution from eternity, without the directing will of a Creator, still the necessity of a verbal infallible accuracy and unchangeable fitness remains; for without it every thing might go to ruin at any moment. If spiritual truths were merely evolutions of material forces, still they are confessed to be the highest and most potent of all, and consequently, the formulas or words in which they are conveyed must be infallibly secure.

"The change of men into brutes or brutes into men," says Prof. Huxley, "may hang upon a breath of damp or dry air blowing in the epiglottis. If I alter *in the minutest degree*, the proportion of the nervous force now active in the two nerves which supply the muscles of my glottis, I am dumb. The voice is produced only so long as the vocal chords are parallel, and then only so long as certain muscles contract with exact equality, and that again depends on the equality of action in the two nerves. *The minutest change would render us all dumb. But dumb men would be little removed from the brutes.*"

"What constitutes and makes man what he is? What but his power of language? that language giving him the means of recording his experience, making every generation somewhat wiser than its predecessor, more in accordance with the established order of the universe? This power of speech, which enables men to be men, looking before and after, in some dim sense understood, is the working of this wondrous frame, and which distinguishes man from the whole of this brute world."

"Let me," says Prof. Huxley, "slightly crush together the bearings of the balance-wheel of the watch, or force to a slightly different angle the teeth of the escapement of one of those bearings, and the watch will cease to go. Let me puncture the jugular vein, and the result will be that life ceases. *The brute and the man are no more different, than the watch with and without a main-spring.*" *

Now then we rightfully apply this proposed material demonstration to the spiritual world, and the necessity of a plenary verbal inspiration there. For the words are as the molecules, magnetic and attractive, the combinations of which produce organized thought, and the certainty and command of which are essential to exact and accurate thought, reasoning, and expression. The inevitable certainty follows (a Creator being admitted) of as minute and plenary a guardianship, protection and infallible determination by the Father of our spirits, of all the springs and links, the coin-words and key-words of truth, that connect our souls with Him, and govern our eternity. There must be a moral exactness and infallibility as sure at least, as that physical and mathe-

* See Huxley's "Man's Place in Nature," and "Origin of Species," pp. 148, 149.

matical arrangement by which the moon was appointed for seasons, and the sun knoweth his going down, and man his frame and labor until the evening. For a breath of expression, the alteration of a word, may produce all the difference between men and angels, heaven and hell.

Here again opens the whole universe of *penal warnings*, as absolute and certain as the *promises*. And here again is our argument, irresistible, absolute, as to the necessity of all this portion of God's disclosures to sinful creatures being set forth in language as deterring, in words as chosen and exact, as suitable to the infinite realities conveyed, as the other corresponding heaven of inducements, the terms of which are laid by God's angels as coals of living fire from His altar with His Spirit upon the soul. And this is the perfection of an infallible revelation spoken "not in words which man's wisdom teacheth, but which the Holy Ghost teacheth," comparing spiritual things with spiritual, nothing kept back that was profitable, no declaration of the whole counsel of God shunned, or made doubtful.

"The power of speech in some dim sense understood," Prof. Huxley argues, "*enables men to be men,*" although in reality mere machines of intricately organized and magnetized matter. But if they are to be angels of the resurrection, sons of God, in the likeness of His incarnate glory, then how much greater the necessity of an infallible divine care and workmanship in the word-thought machinery, by the working of which this infinite and eternal spiritual transfiguration is to be accomplished. For it is only by "*obeying the truth through the Spirit*, by the Word of God which liveth and abideth forever," that sinful men, believing, are thus "born again," and *enabled* to praise their Redeemer and New Creator forever. Only so, that by learning as little children their alphabet in words of two syllables in the nursery of Christ on earth,

> "They, in a nobler sweeter song,
> May sing His power to save,
> When this poor, lisping, stammering tongue
> Lies silent in the grave."

The necessity of a verbal inspiration may therefore be seen not only in the nature of the minutest escapements and nerve-connections of language, but much more in the concentration and comprehensiveness of thought contained in those phrases, in which are conveyed the grandest mysteries of God, Christ, the Moral Universe; God's plan, from the beginning through the never-ending ages. These phrases are the prisms through which alone the Divine Light falls upon our understandings, and so in God's light we see light. Only the Spirit that revealed the thoughts, could com mand the forms of words suitable for them, the garments in which they can be made visible, intelligible. Paul's words may be taken as illustrations; describing his own experience, his incommunicable revelations from God, and his consequent agonizing conflicts in prayer for others, and the method and glory of God's love for lost dying sinners, raising them, by the disclosure of that love in Christ's death, from their death in trespasses and sins to the throne and likeness of their divine and infinitely glorious Saviour, new created in his image.

So the two vast and magnificent prayers of Paul contained in Eph. i. and iii., and Philippians iii. 8-12: —the combinations of an infinite survey of the nature and riches of redemption in Christ, by laws extending to all worlds, with the means of the personal realization of such redemption, and its infinite prize of glory everlasting in Paul's own case; "that I may know him, and the power of His resurrection, and the fellowship of His sufferings, being made conformable unto His death."

Every phrase has to be studied and translated by other correspondent shafts of light; every one being a painting in itself, a Parthenon of divine revelation. Let any man enter amidst these expressions, and ponder them, and ask if it be possible that Paul, or any other man, without a verbal inspiration, could have written them. An infallible writer of such communications from God must have had God to choose His own words for him.

The imagination is taken by these divine talismanic word-gems, of burning light, and carried from point to point in an infinite range of conceptions through the universe. The soul of the believer may be thus on fire and active at the sight of a dome of the Celestial City, photographed by John; or a text of the gates of pearl; or a mention of the sardonyx, the ruby, the chalcedony; the strong and ardent regenerated affections leaping up as a festal pyrotechnic at the touch of a match in the hand of the master. But in Paul's words the thoughts are always conducting us from all our wanderings to that life-giving sacrifice of Christ, whose offering on the Cross made thought and language for us a blessing, not a curse; we ourselves, through the grace of His dying love, becoming "dead indeed unto sin, but alive unto God, through Jesus Christ our Lord." Every part of God's Word, intended for this divine result, or bearing upon it, in Law, History, Prophecy, Miracles, Types, Ceremonies, Sacred Songs, and records of Faith and religious experience, must have been, as ordered of God, infallibly and verbally true and important.

XLIII.

THE EXACTNESS AND FULNESS OF DIVINE INFORMATION AND SPIRITUAL LAW—"IF IT WERE NOT SO, I WOULD HAVE TOLD YOU"—THE GREATEST OF MIRACLES, DEPENDENT ON WORDS.

Spiritual things with spiritual. Take, for example, the contrast between death and life, in Rom. v. 21, and the characteristic, inevitable, respective results as stated in ch. vi. 23. "For the WAGES of sin is DEATH: but the GIFT of God is ETERNAL LIFE, through Jesus Christ our Lord." *What kind of death,* to answer for a spiritual comparison, since the death of the body is as inevitable as its life, for all creatures?

God's Word is kept, to use the sailor's phrase, *close hauled* to the wind from eternity. There are calms, lulls, catspaws, gales; but the steady set of the aerial current of thought and language is towards immortality and eternal consequences; and there are days when a very little disarrangement between the sails and the wind would provoke shipwreck. There is no carelessness with God; no possibility of random words, or want of forethought.

It is instructive to consider the effect upon the whole Word of God, if instead of admitting the significance of *eternity* upon its *warnings* as well as its promises, we deny the reality of a retributive harvest in the future world from men's sowings in this life. Carry such denial through the Scriptures, and apply it as the measure, the test, of an opinion or belief of the final salvation of all men, and it would be like running a subsoil ploughshare through an acre of medicinal plants and flowers, every furrow strown with herbs torn up by the roots.

Take the words of Christ, "*If it were not so, I would have told you.*"—John xiv. 2. Applied as He applied them, *to what we are to meet in the future world*, they are of intense and infinite grasp and importance. They show incontrovertibly that *no truth of eternal bearing on our faiths and habits of character and action would be left out, or doubtful in a revelation designed to prepare us for a future existence.* " In my Father's house are many mansions," enough for all who come to the Father through Me. They shall never perish, neither shall any power pluck them out of My Father's hands. Where I am there shall My servants be, and BECAUSE I LIVE, THEY SHALL LIVE ALSO. Oh blessed assurance!

What was the converse of these propositions, or the wanting of a mansion in the house of His Father, or the perishing of those who did not come to Christ, or the abode of those who would not live with Christ, and yet would be found existing somewhere without Him? If there was not such a perishing, such a

DEATH IN LIFE, out of Christ, if there was no danger of such eternal death, and no possibility of it, *I would have told you*, and you need never have been terrified with falsehoods concerning an imaginary hell.

Now run through the tenor of the Scriptures, and it will be seen at once that there is neither mystery, nor uncertainty, nor doubt, as to men's reaping in eternity what they have sowed in time; but the consequences of sin are as eternal as sin itself is, in every sinful being, who has not fled for refuge to Christ, the soul's only Redeemer. Sin and its everlasting consequences are the realities out of which, and *because of which*, there comes the revelation, the offer, of Christ and His grace. "If it were not so, I would have told you." If none were to be lost, if none *could* be lost eternally, I would have told you. But in that case the whole Bible would have to be written over again, and all that I have taught you of the terrors of the judgment, and the fate of the wicked would have to be expunged.

God has said, in the Scriptures which you confess are His Word, that "the soul that sinneth, it shall die;" and you know that the thing here meant is not the death of the body, or the mere separation of the soul *from* the body, but a *spiritual* death, the consequence and experience of the sins done and habits wrought by the soul in the body in this life. And I have said, and tell you now again, that if ye believe not in Me, as your Saviour from your sins, and come not to the Father through Me for His grace, ye shall die in your sins, and *where I am, thither ye can not come.* "If it were not so, I would have told you." If there were not these eternal consequences hanging upon your reception and belief of My words, or your rejection of them, I need not have spoken. I need neither have warned you, nor died for you. There would have been no adequate reason for My sacrificial expiation, nor any truth in the threatening of dangers to which you could not be exposed. If there were any other possibility of eternal salvation for you than that which is offered to you through a present faith in Me, I would have told you. "I am the door. By Me if any man enter in, he shall be saved. Strive to enter in, for many will seek to enter in and shall not be able, when once the Master of the house hath risen up and hath shut to the door."

"If it were not so, I would have told you." For I came to deliver them who through fear of death were all their lifetime subject unto bondage. But now I tell you, Fear nothing but *that death of the soul,* and him who alone is able to inflict it. "Yea, I say unto you, fear him who is able to destroy both soul and body in hell."—Matt. x. 28.

Oh what an infinite reach of welfare and of meaning, of importance to man, and compassion in God, do these words cover! And if they can and must be applied to the possibility of there not being mansions enough to offer and secure in heaven, for those who are on the way thither through faith in Christ, how much more to the dread vast question, "What shall it profit a man if he gain the whole world and lose his own soul? Or what shall a man give in exchange for his soul?" Can there be any other penalty than that of eternal consequences to be apprenended for those who deliberately, in this world of offered mercy, shut themselves out from such mansions; rejecting from their own souls the grace of a new-created character in Christ, mercifully placed at their disposal by Him, that they may be prepared for heaven, and saved from eternal death?

The believing spirit always sees further than the unbelieving, and nothing can commend itself to the reason as more just than the principle in divine things that to him that hath shall be given, according as he values and keeps what God hath already bestowed. The grace revealed in God's Word as a divine gift to faith, is the only key to the *science of that Word;* the only method by which its treasures can become possessions of the mind. Some men who have denied wholly a divine inspiration of the Scriptures have nevertheless perceived clearly that the supernatural teaching and experience set forth in them are the only perfect method of defending their truth; and they only are consistent reasoners, who *submit their reason entirely, trustingly,* to God's. Deists within the Church of England at one time rejected the supernatural, and regarded all belief in it with as great a degree of scorn as has ever been expressed in our day by what is called "modern scientific thought."

Lord Bolingbroke was one day employed in the morning in his study reading Calvin's Institutes, when Dr. Church, a divine of the English establishment called on him. The deist asked the divine if he could guess what book it was that he had been studying? "Really, my lord, I can not," answered the doctor. "Well," said Lord Bolingbroke, "it is Calvin's Institutes. What do you think of such matters?" "Oh my lord, we don't think about such antiquated stuff; we teach the plain doctrines of virtue and morality, and have long laid aside those abstruse points about grace."* "Look you, doctor," said Lord

* Toplady, in his essay on "Life a Journey," relates the fact that a great churchman, then living (August 1775), said to a lady of quality, "Do not tell me of St. Paul, madam: it would have been happy for the Christian Church, if St. Paul had never written a line of his epistles."

Bolingbroke, "you know I don't believe the Bible to be a divine revelation; *but they who do can never defend it on any principles but the doctrine of grace.* To say the truth, I have at times been *almost persuaded to believe it upon this view of things;* and there is one argument which has gone very far with me in behalf of its authenticity, which is that the belief in it exists upon earth, even when committed to the care of such as you, *who pretend to believe it, and yet deny the only principles on which it is defensible."*

XLIV.

A VERBAL INSPIRATION AS ESSENTIAL AS A PARTICULAR PROVIDENCE—THE SCRIPTURES GOD'S TELEGRAPHIC STATION FOR THE UNIVERSE—THE GREATEST OF ALL MIRACLES—THE HABIT OF CONJECTURES A HABIT OF SKEPTICISM—THE INIQUITY OF MAKING OBSCURITIES THE WEAPONS OF SATAN TO DO HIS WORK.

The demonstrations of a necessary verbal inspiration, in the terms of a published universal law, having Eternity for its range, and all created intelligences for its subjects, are as positive, complete, unquestionable, as those of a particular divine Providence, necessarily extending to all events, influences, and persons. The co-ordination of man's free agency and God's foreknowledge cannot be denied. But the admitted coincidence of the human and divine in the authorship of the Bible, involves the presence and providence of God, supreme in every part, in word as well as thought, as also in the freedom and spontaneity of man, in order that the whole Book may be the whole and infallible truth. For such it must be, if supreme for Time and Eternity.

The places of men's birth, the disciplinary arrangements and tenor of their education, and the consequences of their purposes, thoughts, opinions, and actions, together with the social, political and moral facts and biases, by which their opinions are established, and their characters and powers developed and exerted, are so linked in with the elements and organizations of our globe, with the earth's configuration, atmosphere, climates, clouds and rain, seasons and their changes, vegetable productions and animal races, that the minuteness, omnipresence, and activity of the providence of God, throughout and over all these things, are inevitable. Such providence, connecting and interweaving the spiritual and material, in what is called the "conservation and correlation of forces," morally and physically, must have been universal, infinite, particular; uniting God's spiritual and material kingdoms, and the perfection, government, and protection thereof, in mutual harmony and melody. Every shaft of light, and all the laws of light, every mote in the sunbeams, every raindrop, every variety and degree of strength in all the elements, must have been determined; and their atomic combinations, invisible to us, and incomputable, (save only that we perceive the absolute necessity of their being exactly weighed and measured,) must be providentially ordered by the Infinite Intelligence, that has the care and compounding of them.

There is a sympathy between the physical laws of God's universe and the spiritual, and it may be that God will commission Science to make discoveries at present inconceivable, as to the connections and lessons. All men's sincere researches build better than they know; and even Caiaphases and Pilates, as well as Balaams, may be found again to have prophesied, while attempting to subvert Christ's kingdom. Kings will be nursing fathers, and queens nursing mothers to the Church. Royal Hirams will quarry stones, and fell and float timbers for God's Temple, as in Solomon's time. The scientific observers of the transits of heavenly bodies will be themselves spiritually illuminated, and armed with new instruments, as were of old the Bezaleels and Aholiabs of Judah and Dan.

As God filled the master workmen under Moses " with

the spirit of God in wisdom and in understanding, and in knowledge, and in all manner of workmanship" for the completion of His earthly Tabernacle, so and much more for that not made with hands. The infinite sublimities of the 72d Psalm, and the forty-ninth, sixtieth, and sixty-first chapters of Isaiah, are to be transacted. "The Lord shall be unto thee an everlasting light, and thy God thy glory. For as the earth bringeth forth her bud, and as the garden causeth the things that are sown in it to spring forth, so the Lord God will cause righteousness and praise to spring forth before all the nations."

How infinite the privilege, how blissful the service, of a loving, consecrated workman, in preparing the very least of the instrumentalities of this glory! For it is all ordered of God, to every man his sphere, his errand, and his gift, "and the ministration of the Spirit to every man to profit withal." Every man's heartfelt work upon and for the Scriptures, in every book, in behalf of every verse, every word, is God's providential care and love.

"For that ye ought to say, If the Lord will, we shall live, and do this or that. For every good and perfect gift is from above, and cometh down from the Father of lights, with whom is no variableness, neither shadow of turning." "Of his own will begat He us with the Word of truth, that we should be a kind of first fruits of His creatures;" examples, patterns, first-fruits of the spiritual fruit-tree, "yielding fruit after his kind, *whose seed is in itself.*" And as the Volume is to be used in so many millions of varying cases, and under such infinite variety of circumstances, for the work of regeneration by the Spirit with the truth, every word is important, and must have been, in its connection and meaning, appointed with special design and certainty.

The Scriptures are as a telegraphic station of thought and word for all parts of the world, and all intelligent creatures in it; consequently, every appointed cypher, syllable, signal, arranged and definite; and the Supreme, Only Wise, MASTER-MIND using them accordingly, knowing their absolute exactness and importance. A military commander must not only have his own position, known, but all the distant as well as near correspondences of men and things with it. Every soldier must be in his duty, at his own post, as well as every regiment and officer. Every Word is a soldier of God, not to take the place of another, but having his own sphere, fitness, activity. The genius of a great general is tried by his arrangement and possession of details, in the organizing and handling of an army, compacted, as a building, "according to that which every joint supplieth." The work of coral insects for the building up of an island or a continent; the weaving of an atmosphere for the life of man and the growth of all nature, by exact, invariable, infallible measurements of oxygen and nitrogen; the waves of motion in light and sound, and of the elements that make substance and color, and the correspondences of sense and sight accordingly; all intricate and wise particulars in nature, with their known and immeasurable importance, are symbols or illustrations, assuring a still greater definiteness and certainty in the language of the truths of God's spiritual kingdom for eternity. If the inspiration of the words, events, personages and laws, set down in the record of a divine revelation, were merely human, fallible, uncertain, then none of the securities could be trusted, none could be proved to have been given by God, or their requisitions binding on the conscience.

The greatest of all miracles, the spiritual, are dependent on the meaning and use of human speech, divinely adapted and conveyed, attended by the Holy Spirit in the soul. The heart-felt, contrite conviction of *sin against God* is a miracle; being nothing less than the beginning of Eternal Life, an infinite supernatural work, in a soul dead in trespasses and sins. And then forgiveness is a greater miracle still, through the blood of Jesus Christ. The miracles of grace are greater than those of providence, for the last are kingly servitors to the first; but all in a connection inseparable, and dependent on divine truth; God's truth, expressed in God's word, by God's methods, through human language. The whole kingdom of God is within you, all its miracles, the gift of spiritual sight out of blindness, out of obscurity, (Is. xxix. 18), the first awakening and quickening of souls dead in trespasses and sins; a miracle greater than that of the resurrection of the body.

But all miracles, recorded, taught, known, are wrought through words; "He spake, and it was done; He commanded, and it stood fast;" "by every word that proceedeth out of the mouth of God shall man live."

And what vast consequences may wait upon the use and right interpretation of one word may be seen in the instance of $ἄνωθεν$ (as in the note on page 301), the question whether you will render it *from the beginning* of the history on earth, by enquiries running back through human traditions, and therefore chargeable with uncertainty, or *from above, from heaven*, by direct inspiration and guidance of the Spirit of Christ, in whose name, concerning whose life, and in whose service and love, and by whose infallible guidance, Luke was certainly writing.

"I was well acquainted," said Dr. Witherspoon,

in one of the papers of his DRUID, "with a divine, who began a prayer in his congregation with these words: '*O Lord, Thou art the simplest of all beings!*'—which incensed his hearers against him to such a degree, that they accused him of blasphemy:—whereas, the poor man only meant to say that God was philosophically *simple and uncompounded*, altogether different from the grossness, divisibility, or in learned phrase, discerptibility of matter." His hearers thought he was making God a simpleton. What if the choice of the words for a divine revelation concerning God and man, for time and Eternity, had been left to the culture, taste, knowledge, mental habits, and style of the respective human authors or writers employed in it!

The various idiosyncracies of language and style, characteristic of the writers of the Word of God, demonstrate the perfect freedom of their faculties both in thought and speech; and at the same time the necessity of an infallible divine guidance, and perfect honesty and common sense, in interpreting God's will, and following his instructions. Dr. Witherspoon gives a curious illustration of combined ignorance and obstinacy, in an English naval commander, entrusted with despatches from England for the governors of the provinces of North America. The captain of the frigate had orders to proceed to

Georgia, but first to New York, then to the Carolinas, Virginia, Maryland, Pennsylvania, and the Jerseys. Arriving at New York, and mentioning his orders to the Governor, he was told, "If you will give me the letters for the governors of New Jersey and Pennsylvania, they shall be delivered in forty-eight hours; but by your prescribed route it will take three months." The commander replied, *I shall stick to my instructions.*

And so probably he attempted that impracticable entanglement of sea and land navigation, as impossible as the pretended combination of forgeries and truths in the law-book of the Almighty. The British Admiralty were in those days, before our Revolution, somewhat pardonable for instructions proceeding from ignorance of the colonies, and producing such confusion of provinces, distances, and relations of space. But what can be said of those critics on the Scriptures, and inventors of canons for the overrunning and interpretation of them, who deny the authorship of Moses and the Pentateuch, and send forth orders to set both down in unknown Apocryphal regions, and to visit and overhaul the whole Bible accordingly, by the guidance of a new chart, laying down the whole compass of documents, authorships and chronologies in prophecy and history, between Moses and Malachi, as a region of sunken rocks, to be searched out, protested, and guarded against!

And then the existence, eras, and authority of imagined fragments of history and law are offered as realities, together with conjectured and asserted Books of Origins, and families of manuscripts, and revisions of texts, by "transcriptional probabilities," commended to us as the oracles of God; and the right use of them taught accordingly, by the latest discoverers of the doctrine of wholesale forgeries of the Books of Moses, foisted on the whole Jewish nation more than eight hundred years after his death; and such anonymous forgeries sanctioned as a religious and patriotic habit of the Hebrew literature, acceptable to God, and endorsed, or "accommodated," by the Lord Jesus, as wrought by inspiration of the Holy Spirit!

The conjectures of minds that take the standpoint of their reasoning not within the light of an admitted inspired record, but outside, in the atmosphere of uninspired human nature, denying the existence of any infallible revelation, produce at length *a habit of inveterate skepticism,* "*the holding down of the truth in unrighteousness.*" They are like those *suspicions among thoughts,* which Lord Bacon says are like bats among birds, flying only in the twilight: whereas, the lark soars singing up to heaven in the morning sunlight. No small portion of the modern apologists for the Scriptures, and interpreters of the Bible by analogy of uninspired literature, are hunters after suspicions as if they were discoverers of new truths; or innocent detectives on the wing, robin-redbreasts or heaven-appointed doves, let loose from Noah's Ark to return and report. By them shall there be a new catechism for the children after the flood.

Critical proofs are good for nothing, except as coinciding with Christ's words. Internal evidence is all powerful, because of such established coincidence with the letter and Spirit of the divine oracles, and the purpose of Christ's coming for the redemption of the soul from sin and death eternal. "Concerning the works of men," said David in the 17th Psalm, "by the word of thy lips I have kept me from the Paths of the Destroyer." What a precious divine testimony is this! "And herein do I exercise myself," says Paul, (Acts xxiv. 16,) "to have always a conscience void of offence *toward God and toward men*." And again, "having our hearts sprinkled from an evil conscience, IN FULL ASSURANCE OF FAITH."

It was a demand *ex necessitate rei;* the absolute necessity for any right reasoning in regard to God, heaven and hell, that the information concerning that *which no witness could behold in Christ's bosom*, or in the Eternal World, and return on earth to testify, should be assured by infallible divine inspiration. The messengers and ministers of Christ must therefore, be witnesses by the Holy Ghost, of things which the Holy Ghost only could reveal, and set forth in accurate language. Apart from such inspiration, mere external erudition, however perfect and exact, would be valueless, much more when theories by conjectures and doubts are admitted as postulates of reasoning.

Prof. Stuart, in a note on Hug's Introduction to the New Testament (page 721) remarks that nearly all the writers who, up to that time, had made out theories as to the origin of the three first gospels had left out of sight and consideration *the fact of the inspiration of the authors*. It was not even an element of belief, but denial, with many. Yet this fact in the very nature of the case, was the truth of truths, the very first fact of importance to be considered; the very foundation of all right reasoning; the claim without which the Bible is of no more worth to us, as a witness of things past or to come, on earth or in heaven, than Homer's Iliad. For by that, once determined, we must ever be held, as the final arbiter and interpreter of all truth and certainty.

Our critics are so oppressed by this habit of referring every thing to the impulse and idiosyncrasy of the writer, irrespective of any supreme guidance or suggestion of the words, that the result of their investigations becomes altogether human, nothing divine; a thing of mere natural genius and culture. The inspiration of particulars in language being denied, as also any guidance by the Holy Spirit, of natural peculiarities, tendencies, preferences, everything is left to each individual's education, circumstances, dialect, and native likelihood of error, with ever so great supposed sincerity, in whatever he could not for himself ascertain. Then, of the ascertained things, why he left this, why he inserted that, why he repeated what was already recorded by another, how or why he could have used a new word, or such a pronoun as εκεινος sometimes absolutely, sometimes abstractly; what imagined reason can possibly be asked or given, except on the supposition that the whole is overruled or appointed by God's inspiration? Yet such inspiration is from the outset denied as an impossibility. And this postulate is the banner of the benevolence of Philosophy and Rationalism now unfurled and floating from the teachings of some professors in theological seminaries, and preachers to whom Moses and the Prophets, who spake of Christ, are myths as outworn as the cradle of bulrushes in which Moses once floated, as a new born lily, on the bosom of His mother Nile.

The modern idea of a new progressive theology by the consultation of doubts and obscurities as to the meaning of Eternity and eternal realities, may perhaps lead to the *endowment* of new sacred scientific professorships, for solution of the Nebulæ of God's Word, never yet decyphered, but supposed to contain the key to all former mysteries and difficulties. But this would be like inverting a telescope to look at the stars. Time-calculations in cloudy days might answer for travellers inland: but on the ocean of Eternity, what then? A false compass or chronometer on board ship may be prevented from action and discovery, by the ship itself being employed exclusively on coast or river navigation, and never out at sea. It will be too late to correct mistakes, once the boundary line has been past between this world and the next, Time and Eternity.

XLV.

HALF-TRUTHS WHOLE ERRORS—ABSOLUTE SAFETY ONLY IN THE DIVINE RECORD—THE INADEQUACY OF MERE HUMAN LANGUAGE—PAUL'S EXPERIENCE OF POWER AND WEAKNESS.

From any revelation which was half divine inspiration, and half natural light, or mere human investigation by common reason, common sense, and what is called profane history, nothing but half-truths could have come; and the mere *human* would have been preferred to the *divine*, and enthroned as the last appeal, because the first discovered certainty. If thine eye be single, then indeed thy whole body shall be full of light; but if evil, darkness; and how great *that* darkness! So great, so complete, that a man, and even a corporation, shall contend with the utmost fierceness, that it alone is light, and the only perfect light. See a wonderful illustration in Plato's description of the Cave, and the fire-light, and the men reasoning according to it. And yet the same men may have all their faculties of mind and body in what they regard as perfect simplicity and soundness, so that they will burn at the stake those that differ from them.

It is a truth of physiology that a wound in the eye may so draw away the aqueous humor, *without any injury to the general health,* as to produce utter blindness, as effective as if the whole external world were covered with a veil. Such was the veil upon the heart of the old unbelieving Jews, in full health in regard to this world and all its interests, but utterly blind as to Christ and the Life Eternal. In this mischief all men are "Jews by nature, and not sinners of the Gentiles."

The minutiæ and particularities, so extreme, so rigid, in the Hebrew laws, were all necessary, and all had their individual meaning and application, for the training of the conscience toward the invisible God, even by visible realities of form and figure. They were as the spongioles of roots, entering into the hidden fountains and elements of eternal principles, to carry up those principles into a trunk, and branches, and fruits, individual and national. When the rules are grounded in principles, and grow out of them, they produce buds and blossoms, leaves and fruits, for the concentrated nourishment and life of the soul, and their seed is in themselves, in their kind.

But if the ritual of God's service, or selected parts of it, are set up to be the lords many and gods many over the conscience, instead of a guide to God and the teacher of His love, then they become as the Brazen Serpent, which the heroic Hezekiah destroyed as Nehushtan, *the piece of brass*. The conscience towards law must be first of all towards God, enlightened by His word, and Spirit, and thus authoritative and supreme. For unquestionably there may be a conscience towards evil, an evil conscience, seared as with a hot iron; a conscience towards idols, a warped yet sincere conscientiousness, which is the very perfection of the despotism of Satan, first blinding the mind against the truth, then hardening it, fossilizing it in error as the truth; with strong delusion to believe a lie, having pleasure in unrighteousness, and being self-wrought into the nature of that which they voluntarily believe and choose.

It is not intellectual discernment, nor any mere intuitions of genius, that can create in the soul the knowledge and love of Christ, as the soul's light, life, and Redeemer. Take for illustration the German poet Goethe's account of his first acquaintance with Shakspeare. "The first page of his that I read made me his for life; and when I had finished a single play, I stood like one born blind, *on whom a miraculous hand bestows sight in a moment.* I saw, I felt, in the most vivid manner, that my existence was infinitely expanded, everything was now unknown to me, and the unwonted light pained my eyes. By little and little I learned to see, *and thanks to my receptive genius*, I continue vividly to feel what I have won. I sprang into the open air, and felt for the first time that I had hands and feet. And now that I see how much injury the *men of rule did me in their dungeon*, and how many free souls still crouch there, my heart would burst, if I did not declare war against them, and did not daily seek to batter down their towers."—

Compare this enthusiasm and worship of a human production with the great German poet's treatment of the gospels. It was not any want of susceptibility to be moved, nor of power of perception, where honor one of another was concerned, that prevented the same ardent admiration of the words of Christ, but Christ's own sad question, "*How can ye believe*, which receive honor one of another, but seek not the honor which cometh from God only?"

The demonstration itself, to us, of His being for us that Way, that Truth, that Life, rests therefore in this, His perfect conformity with the original draft, in the body of that writing, which, by such conformity, He proves irresistibly to be from God; and which we can prove to our own satisfaction and full assurance of understanding, *only by coming personally ourselves to Christ*, and trying His life, His love, upon and within our own souls. I KNOW WHOM I HAVE BELIEVED. How can any man otherwise ever come to the knowledge, by experience, of life eternal, in God, in Christ, in time or eternity?

It is only *by faith* that this knowledge is ever *possible*. He that believeth on the Son of God hath the witness in himself, in Christ, within him, the hope of glory, the Author and Finisher of faith. He that believeth not God's word, hath made Him a liar, because he *believeth not the record* that God gave of His Son. And this is the record, that God hath given to us eternal life, and this life is in His Son, HIMSELF THE LIFE. *He that hath the Son hath life; he that hath not the Son of God hath not life.* These things have I written, that ye *may know that ye have eternal life*, and that ye may believe on the name of the Son of God.—1 John v. 13.

This is the style of ineffable divine certainty—*what the Spirit saith unto the churches*. He that hath an ear let him hear this, even according as Christ Himself heard and obeyed unto death, this formula of God's covenant and will, IT IS WRITTEN.

How many men, striving to enunciate what they did not clearly comprehend, have lost themselves in verbiage, so that the reader or hearer has to cry out for an interpreter, or even a pilot with a *foghorn*, to guide him out of the confusion. Except a man can interpret, of what avail are his volubilities of tongues? Paul himself, and his fourteenth chapter of First Corinthians, are proofs of the necessity of a verbal inspiration in the ministry of divine, soul-saving truths for all souls through all ages. "I thank my God that I speak with tongues more than ye all. Yet in the church I had rather speak five words with my understanding, that I might teach others also, than ten thousand words in an unknown tongue." Therefore, "Let him that speaketh pray that he may interpret."

Paul himself could speak with tongues and interpret, only by the Holy Spirit in his own heart and mind, guiding him for that very purpose, in words that the

Holy Ghost teacheth. For that let every minister of Christ pray. But he cannot even pray aright, except by the Holy Ghost teaching him how to pray. And the Holy Spirit will thus go with His words from his heart, and will be the living and illuminating fire, the heavenly magnetism. What are even the best words without that? Do we not know that when this physical frame of our earthly nature is charged with electricity, we can light the gas by the touch of our knuckles? And even so, when a man's own soul is charged with the fire of God by the Divine Spirit, he can set souls on fire; but not otherwise. How much more at the foundation of the Christian faith for all ages and all souls, must there be the words of eternal truth, burning with and by the Spirit that indited them, and as absolutely true as God is true; words coined by God, because omniscience alone and infinite Love could inspire them, and the pulses of the same love in human ministries are to beat with them.

How often do writers of the greatest power find extreme difficulty in putting into language satisfactory to themselves the conceptions, the thoughts, which they desired to express, but have found themselves almost in despair at the confessed inadequacy of their own expressions. Plato, John Foster, De Quincey, Coleridge, Pascal, Locke, Stuart Mill, Kant,

John Howe—men of all languages, researches, beliefs, pursuits; naturalists, philologists, psychologists, anatomists of body and soul, metaphysicians, biologists, theologians, poets, mathematicians, confessing that language itself is one of the greatest of mysteries, and perfect simplicity, profoundness and exactness in the use of it an impossible attainment. But in "THE VOLUME OF THE BOOK WRITTEN OF ME" there is this tri-unity of qualities; simplicity in word, infinitude in meaning, and exactness in expression; so that he may run that readeth, or read running.

They are words that shall never pass away, though heaven and earth shall pass; a judgment, and truths, and modes of reasoning, that are *made to rest for a light of the people;* words of God in the mouth, and His Spirit in the heart, even of babes and sucklings. The simpler the words, the more perfect and absolute the proof that God Himself chose them and inspired them; as in the Gospel of John, perhaps the most radiant with divine demonstration of all the volume, and yet the most childlike and artless; simple and transparent as the air, profound and measureless as space. Who can account for the miracle, or who can deny it?

If this be true in regard to men's efforts to catch and flash upon the screen the variations and almost infinite excursions of their own minds, uninspired, so that they cry out of the depths, O for a supernatural dialect, as swiftly at command as the lightning-like revelations that encompass and outrun all our powers of expression!—how much greater the necessity of a verbal realization, an inspired conveyance, for those divine thoughts, that as the heavens are higher than the earth, so are higher than man's thoughts, and are *not* man's thoughts at all, but only God's revealed to man for his study and obedience! And so is the word that goeth forth out of God's mouth, not in cataractical confused masses, but gentle and gradual, as the drops of the rain, to accomplish that which He pleases; jewels of expression, framed for His own thoughts, and accompanied by His own Spirit.

One would give a million pounds sterling, if he had it, for the invention of a *psychograph*, or photograph of thought, in accurate and adequate language, as the flash of light first rises in the soul. What an infinitude of labor it would save, and wrestlings of second thoughts, against the first, or of doubts against realities; what instant visions it would give of the nature of plans or purposes of good or evil, half-formed; but if evil, then, the moment they are thrown upon paper, arrested, and remaining only as evidence of what would have been reality, if not seen and known as soon as existing, and perhaps annihilated as soon as seen. "Thou understandest my thought afar off. Thou compassest my path and my lying down, and art acquainted with all my ways." God *must* do this, and judge mankind accordingly, or he would not be God. And there must be some kind of telephone playing into the eternal world, with intelligible cyphers dotted in the book of judgment, disclosing what is going on here. The conscience toward God is such a faithful and infallible witness, and even in its earliest glimmerings what a power of language and coloring it possesses! What worlds of refuse, and of lumber, fit only for the chaos of Gehenna, might be prevented, if each man's soul were such a stenographic recorder, or reporter aloud, in plain language!

A *cardiphone*, an utterance of the heart, a *detectiphone*, reporting at once to the self-consciousness and to God! What a shield it might be against the malignities and fiery darts of the Wicked One! And what a gift of divine power would a good man have, if his incommunicable, inexpressible revelations, aspirations, presciences of the unseen and eternal, could be written down at the very instant of their momentary consciousness! For we often have a conscious insight of such profound immeasurable power and glory, of such irresistible, all-compelling demonstration of truth, as, if completely uttered, and conveyed as soon and as distinctly as a flash of lightning at midnight, would overcome all oppositions, of all minds, all worlds. But we lose it in the very attempt to describe it, or translate it into language. And all efforts are vain to satisfy even our own ideal of it. But an infallible revelation from God must possess these commanding qualities of thought and utterance, to justify God in hanging upon its words an eternal judgment of His own character, and that of His intelligent accountable creatures, in His own sight and in theirs. "That thou might be clear when Thou judgest, and be justified when Thou speaketh."

"Men owe it to God," said Pascal, "to receive the religion which He sends; God owes it to men, not to lead them into error." (Pascal's "Thoughts," ch. 20.) "To lead into error," Pascal adds, "is to place man under the necessity of assuming and approving falsehood. This God cannot do; and yet He would do this, if in an obscure question, He permitted miracles to be wrought on the side of falsehood." This is absolutely impossible. God Himself therefore is ever with us, the Interpreter and Guardian of His own Truth.

XLVI.

PRAYERS AND PREACHING OF THE APOSTLES—DEVELOPMENT AND INCREASE OF ILLUMINATIONS IN GOD'S KINGDOMS OF NATURE AND GRACE—INCALCULABLE MINUTENESS AND GRANDEUR IN WORD AND WORKS —OUR LORD'S EXAMPLE OF A PRIORI REASONING— ARCHBISHOP LEIGHTON'S EXPERIENCE.

There is no report on record, no inspired account of the words of the early preachers, nor example of their power in preaching or praying, save only in two or three chapters of the Acts of the Apostles, and in the prayers of the Apostle Paul. And though these are great masses of truth, shafts of light concentrated, yet all the rest has to be imagined, all the work of the divine Spirit in the men going forth from Pentecost, under the power of the first baptism, and all the fervor and power of their successors. The superhuman electricity, awakening vividness and persuasion of their eloquence, the divine lightning, the phrases condensed with thought in the words taught by the Holy Spirit, and piercing through the soul; the startling earnestness, the flame of knowledge from infinite depths of anguish and of joy in their own experience, the pleading, the tears, the weeping fervor and fire, the infinite ·compassion and love, the celestial radiance of the soul in its peace and blessedness of Christ; the realities of sin, death, the judgment, heaven, hell;—all these creations to the sight, of spiritual worlds, spiritual thought, scenery, experience, things seen and known of Christ, and spoken forth from His indwelling and inspiration in the soul, and in words taught by the Holy Spirit;—constituted a whirlwind flame of eloquence, a winged burning chariot, full of eyes and voices, as in Ezekiel's vision, drawing hearers and seers within the sweep of its attraction, rolling through the cities and neighborhoods of the Jewish and heathen world, as apocalyptic orbs of celestial fire and glory.

There is no description of it, but it was the outpouring of a divine life, in suffering and redeeming intensity, and the rapid diffusion of Christianity followed in its train. They that wielded this power, out of Christ's love constraining them, were filled with divine consolation in the use of it; it was the life and blessedness as of angels to them on earth, to speak thus of Christ and His love; and for all that they had relinquished or suffered in this world they received a hundred-fold, in the bliss of this very service.

Think of the multitude of illuminations and illustrations of the Scriptures, flashing as a sea of diamonds mingled with fire, now coming into knowledge almost universal, through periodicals and papers in every tongue, and demonstrated by increasing millions of Christian minds and hearts out of their own blissful experience. This is God's progressive work, how gradual, yet how irresistible! And the law and condition of all this growth, with all and in all that receive it from the Scriptures, is that of God's providence and light, interpreted and applied by the Holy Spirit in the soul. The infinite wonders brought to view through the telescope and microscope, in material worlds, are but an approximative illustration of what God is doing in the spiritual universe.

Consider the working of light within the atoms of different substances, according to positions and angles of incidence, refraction, reflection, medium, polarization, repetition. There is as great a variety in unity, by the working of spiritual light in more minds, than atoms. The discovery of the polarization of light was as a new creation. And such is the revealing effect of the rays of spiritual truth upon the inward texture and organization of souls; lightning like, so sudden, but Godlike, so immutable and eternal.

We have experience of polarized light, even in our hours and moments of prayer, and in the revelations to faith produced by it. For prayer by faith ("praying in the Holy Ghost"), is to the soul as Lord Rosse's great

Telescope; and as the vision sweeps round the infinitudes, it opens new unfathomable abysses, that in their very darkness show the unsearchableness of the light itself that discovers them, and new immeasurable continents of worlds, as islands, in eternal boundless space; and still, light reflected from all; apocalyptic light, constructing, organizing, living, growing, weaving, renewing, changing. It is God's light and God's providence that opens all this glory in and upon His creatures. "In Thy light shall we see light." Material astronomy is counterparted and illumined by the other infinite spiritual universe, under God's law of Love.

And now, if it has taken so many thousand years to discover and apply by genuine mathematical calculations and evidence, some of the laws of matter in God's visible tangible universe, how much more must it require of diligence and time, with spiritual humility and waiting upon God, to discern the times and seasons which the Father hath put in His own power; and the visitations, workings, limitations, and possible spheres and conquests of thought, through the patient study and application of His Word, by faith and prayer;— and all this in a state of being and action, where the voluntary exercise of these qualities, and improvement of these gifts, are offered as the securities of an eternal progress in the beatifying knowledge of God.

God's Timepiece for Man's Eternity. 371

Our Lord Jesus was certainly the Master of *à priori* reasoning in regard to the Word and attributes of God, "Ought not Christ to have suffered these things and to enter into His glory?" What a mountain-mine of intelligence in that question! The *ought not*, was grounded on what had been written of God beforehand in the Scriptures, and was not here expounded merely of any moral necessity or propriety in the nature of things, or in God's attributes, but *because it had been so set down in God's Word*.

The Lord Jesus showed His disciples, by the revelation of His own nature, how to see His foreshining radiant image in the Scriptures. It was as if He had taken a steel mirror, which had been overclouded and stained by using it for pressing herbs, or for hairdressing, (for even thus had the Jews abused and perverted their own Scriptures for the uses of this world;) as if He had taken such a mirror, and wiping it clean, and making the reflection pure and perfect, had bent His own face over it, and then called His disciples to look at the image of His whole being in its depths.

For so it was, that in all the Scriptures, after His death and resurrection, He showed them Himself, in His sufferings and glory; Himself, in the human and divine; Himself, as the teaching, miracle-working, crucified, dying, Self-existent Lord; Himself, the buried and risen, ascended and enthroned Almighty Saviour ;—all now as clear as the sun ; His whole foreshown and afterwards reflected attributes, through eternity, the same, yesterday, to-day and forever.

And the same divine Spirit of Christ which was in them foretelling and instructing, must be with and in us, showing what they saw, showing the fulfilment, clearing and quickening our vision, removing our errors, correcting our mistakes, preaching unto us the gospel with the Holy Ghost sent down from Heaven. The angels desire to look into these things, fellow-students with us; and the Holy Ghost from Heaven is as necessary for our enlightenment as for theirs. God grant we may neither despise nor reject nor deny it.

But we are dependent on the Holy Spirit, and on the presence of Christ dwelling in our hearts by faith, for the climate of our souls, through the breathing of a Saviour's love.

The climate of our souls! A world of illustrations from the physical to the spiritual creation is opened before us by this expression. Take some of the instances of truth reverberating from the material to the immortal. "In that aerial ocean," says Humboldt, "on the shoals of which we live, the climate of our own region depends on the variations of the atmosphere as to temperature and moisture, density, pressure, oxygen, and electricity, polarization, magnetic resonance and purity; "but greatly also on the degree of ordinary *transparency and clearness of the sky,* which is not only important in respect to the increased radiation from the earth, the organic development of plants, and the ripening of fruits, but also with reference to *its effect on the feelings and condition of men."* Out of the laws of the visible and tangible creation of God, the invisible and eternal may be known and illustrated, or impressively typiped. The spiritual atmosphere of our own heart and life depends on Christ in us the hope of glory, and on the inspiration of His love, producing all that we ever possess of sincerity, freedom from selfishness, a single eye, a contrite mind, a regard to the divine approbation, through the love of Christ constraining us.

Thus the invariable transparency and clearness of the firmament of God's Word (forever, O Lord, Thy Word is settled in heaven), and the exceeding and eternal brightness of divine truth and glory, shining in the face of Jesus Christ, down into the heart,

---

* See the illustrations in Humboldt's Cosmos, Vol. I. pp. 292-369. "A physical delineation of Nature terminates at the point where the sphere of intellect begins, and a new world of mind is opened to our view." "Language, more than any other attribute of mankind, binds together the whole human race," and carries our thought into eternity.

through the atmosphere of the love of Christ, will produce a gracious and fruitful experience, filling the soul, and at length the whole earth, with all the fulness of God. Thus God and the universe, heaven and the world, are mutually illuminated; and so is the only way of knowing God's spiritual kingdom in all worlds, and becoming heirs of God and joint heirs with Christ, by His own new-creating Spirit of love and of power and of a sound mind. Again, take the illustrative fact that "every part of the earth's surface absorbs and radiates heat at the same time, and that the power of radiation is always equal to the power of absorption." Even so the power of magnetic radiation in the soul, the power of communicating divine truth, is always equal to the power of faith in receiving and absorbing the light and love of Christ in His Word. And both are dependent on the habit of obedient and constant working by love with the truth as it is in Jesus, committed to the heart for this purpose. As it is used, so it increases, both in depth and intensity, in volume and in power.

We are better prepared for a childlike faith in every jot and tittle. of God's Word, than those children in the market place could have been, to whom Christ preached concerning the lilies of the field; since, through the microscope, "organized beings, possessing life, and exercising all its functions, have been dis-

covered so minute, that a million of them would occupy less space than a grain of sand; so that what before were imaginary things are now real beings, with definite weights, and uniting by fixed laws."*
With what intense interest and reverence, must every intelligent being ponder the progress of Science, in the light reflected from and upon the sublime questions of natural and spiritual Theology in Job. "Dost thou know *the balancings of the clouds*, or the way in which *light is parted*, and the firmament spread abroad, and the dust of the orbs of heaven weighed and measured by Jehovah's counsels, judging and governing the earth and the people, *the wicked and the good, by them?*"

The possible dependencies of nations on a word and its wrong or right pronouncement, are illustrated in the Book of Judges, xii. 6 (whether Shibboleth or Sibboleth), the tribe of Ephraim being almost annihilated by a slip of the tongue. Was it accidental? Can anything be accidental under God's government? Was there not a wise, holy, and retributive providence there, connecting heart and tongue, syllables

---

* See Mrs. Somerville's "Physical Geography," chapters xxi. and xxii., and pp. 268, 299. Compare also Arnold Guyot on the "Earth and Man," together with Mary Somerville's instructive volume on the "Connection of the Physical Sciences," Harper's Edition, from the seventh London.

and moral habits and consequences? Such an event is but one of God's prisms for analyzing light, and throwing its responsibilities of knowledge into eternity. The minuteness of causes is an infinite and solemn wonder. What a world of spiritual lessons in the study of atoms and their combinations, in physical and mental organizations, and in the elementary chemistry of the earth and man! What warnings in the investigations of *miasma* on the earth or in the air, and in accepted hereditary beliefs, in currents of opinion and prejudice, in pregnant false axioms and seeds of error and misery! The very hairs of our heads are all numbered. And so one half of God's universe looks down into the other as a mirror of its meaning and its laws.

How then can a verbal inspiration in God's BOOK OF THE SOUL be denied, when it is not only admitted, but woven into the very demonstrations of science, in the BOOK OF NATURE, and taught by scientific men as a postulate of philosophy? There must be an omnipresent, all-determining and arranging Providence, in Nature as well as Man, in the letters and syllables that spell and mean Eternity.

For God hath "set one thing over against another"; and the world, which is man's birthplace and standing stool, is full of educational analogies, "and whatsoever God doeth, it shall be forever"; it hath that meaning for man, "That men should fear before Him"; and for that, "every thing is beautiful in His time." The Book of Ecclesiastes is full of these disclosures of Time for Eternity, and of God's work for man's Immortality. But we are carried back into the first volume of science ever written or known on earth, for man's guidance, by the culmination and comparison of the discoveries of five thousand years. The treasures of information, and the vast and profound generalizations, brought together in modern works on the Connexions of the Physical Sciences, the phraseology and the proofs of the laws weighing, measuring and balancing the globe and all its elements, with the definite and relative proportions of atoms, and the processes of light, heat, combustion, magnetism, electricity, temperature, in the earth and its atmosphere;—all these disclosures are just a providential commentary on the Scriptures, as unintentional, many times, from mount to mount, from altar to altar, as Balaam's majestic prophecies; yet all concluding, What hath God wrought! and teaching, Let me die the death of the righteous, and let my last end be like His!

"Heaven is My throne, and the earth My footstool, saith the Almighty; but I create new heavens and a new earth, and *to this man will I look*, even to him that is poor and of a contrite spirit, *and who trem-*

bleth at My word." Compare with this, and understand by it, our Lord's first benediction, "Blessed are the poor in spirit, for theirs is the kingdom of heaven."

The soul to be saved from eternal death, and CHRIST, *the only Being that can save it*, are the combination key for our commanding and opening of the Spiritual Safe given to us in the Scriptures. A man may err in many things, but if he keep those two, he is honest and safe, and gets into the heart of God's Safe in Christ, and there God will keep him. "For *whatsoever things were written aforetime* were written *for our learning*, that we, through patience and COMFORT OF THE SCRIPTURES, might have hope." THE SOUL TO BE SAVED BY FAITH IN CHRIST, is the all in all, from Genesis to the Apocalypse.

Archbishop Leighton used to say, "I prefer an erroneous honest man before the most orthodox knave in the world; and I would rather convince a man that *he has a soul to be saved*, and induce him *to live up to that belief*, than bring him over to my opinion in whatever else besides." He could say, Whatever else I leave undone, one thing I do; *seek for souls*, that they may be saved, not lost forever. And these he sought among men of all persuasions. A friend, calling upon him one day, and not finding him, learned that he had gone to visit a sick Presbyterian minister on a horse which he had borrowed of the Roman Catholic priest. The skepticism which he sought to cure in others he had known within himself; "all sorts of skeptical and doubtful thoughts on the great points of religion he said, having not only passed through his head, but stuck fast and painfully in his mind, till the mercy of the Lord dispelled them." And so his direction to other souls was just this, "Wait patiently on the Lord, and hope in him, for you shall yet praise him for the help of his countenance. That alone can enlighten you, and calm the storms that are raised within it. In the midst of these assaults, throw yourself down at his footstool, and cry, "O God, Father of mercies, save me from this hell within me! I acknowledge, I adore, I bless Thee, whose throne is in heaven, with Thy blessed Son and crucified Jesus, and Thy Holy Spirit, and though Thou slay me, yet will I trust in Thee."

XLVII.

THE POSSIBLE SPOILING OF A PREACHER BY PHILOSOPHY—SPIRITUAL DISCERNMENT AND POWER VINDICATED AS GOD'S ONLY — INDEPENDENCE ONLY BY FAITH AND SUBMISSION.

There is no possibility of independence, or any true method of science in man, or security against error, without dependence on God, the Creator of man and of science, and of man's relations to Himself and to all knowledge. Measuring themselves by themselves, and comparing themselves among themselves men must forever remain mere imitators of one another's mistakes; relying on human authority, yet denying universal experience of guilt and ruin as a libel, and individual experience of regeneration and spiritual life as fanaticism. So have men used the Word of God rather as an external lamp contrived, than an inward fountain of holy consciousness and joy; and so have come weakness, and superstitions, and fears, and the mere belief of the devils, who tremble, instead of the freedom and fearlessness of the sons of God. For nothing tends so much to produce a manly independence, confidence, and genuine liberty of thought and feeling, as a simple reliance on God's Word, and an unconditional submission to it. "Let them destroy my works," said Luther; "I desire nothing better; for all I wanted was *to lead Christians to the Bible*, that they might afterwards *throw away my writings*. Great God! if we had but a right understanding of the Holy Scriptures, what need would there be of my books?" God has provided for us this divine independence of all human authority; "not in word only, but in power, and in the Holy Ghost, and in much assurance."

But assurance is a thing which can not be got from other minds, any more than the power of sight can be got from spectacles. There must be the seeing eye, before any spectacles can help it. There are schools and phrases of philosophy, as well as religion, to which a man may be in bondage, and the power of the pulpit may be greatly hindered or diminished in that way. "Beware lest *any* man *spoil* you through philosophy and vain deceit, after the traditions of men, after the rudiments of the world, and not after Christ." Schools may spoil you, if philosophy and the traditions of men are taught in them, rather than the Word of God by the Spirit of God. Philosophic views of the spiritual life itself, as organic and successional in and through a visible organization, indestructible even by the most radical corruption and apostasy, so as to embrace even the Church of Rome as an appointed and legitimate development of that life; inspiring on the one side a false and most immoral liberality, and on the other a presumptuous and immoral exclusiveness; such views prevent the development of power. That which is successional is depravity, rooting us in the race, in the wild olive tree, out of which grace cuts us, and grafts us into Christ; grace, which comes not by organic succession, but constant divine interposition and new creation. Second causes multiplied in spiritual things cut us off from God, and from the belief and experience of divine power; and the Church, in some systems of spiritual philosophy, is a vast second cause, endued with divine attributes, and preventing direct access to God, almost as fatally as the "practical eternity" of a succession of eras and causes without God's intervention, in the scientific philosophy of an atheistic evolution.

Philosophic views of penalty, as bringing all creatures at length into the bosom of God; philosophic views of the divine attributes, tending to pantheism; philosophic views of faith, disconnecting it from God's truth, which is its only legitimate foundation; philosophic views of history, exalting it to such a position as to make the authority of God's Word dependent upon it; the very vagueness, doubtfulness and subtlety of philosophic views or speculations generally;—all this may just leaven a man's theology so far as to spoil it, render it unfit for use, deprive it of regenerating efficacy, and render power in the pulpit impossible. Some of the most approved German writers are illustrations of theology so spoiled. In the system of Nitzsch, for example, much applauded for its orthodoxy, and philosophic exactness, it is maintained that as to logical position, by the letter, the tenet of absolute, positive, eternal punishment is *undeniable*, but as to reality, *irreconcilable with the philosophy* of the divine nature, and therefore *impossible*. The logical letter is a falsehood; the spiritual truth is that of final universal salvation. There can be no such thing as power in the pulpit, in proportion as such views have place in the preacher.

Again there is the paralytic weakness and bondage attached to low and uncertain views of divine inspiration. Here is a great secret of rottenness and feebleness. Every reader of history remembers the anecdote of Mirabeau's impression on first hearing Robespierre, then an unknown young man, speak in convention. "That young man will yet be heard from; he will make himself known and felt, for he *believes every word he says.*" The very opposite impression will be made by the pulpit-orator unless he is profoundly grounded in an impregnable experimental assurance of the Scriptures as the Word of God. But an assured and steadfast faith in the Word of God is the gift of God's own Spirit. Consequently, it depends on the degree of earnestness with which the preacher himself seeks God. If, day and night he follows hard after God, if he makes it his delight to find Him and commune with Him, if he supplicates like Moses, "I beseech thee, O Lord, show me Thy glory," then will God shine into his heart to give him the light of the knowledge of the glory of God in the face of Jesus Christ, and will give him that glorious ministration of the Spirit which exceeds in glory, that revelation by the Spirit searching the deep things of God, that Spirit of wisdom and revelation in the knowledge of Christ, and that earnest of the Spirit in the heart, which makes the Word a vivid flame, a burning life, an irresistible experience, a fire infolding itself, an electric light penetrating the whole being. God causes those who sow in tears to reap in joy; He gives the latter rain to those who avail themselves of the early; and so He blesses the springing of His own seed unto life everlasting.

The knowledge and assurance of a divine inspiration are not to be gained by study in the schools, not even on the highest theory, but only from God Himself, only from the same Spirit, by whom the Word of God is itself truly inspired. This power belongeth unto God. Archbishop Usher, with his boundless learning, before the modern German *exegetes* began their studies, wrote out, with a piety like Paul's, a profound logical and holy demonstration of our dependence on the witness of the Spirit. That witness was the secret of his own power, as it was of Bengel's. If men throw themselves on the knowledge and assurance of the schools, it fails them, as when in a critical moment a revolver misses fire; it fails them as power, for God vindicates that for Himself alone; and "cursed be the man who trusteth in man, and maketh flesh his arm, and whose heart departeth from the Lord;" he shall be, and his proofs shall be, like the heath in the desert, like the parched places in the wilderness, like salt and ashes instead of verdure. All the arguments may seem to be the same, but the life, the power, the assurance of the Holy Ghost are wanting, and under the firmest creed there will be faltering and doubt. When the schools of the prophets, and all the apparatus of their colleges, were multiplied in Israel, then false prophets were multiplied, men educated, but not baptized, heirs at law, but not at equity, graduates at the schools, but not commissioned of the Lord Almighty.

But how much more, if the theory itself be based on doubt instead of certainty. There may be such theories of inspiration as inspire nothing but anxiety and unbelief; theories so discrediting and questioning, so dishonoring to God, His Word, and His Spirit, that the experience of divine power is rendered impossible. If a student has been so unfortunate as to come into the ministry under such a discipline, he comes as one with a palsy; he comes distrustful and afraid, inexperienced and ashamed; he can not develop power, for he does not feel it, does not believe it.

If a man is doubtful about a bill, a draft, a signature, he can not use it with confidence; other people will not take it, but with a private mark to return it; commercial operations can not go on. If a physician is doubtful about a medicine, whether, for example, it be quinine or oak-bark, and the patient too is doubtful, little good will the prescription accomplish, for there will not be the power, even if the medicine be genuine; so much does even nature depend for the efficacy of her real causes upon faith. But how much more the divine nature, that operates only by faith, new-creates by faith, produces the experience of life by faith.

The Word of God is self-dependent, containing all

things necessary for its proof, confirmation, and energy, within itself, by virtue of the inseparable presence and life of the Divine Spirit; and so completely independent of all history, all human testimony, that if all such were annihilated, all the books and records containing it burned, the Word of God by the Spirit of God would have the same power as ever.

And yet, there is nothing that in and by history has more perfect infrangible proof, accumulated and germinating forever. But that proof alone a man can not stand upon, for with all its perfection, human testimony alone by itself has the quality of a lie; let God be true, but every man a liar. Every preacher is bound to know and possess the power of God by the Spirit of God, and to depend on His Spirit and not on man; then and thus only will he know how to apply human testimony in its proper place, and how to appreciate the combination between human and divine. The human testimony to which Christ refers as true ceases to be fallible, and by His endorsement becomes divine. Just as His own incarnation, constituted a fleshly tabernacle as divine and incorruptible as His own divine Spirit from eternity, so the words sanctioned and employed by His Spirit become themselves Spirit and life; infallible, incorruptible, divine. The personality of Christ carries every believer, as it did the thief upon the cross, and Paul the persecutor.

From Genesis to the Apocalypse we know *whom*, and therefore *what* we have believed. "Whom, not having seen, we love, and in whom though now we see Him not, yet believing we rejoice with joy unspeakable and full of glory, receiving the end of our faith, the salvation of the soul."—I Pet. i., 8, 9. Of which salvation the old prophets and reasoners in the face of death inquired and searched diligently; kept, like ourselves, by the power of God through faith unto salvation, *ready to be revealed*, through a Saviour, *ready to appear*, yet neither of them among the things then visible, but ministered through them to future ages, as a grace to be hoped for at the revelation of Jesus Christ; and meantime the hope itself to be acted upon and acted out in holy fear, prayer, and conversation, obeying the truth through the Spirit, for the regeneration of the whole world. Such is the sanctifying faith created and sustained by these gospels and epistles.

They carry such a charm of deep sincerity, such profound sense of integrity and truth, such disinterestedness, such uninterrupted and uncorrupt appeals to the highest motives of gratitude and love; there is such undisguised absence of all offers or promises of gain in this world; such assurance, on the contrary, of loss, affliction, tribulation; such delighted and grateful recognition of obedience and faith in others; such gratitude for kindnesses received; such fervor of the spirit of beneficence, forgiveness, charity; such lowliness, poverty, self-restraint and self-denial out of love; such freedom from asceticism, superstition, formalism, spiritual despotism, severity and cruelty; such communion both of joys and sorrows; such consolations imparted and shared; such compassion for them that are wandering; such an earnest imitation of Christ in all points possible on earth; such a constant thoughtfulness and beholding of His love and care and glory in heaven; such entireness and supremacy of living for Him, yet not as penance or painful duty, but by sweet and cheerful constraint of grateful love; such artlessness in the narratives; such entire absence of the consciousness or vanity of authorship, or seeking of the praises of men. It is unaccountable by any thing but a divine inspiration. It is the work of nothing less than an inspiration infallible, and a sanctification that could come only from the Spirit of God.

And still we might go on with a volume of the characteristics of saints, and challenge any one to add a virtue or proof of divine goodness which is not plainly manifest, or to mention any thing omitted; yet all manifested unconsciously, unintentionally, as the lilies of the field grow and blossom. Fulfilling constantly, as never before or since, the command of the Lord Jesus, Let your light so shine before men, that they may see your good works, not you, and may glorify, not yourselves, but your Father in heaven, being drawn to Him by love, and inspired by Him, and endowed by Him, the Author and Giver of all this light and glory.

The evolution of such a book of narratives and letters, such reasonings of divine logic and truth, *from the sole premises of love*, is more than human, is beyond all the possibilities of the natural man. It is infallible omniscient wisdom and love, working, patient, long-suffering, immutable, through vast and varied dispensations, interruptions, rebellions, perversions, idolatries, and fathomless gulfs of depravity; an unceasing system of instruction, education, and pardoning mercy, from Adam to Christ, the same, yesterday, to-day, and forever.

Now at every stage of this wondrous body and growth of divine revelation it was absolutely impossible for any forger to have understood what went before, or imagined or contrived an after-piece corresponding. Stand at the closure of the book of Malachi, and gaze into the gulf of the future four hundred years. It is impossible for human power, wisdom, wit, prescience, to invent or imagine the beginning of the gospels, or the incarnation and life of Christ.

Stand at the close of the gospels, those simple exclusive portraitures of the divine Saviour of our race, His mercy and love, His words and miracles, His sufferings and death. It is impossible for the human mind to imagine or invent from these biographic data, the Acts of the Apostles, from the Pentecostal miracle of tongues to the conversion of Saul and the establishment and visitation of the churches, ending with Paul in his own hired house preaching freely in Rome.

Stand at the last trace of intelligence in the book of the Acts, and again it is absolutely impossible for any man to contrive the Epistles;—the chain of doctrine, fruits, practice, development, interpretation; the divine lights thrown back from regenerated lives over all past revelation, and forward till this mortal shall have put on immortality.

And once more, stand at the close of the Epistles, at the ascription of Jude, "To the only wise God our Saviour," and look forth into the untried eternity, the field of all prophecy in fulfilment. It is impossible for any human being, any forger, any uninspired soul, of that age or of any age, to imagine or contrive such an APOCALYPSE from the Lord Jesus Christ, on the throne of the Almighty. Such an opening of the future, and of heaven and hell, with such startling supernatural disclosures, such an aurora over the whole heavens of embattled squadrons of flame and lightning and thunder, and yet not a contradiction nor incongruity of thought or words, but a perfect symmetry and fulfilment of all previous seeds of thought and prophecy. More impossible than for a man contemplating a seed which had been discovered in an Egyptian mummy three thousand years ago, to describe what would grow out of it in the coming spring resurrection, to tell beforehand its form and development, whether a tree or a vegetable, a flower or a cedar of Lebanon, a lily of the valley, or a *California Gigantea*, five hundred feet high.

XLVIII.

THE IMPOSSIBILITY OF A PRECONCERTED FORGERY —BUT IF INCREDIBLE BEFOREHAND, ITS SUCCESS YET MORE IMPOSSIBLE—A VERBAL INSPIRATION NO MORE IMPROBABLE THAN A SPECIAL PROVIDENCE.

The supposition of a Corliss steam-engine contrived with all its parts, provisions, steam-chests, cylinders, motors, condensers, shafts, safety-valves, ages before the force of steam was ever known, by pre-existent savages before they had learned to talk one with another by imitation of the cries of brutes, would be a probability of common sense, worthy of being believed and acted on, in comparison with the supposition of an uninspired human being first imagining the story of the creation, temptation, and fall of Adam and his posterity, and then, out of these imagined elements, contriving the forgery of a Divine Revelation, with disclosure of the plan, possibility, mystery, and history of the redemption and regeneration of mankind, by a Saviour to come.

But if the forgery, with its predictions and its planted seeds of spiritual thought and promise for faith, were deemed an incredible performance, what shall be said of its success by the fulfilment of those predictions demonstrating its truth by successive developments through the march of centuries, successive minds and events through intervals of distant ages entering into, and setting at work, and enlarging the fictitious scheme of the world's regeneration from sin and misery? By the supposition of its being a forgery, not one of the successive unconscious agents of this vast engine of intricate spiritual machinery could ever have had a conception or belief of that supernatural and new-creating design in the execution of which it is in reality employed, and by force of which it does in reality change and govern human society.

So that we have such a forgery performing for thousands of years the actual spiritual work, which the very accusation of forgery against the books of the Bible denies ever to have been designed or contemplated in them; and if the contrivers of those books *were* forgers, *as accused*, then they never could themselves have intended, much less believed, such a divine result.

And now the ideas of a Personal Creator, Lawgiver, and Providential Governor, and of sin, and consequent eternal death, and of an Incarnate Divine Saviour, made known by inspired Scripture are presented by Herbert Spencer's "First Principles," as a vast compound lie, ordained to be excogitated by the human reason *as a sheathe for necessary truths otherwise impossible to be fastened on the human intellect!* And all this, the foundation of a system of "sociological secularism," to be taught in our common schools and colleges, for the perfect infallible guidance of a race of future angels!

These philosophers and higher critics, rejecting the argument from design, and a plenary authoritative inspiration as incredible, propose for our belief a deity of NATURAL SELECTION and scientific experimentalism and evolution, clothed with the authority of "Nature's pluck," and designing, contriving, and experimenting for millions of years the construction of a human eye for the use of the human being, before the frame, organization, or actual existence of that being shall have been imagined, or the possibility of language or of sight provided for!

A *pre-existing* race of men before Adam is also postulated, for hundreds of thousands of years left without the knowledge of God, and therefore certainly without any claim ever made by Him, of having been their Creator, and without any provision for those spiritual wants, which alone can pronounce the man a man, in any way different from the brutes, or his organization a fit temple for the incarnation of the Son of God!

An evolution from the monkey is proposed as an escape from the difficulties of the Creative Genesis, and an insurance against the consequences of our yet possibly finding a fossil man just in the attitude of emerging from the likeness of his Simian parentage! If any future age *should* discover such a *birth-process* engraven in the rocks, what in the name of truth could men do with the book of Genesis or the theory of an infallible inspiration? Let us have mercy upon our posterity beforehand, and not expose them to the hazard of such a shipwreck of their faith as must ensue if they ever discover the missing link between the man and his monkey anteriors.

A verbal inspiration of the Scriptures is no more

improbable, nor beset with difficulties, if a divine revelation be admitted at all, than the particular providence of a Creator and Father, overruling all things, according to His own foreknowledge from the beginning of the world. Far greater objections may be urged against the particular providence, than ever have been against the particular inspiration. The two things are probable by science itself, examining the buried strata by which the construction of a world is proved. It is not denied that the print marks of a rain-storm may be detected on the sands of an antediluvian ocean. To-day we may examine and test the proof-sheets of photographic impressions of the form and motions of animals engraven with the rapidity of lightning. We may do the same with reminiscences of scenes, transactions, and words forever gone, yet capable of being renewed with infinite exactness, even as God Himself is said to require that which is past. The shadow of a humming bird flying between oneself and the sun could not be lighter, swifter, more evanescent than idle thoughts and words; yet they are engraven on the mind; a passing cloud could not change more silently; yet there is the image, its word, its lesson. As the vision of Eliphaz the Temanite, a spirit passed before my face; it stood still, but I could not discern the form thereof; an image before mine eyes, silence, and a voice, a still small voice. It is gone, but it is a presence forever. Shall mortal man be more just than God? Shall a man be more pure than his Maker?

Is any right conception of truth or duty possible, that is not first of all and above all, responsible to the Author of truth, and of our own being and immortality? We are treated from time to time to critical speculations, assuming a disinterestedness in the pursuit of truth, higher and more divine than that of Christ our Saviour—just as if, indeed, the search after truth made us superior to the fear of God Himself, because Science has not yet demonstrated through Sense to Reason that there is a Supreme personal Creator and Governor of the universe. Our responsibility and duty, in the province of education (we are told, in certain quarters), is therefore *first* to TRUTH, *not* to CHRISTIANITY.

If Christianity be indeed the truth, it is the divine fountain of all truth, the highest heaven of science; and all scientific truth is only the servant of Christ its Author; and all discoveries of science are only Christ's Supreme Providence, as Head over all things unto the Church, which is His body, His spiritual kingdom, the fulness of Him who filleth all in all.

But if Christianity *were not* true, then there is no such thing *as truth*, no moral nor spiritual reality, nor kingdom, nor fact, nor any responsibility either to

God or natural law, which is only evolution from a "practical eternity, without Creator, Lawgiver, Governor, or design." We are thus plunged in a boundless chaos, such as neither Lucretius nor Democritus ever in the gloom of paganism imagined.

Pilate himself, when scourging and crucifying Christ, asked Him to His face, *What is truth?* As if he had affirmed, "That is my sole object. My obligations are to Truth, not to Christianity, nor to the Jewish Scriptures, nor to any God proclaimed by any thing written in them; but to whatever truth, at whatever cost, a scientific investigation by the senses may discover. I crucify the pretence of an infallible inspiration in the Scriptures, for the sake of Truth; making myself heroically naked of all prepossession in its favor, that I may wrestle with it, regardless of consequences. I abjure all justification by faith, even in God, and admit nothing on authority even of God's assertion, but go by fact made known by mine own senses."

Had Prof. Huxley been there, he might have said to Pilate, "If thou have the courage to stand alone, face to face with the abyss of the Eternal and Unknowable, be thou content, once for all, not only to renounce the good things promised by infallibility, but even to bear the bad things which it prophesies; content to follow reason and fact in singleness and honesty of purpose, wherever they may lead, in the sure faith that a hell of honest men will be to them more endurable than a paradise full of angelic shams."* Is this a suitable language even for what is called natural piety? Is it not rather the most transparent pride, while a Divine Creator is denied and the word of His inspiration ridiculed?

XLIX.
THE FINAL ARGUMENT, AND ITS PERFECTION—ILLUSTRATION FROM THE VISION AND INSPIRATION OF THE WORD OF THE LORD UNTO EZEKIEL.

"*He was clothed in a vesture dipped in blood*, and His name is called THE WORD OF GOD: a name WRITTEN, that no man knew but He Himself: KING OF KINGS AND LORD OF LORDS."—Rev. xix. 11, 12, 16. This answers to the announcement of Christ in John xiv. 6. " I am the way, the truth, the life: no man cometh to the Father but by Me." It is that testimony of Jesus which is the spirit of prophecy: by which heaven is opened, and He that is called faithful and true judgeth in righteousness.—Rev. xix. 10, 11.

Here we discover an analogy, vast and indisputable, between the divine and human personality of Christ, made flesh and dwelling among us, and the

* Huxley's "Critiques and Addresses," p. 240.

divine and human personality of the Word, the Scriptures given by inspiration of God, πασα γραφη θεόπνευστος, CLOTHED IN A VESTURE DIPPED IN BLOOD, and conversing with us, as we converse one with another, but with absolute infallible truth. The infallible perfect inspiration of the whole Word of God, in all its parts, is as sure to human reason as the central truth of the incarnation, without which the whole moral universe, and the proofs of God in it, fall asunder.

Every step in that incarnation, every *crepusculum* of its dawning, every new shaft of light, every increase of divine revelation looking towards it, was a ministry of glory instrumental even in the process of condemnation, to the manifestation predicted in Romans viii. 18-23, and Eph. iii. 9-11, and iv. 7-16, and i. 17-23; a manifestation of boundless glory and power, till this mortal should put on Christ's immortality, and death be swallowed up in victory. And all things after, as well as before the annunciation of this mystery by the Holy Spirit to the mother of our Lord;— the babe in the manger, the miracles, the temptation, the voices of God and of Christ, the baptisms of blood, the cross, the forsaking of the Father, the forgiving parables and prayers, the salvation of the dying thief, the resurrection, ascension, Pentecost, and all the following presences of Christ in His gospel throughout the world ("Lo, I am with you always even unto the end of the world "), have been only successive manifestations and workings of the omniscience and omnipotence of that incarnate incomprehensible love, by which, through Christ dwelling in our hearts by faith, we begin to comprehend that which passeth knowledge, and are prepared to be filled with all the fulness of God. "For God, who commanded the light to shine out of darkness *hath shined in our hearts*, to give the light of the knowledge of the glory of God in the face of Jesus Christ."—II Cor. iv. 6. "The Son of God was not yea and nay, but in Him was yea."—II Cor. i. 19, 20. An infallible inspiration may be demonstrated from the first six chapters of this Epistle of Paul to the Corinthians. These things saith the Son of God, who searcheth the reins and the hearts.

What train now, for the completeness of our argument, in tracing the inspiration, divine life and authority of the Scriptures can we pursue, other than this very line of light, flashing from the indisputable revealed fact of the *divine-human, human-divine?* This mystery of the Root and Offspring of David in one person, is "the KEY OF DAVID, *that openeth and no man shutteth*, and shutteth and no man openeth:"—Revelation iii. 7.

Comparing Isa. vi. 1–8 with John xii. 37–41, and the first and tenth chapters of Ezekiel, we have a demonstration of the human and divine in one, and a vivid illustration by the prophetic imagery.

We permit ourselves to be taken up, as it were, into the chariot of Christ's deity, and to observe how the truth is shot from the wheels, full of eyes, and from the living creatures, and from THE SPIRIT OF THE LIVING CREATURES in the wheels. For Ezekiel's vision, in the first chapter of his prophecy, is a sublime and graphic description of the Word of God, as at once the abode, vehicle, and manifestation of the divine glory.

When the living creatures moved, the noise of their wings was like the noise of great waters, as the VOICE OF THE ALMIGHTY, THE VOICE OF SPEECH, as the noise of an host. And there was the form of a man's hand under their wings, and the living creatures had the likeness of a man, and above the firmament which was over their heads, the likeness of a throne, and on the throne the appearance of a man above it, and a rainbow round about His loins, the likeness of the glory of the Lord. The living creatures and the wheels were filled with one and the same spirit, and ran and returned as the appearance of a flash of lightning; their whole body and their hands and the wheels being full of eyes round about. Whither the Spirit was to go they all went, as inseparable personalities. And this, says Ezekiel, is the living creature that I saw under the God of Israel.—Ez. x. 20.

The Scriptures are thus a divine incarnation of infallible truth in human language, "in words which the Holy Ghost teacheth"; and so, as the Saviour was partaker of flesh and blood, and in all points tempted like as we are, yet without sin, the Word of God, for the Holy Spirit's use, and for our belief unto salvation, is in all points like our natural word, yet without error or imperfection: never the human without the divine, but always the divine in and through the human, assumed for the sake of manifesting the divine. The two things are one, and yet so manifestly two in form, that unreason and unbelief may separate them, and contemplate only one, and at length lose sight of the other.

A stained and storied window may be so constructed that you may look through it, if you will, and behold the heavens; or you may stay your eye upon the coloring and the figures, and may see nothing beyond, because you do not look at the window with any such purpose; and even in a window with plain glass, a man might stop his sight at the sashes. So with the Deity of Christ, and the Godship of the Word,—men *may* not see it, if they *will* not. When John announces that the Word was God and became flesh, he adds, "And *we* beheld His glory," but others did not. Others beheld nothing but the flesh, nothing of the glory; they saw Him indeed, and yet believed Him not, because, being in the form of man, they might, if they chose, have their eyes holden, that they should not see Him in the form of God, should not behold, feel, acknowledge, the majesty and power of His Divinity.

And precisely so it is with His Word in its human dress, language, imagery. The Scriptures being God-man, as Christ is God-man, in our right mind we behold their divine glory. And yet, if men choose, they may be blind, they may really behold nothing of the divine, nothing but the human, just as they were blind on earth who beheld in Christ Jesus nothing but a man like themselves. Is not this Jesus of Nazareth, whose father and mother we know? Is He any other personage than the son of the carpenter?

L.

THE NEW-CREATING LIFE AND MEANING OF DIVINE INSPIRATION AS INHERING IN THE INCARNATE PERSONALITY OF CHRIST THE SAVIOUR.

The inspiration is not only divine, as Christ is divine, but its prismatic elements are the very attributes of Christ. The colors that constitute every rainbow of truth in the Scriptures, and the active quickening powers of all the rays of light, all the doctrines, all the providential and restraining interpositions of mingled truth and discipline, are the workings of the incarnate new-creating personality of the Son of God, by which, in human language, God informs, awakens, convinces, and inspires the soul. The qualities of divine gravitation by which God works in us both to will and to do, are the varieties of righteousness, grace and peace "*multiplied unto us,*" and acting upon and within us, "*through the knowledge of God and of Jesus our Lord;* according as His divine power hath given unto us all things that pertain unto life and godliness, through the knowledge of Him that hath called us to glory and virtue"; by whom, are given unto us those exceeding great and precious promises, the perfection of which will then only be known when the justified and glorified soul is presented without spot or wrinkle or any such thing before the throne of God in Christ's likeness.

In all the dispensations preparatory to the raising of this Living Temple, not a truth was ever omitted which was requisite, not a measure ever ordered which was redundant, or unimportant. If in the typical and temporary ancient tabernacle, every loop and pin was necessary to its perfection, and every thing *ordered in writing by God Himself to Moses* (" See," said He, "that thou make every thing according to the pattern showed thee in the Mount ") much more in the structure of the Scriptures consigned to the Church for perpetual use and instruction for eternal life; every text must be arranged by and for its author. This train of demonstration is pursued by Boyle in his "Work on the Style of the Holy Scriptures." (Fourth edition, 1625, in London.) He argues from the omissions as well as the particulars, and says with an originality and beauty afterward imitated by others, that "as to things of this nature, there is such a fulness in that Book, that oftentimes it says much by saying nothing, and not only its expressions but its *silences* are *teaching, like a dial,* in which *the shadow as well as the light informs us.*"

This harmony of the opposite poles of truth, infinitely distant from the capacity of human thought, yet infinitely true in the divine unity, and in that through the whole created universe, is the incomprehensible mystery of pantheism and personality in one: to admit which requires the simplicity of a little child, the mind of babes and sucklings, contemplating Christ's own childhood in the 8th Psalm, and in Rom. xi. 36, and I Cor. viii. 6, and Col. i. 16, and Heb. chs. i., ii. In the most exalted and divinely inspired strains of our Christian poetry we find the reflection of these truths; imagination and a grateful adoring faith united in the exquisite expression of them. So in Cowper's "Task":

"One Spirit, His,
Who wore the platted thorns with bleeding brow,
Rules universal nature. Not a flower
But shows some touch, in freckle, streak, or stain,
Of His unrivalled pencil. He inspires
Their balmy odors and imparts their hues.
The Lord of all, Himself through all diffused,
Sustains, and is the life of all that lives."

And so the poet Wordsworth:

"From worlds not quickened by the sun
A portion of the gift is won,
An intermingling of Heaven's pomp is spread
On ground which British shepherds tread.
This silent spectacle,—the gleam,—
The shadow—and the peace supreme:—
A presence infinite, a sense sublime
Of something far more deeply interfused,
Whose dwelling is the light of setting suns,
And the round ocean, and the living air,
And the blue sky, and in the mind of man.
A motion and a spirit that impels
All thinking things, all objects of all thought."

All objects of all thought: every *variety* of truth being essential. Every sheaf that Christ Himself harvested, out of the Old Testament, and out of which, passing it through His own heart's blood, He formed and inspired the New;—*all things*, not one jot or tittle superfluous or trifling, all divine, as Himself divine, in His own eternal being and right; and *divinely poor, self-mortifying*, humiliated, despised and suffering, for the purposes of His own dying love, and for the création of those omnipotent instrumentalities and magnetisms of that love through the cross, in the sacrifice of Himself as "the propitiation for our sins, and not for ours only, but for the sins of the whole world."—I John ii. 2. "For their sakes I sanctify myself, *that they also may be sanctified by the truth.*"

These truths are fully understood only in their complex unity and intercommunicating power being fitly framed together, as magnetic creative pencils of light to be employed by the Divine Spirit, taking of the things that are Christ's, for man's transfiguration into Christ's likeness; that as Christ was the brightness of the Father's glory, and the express image of His person, upholding all things *by the word of His power*, so also He should be revealed as the Lord, and First-born, and all-quickening new Creator and Possessor of His own *inheritance of saints in light;* Head over all things to the Church, which is His Body, the fulness of Him that filleth all in all.

We can not find out the melody of a Psalm in sacred music, but by practicing the notes, which, running together, are at once the keys and the unlocking of the presence chambers of a divine inspiration. Playing the organ, a master of the instrument draws forth the whole meaning:

> "Untwisting all the chains that tie
> The hidden soul of harmony."

But he can do it only by an accord with the soul of the composer, an inward harmony of faith and love, to find out what is in the Bible, by experiment; testing the notes by touching the keys; the inspiration by contact with the written words.

Here we see God's own right of way established through the Scriptures for all believing souls, that through His Word, and the infallible divine inspiration and light inseparable therein, men watching and trusting, may be kept from the paths of the Destroyer. "The Lord thine everlasting light, and thy God thy glory; that he who blesseth himself in the earth may bless himself in the God of truth, and he that sweareth in the earth may swear by the God of truth." "A word in season to the weary, a light to the Gentiles, a way in the wilderness to him that walketh in darkness and hath no light, but feareth the Lord and obeyeth the voice of His servant." "I have put my words in thy mouth, and I will bring the blind by a way that they knew not; I will lead them in paths that they have not known; I will make darkness light before them, and crooked things straight. There shall be a way and a highway, the way of holiness; the way-faring man, though a fool, shall not err therein." "In that day shall the deaf hear the words of the book, and the eyes of the blind shall see out of obscurity and out of darkness. They also that erred in spirit shall come to understanding, and they that murmured shall learn doctrine."—" Now go, write it before them in a table, and note it in a book that it may be for the time to come FOREVER AND EVER." (Isa. xxx. 8.)

LI.

THE SOUL LED AND INSTRUCTED BY SUPPLICATIONS —UNIVERSAL TRUTH DISCOVERED AND RECORDED BY PRAYER—TESTIMONY OF ANCIENT LITURGIES— TREES OF LIFE, NOT MERE TENETS OF THEOLOGY.

The beautiful hymn of Cowper, on the unborrowed majesty and glory of God's Word is another sweet memorial of these truths, the work of a divine experience.

> "The Spirit breathes *upon the Word*,
> And brings the truth to sight;
> Precepts and promises afford,
> A sanctifying light.

> "A glory gilds the sacred page,
> Majestic, like the sun,
> It gives a light to every age;—
> IT GIVES, BUT BORROWS NONE."

There is also a second breathing of it *into the heart, by the Spirit* accompanying and applying it, revealing its meaning *through its effects in love,* in the affections, in drawing forth the intensity of our desires after God. God gives us disclosures and possessions of the truth in prayer, imparting His strength in and through our own soul's wrestlings with Him. "*In the day when I called,* Thou answeredst me, and strengthenedst me *with strength in my soul.*"—Ps. cxxxviii. 3. Our best and deepest knowledge of the truths of the gospel is wrought out and burned in through this exercise by importunity of spirit; ("They shall come with weepings, and with supplications will I lead them." —Jer. xxxi. 9). And our power to enlighten others, and make the truth burn in their hearts, increases in the same way. Through prayer Paul was made to know the infinite meanings of Christ's appearance and words to him in the way to Damascus; and through conflicts of prayer and love was enabled to communicate them. Compare Eph. i. 16, 17, and iii. 16, 17, and Phil. i. 4–11, and Col. i. 9–11, 28, 29, and ii. 1–3, and I Thess. iii. 10–13. Through such incommunicable strivings for others, ("I would ye knew what great conflict I have for you"), ἡλίκον ἀγῶνα, *striving according to his working which worketh in me mightily,* ἀγωνιζόμενος, Paul learned still more for himself of the unsearchable riches of Christ; and then, through the divinely directed and inspired writing out of some of those petitions, the Holy Spirit recorded for all ages those infinite masses of truth, those orbs of light, thus bowled through the firmament by the Spirit of wisdom and revelation in the knowledge of Christ.

A record by the Spirit, *a supernatural revelation and command* of ideas and phrases beyond reach of the human mind, discoverable only by immediate divine inspiration. And yet how natural!—neither suggestion nor command mentioned, that Paul should make this record, but just the irrepressible out-pouring of his own heart in love and prayer, that the same baptism with those truths in Christ that transcend all knowledge, and yet are to be the fountains of infinite spiritual power and glory, may be vouchsafed to all the disciples. And so, in this wonderful way of teaching in prayer the master-truths that could be comprehended only by the same personal discipline and experience, we are let into depths of thought, and an apocalypse of Christ's supreme dominion over the universe for the new creation of souls, the conception of which, and the concentrated telegraphic expressions, words, phrases, necessary to convey them, could be taught and reported only by that same new creating Spirit, "which is Christ in you the hope of glory," and which creates the power of comprehending an incomprehensible mystery by an indwelling personality of Love, and by our thus being "filled with all the fulness of God," which itself is an impossibility to natural reason.

"As the soul in prayer gets nearer to God and His truth than any other way, so *the voice of the Church in prayer in all ages is the most living and perfect creed.*" * It is truth on fire, truth expressed by the Spirit in the wants, desires, and adoration of the soul; for it is the Spirit that maketh intercession in the soul with the groanings that can not be uttered, the Spirit inspiring and offering up the oblation of truth passed through the life of the believing soul in prayer and praise and love. As the soul prays, so it believes, so it knows; its convictions, its intuitions by the Spirit, its vision and sense of things divine, *the things of the Spirit*, are clearer, brighter, of vaster compass, of greater purity and strength; for it is the Spirit that takes of the glory of Christ, the things that are Christ's, and shows them to the soul. The work of the Spirit is to penetrate the soul with Christ's own glory, and absorb it in His love, set it on fire with His love, complete in His dominion and image.

* See the volume of "Bright's Ancient Collects, or Prayer from Ancient Liturgies." The author remarks in his preface, that "to separate the morals from the mysteries, the practical element, as it is called, from the element of SUPERNATURAL FACT, and of pure doctrine, is simply to destroy the whole fabric."

The great power in theology, the only effective power in the teacher and the preacher, is the learning and possession of Christ's divinity in this practical experience of His love. For thus the soul's sensibilities are all entwined with the divineness of his being, taking their life from that; even as the sap from the root runs up through the tree to the fruits; his divineness vitalizing all His precepts, words, instructions, in the soul, and working therein a permanent, triumphant, constraining conquering life.

"Who is he that overcometh the world but he that believeth that Jesus is the Son of God?" If the power of the soul over the world is lost, it is because this divine Christ is lost out of it, or the tenet is separated from the love, or perhaps the love itself is suffered to die out, and the dry tenet only remaining, becomes inefficacious for life, and if so presented or used, it is as a mallet or maul, of dry tough wood, beaten on the human reason as on an empty unfeeling drum.

For indeed all tenets of theology become mere clubs, instead of being trees of life for the healing of the nations, if they are brandished without the life of love.

And on the other hand, to present Christ as a teacher merely, or a great human philanthropist, by virtue of his manliness, without the divineness which bases and holds all His authority, majesty and new creating power, is to mock and deny Him, even while naming Him; is to apply ice instead of fire to the soul. The seven sons of Sceva undertook the name of Christ as an exorcism, a tenet brandished at second hand. Nothing but contempt followed, and the manifestation of evil spirits, so that these vagabond Jews fled out of the house where they had attempted their adjurations, naked and wounded.

LII.

THE BIBLE THE MOST NATURAL AND YET THE MOST SUPERNATURAL OF ALL BOOKS—DIVINE LIGHT ITS GARMENT, DIVINE LOVE AND LIGHT ITS SUBSTANCE—A CHILD'S BOOK FOR ALL AGES.

We come then to this proposition, namely, THAT THE WORD OF GOD, BEING THUS BOTH HUMAN AND DIVINE, *what is natural and human in it is as free and perfect as if there were no supernatural inspiring it; but as truly inspired of God, and free from error and imperfection, as if there were nothing in it human, but all supernatural.* This covers all the questions of verbal, plenary, doctrinal, circumstantial, every thing. Error in man is natural, and infallibility supernatural. Now with infallibility, error is impossible; and yet, the Word is not less natural for there being no error in it, even as the Lord Jesus was none the less a true and real man, for His being a perfect man. But error is unnatural and impossible to the Divinity; and error would render the Word more unnatural and impossible as a divine product, than absolute and unmingled truth renders it unnatural and impossible as a mere human product.

The argument is so plain and familiar in regard to Christ our Saviour, that no critic questions it, as to the elements of His incarnate being.

Our Lord Jesus, as a man, had all the natural and innocent weaknesses of a man, just as, when He was a babe and a child, He had a child's helplessness, not a man's strength. He was fatigued and needed rest. He was fast asleep on a pillow in the stern of a fishing smack. Early in the morning He was hungry, and came to a fig-tree, if haply He might find fruit thereon to serve for a breakfast. These are no proofs that he was not divine, but demonstrations absolute that besides being divine, He was also human. "In Him dwelt all the fulness of the Godhead bodily." He *took upon Himself* our nature, not changing it into part of His divinity, but shining through it, and making it divine, as God the Father who *is* light, is said to have clothed Himself *with* light as with a garment.

The same argument applies with the same indisputable force to the Word of God. It has all the marks of nature, except error and sin. There was Paul's cloak at Troas; he forgot it, and had to send for it. A most singular thing that his inspiration should permit him to forget what afterwards it would be thought worthy of inspiration to make him remember and mark in a divine record! And yet, this is no indication of that Epistle to Timothy not being God's Word, but simply proof that it is man's word and natural, as well as God's Word and supernatural. But everywhere the natural is an enshrinement of the divine, and the supernatural adopts and transfigures the human, so that we can never draw the line, nor say at any point, This is human and uninspired. For the moment we admit this, all is uncertainty and darkness; we need another and higher divine revelation to teach us infallibly what in the first is divine, and what merely human, what is authoritative, and what of no authority at all. It is essential to a revelation for the soul of man, born and educated in this world, but travelling to the eternal world and to God, that it be all human and natural in the dress, the language, the imagery, the play of genius and of reason; but all divine in the inspiration and authority, and no uncertainty whether one part may not be pronounced merely human, and only some other part divine.

The Bible is the most natural book in the world,

and yet the most supernatural, the only supernatural. It is natural, without that being an object or effort; in all things exquisitely simple, unostentatious, inartificial, unelaborate, a spontaneous ease and beauty no more produced by human art or training, and no more to be judged by that, than the graceful motions of a little child are to be learned at a dancing school, or governed by its rules. The primeval wilderness could not grow more wildly free and varied, and yet the tiniest flowers and mosses in that wilderness are wrought with a care, skill, perfection, such as God the Creator could alone impart; thrown by quantities lavishly and carelessly abroad, yet each the production of infinite divine power and wisdom. Just so it is with the variety in God's Word, and yet the minutest fragments evince both in themselves and in their places, an equally microscopic intelligence and care. "As there is a reason why a fern grows here and a flower there, why pine and not oak crowns yonder headland, a reason for every wind that blows, a reason for the shape and color of every cloud, a reason for every thing and for the place of every thing in the world of Nature, even so it is in the world of Scripture."*

* "The Star of our Lord," by F. W. Upham, author of the "Wise Men and who they were." p. 101, on language and inspiration.

The Bible comes to us in the most natural shape and manner possible, that it may be with us and in us, as at once a friendly companion and teacher, and a spring of life. Just such was our Lord's example and work of gentle, instructive, patient humility, poverty, affectionate lowly service, and attractive, animating, reproving, yet ever encouraging and joy inspiring conversation. "I am with you as one that serveth; and these things have I *spoken* unto you, that *My joy* might remain in you; and I have called you friends, and lay down My life for you." So, the divine Word is compared to the dew and soft rain descending on the mown grass, and it runs like a brook in green pastures, playing and laughing like the children, singing as the birds, a pure river of the water of life, by which we may abide, and of which we may drink; but it does not thunder from the sky, a stupendous fixture like a cataract, nor stand like a water-spout between earth and heaven.

This neighborhood and familiar harmony of infinite mystery and majesty with childlike unconscious simplicity, and tragic awful sublimities with homely, every-day occurrences; the mountains trembling, the sun and moon standing still in their habitation; Omnipotence rending the rocks, parting the sea, blasting armies with the sweep of an angel's wing;-- and side by side the gardens of the little ones, the playgrounds, domestic interludes of an infinite landscape:—

> "These hedge-rows, hardly hedge-rows, little lines
> Of sportive wood run wild; these pastoral farms,
> Green to the very door; and wreaths of smoke
> Sent up in silence from among the trees."

And this Incarnate Divine Teacher, walking with us through the cornfields, pointing out to us the lilies, that we may rejoice in their divine array, and learn their loving lessons of adoration and confidence from Him, who Himself made them for the introduction of our worshipping childhood to our Heavenly Father. And this familiar, loving companion of our souls, speaking as never man spake or taught, by His own example of love, obedience, and trust, even unto death, in His Father and our Father, His God and our God, and leaving us His own example in dying, "Father, into Thy hand I commit My Spirit," so that even in crossing that narrow sea our hands are held in His. So infinitely childlike, affectionate, divested of all terror, clothed with all joy, is this life-giving gospel to attract our souls! Hence too, not angels, with their telegraphic banners and lightnings, or a procession of apostles from heaven's holiness and glory, but men out of the "back slums" of creation, fresh from the fall, "clothed with filthy garments," "brands plucked from the burning," chosen as its *preachers;* sinful men, made believers, blind men once, but restored to sight, men once dead in trespasses and sins, but "quickened" and living in Christ, and able to speak, from experimental knowledge and with intensest sympathy, compassion and love (as in Ps. xxxii. and cxvi., and Eph. ii. 1-7), both of the ruin and the remedy, both of the evil and the cure, both of the death and the life. Earthen vessels for such treasures, that the excellency of the power might be manifestly only from God, not man. Thus, both in the revelation by God, and the preaching by man, the testimony is that of God, the witness is the witness of the Spirit.

With this combination of the natural and the supernatural, the Bible is distinguished from all other books by its simplicity, and its perfect freedom from exaggeration. It never colors too highly. You may say it would be impossible to do this, where truths respecting God and eternity are the subject-matter; for neither human thought can reach the measure, nor human language the expression of their sublimity and importance. This is true. And yet, they may be spoken of in a style of bombast and exaggeration. Where there is not real feeling, but the resemblance of it, this is very apt to be the case. The language of reality, the language of deep feeling, is always that of simplicity; but genuine feeling is on the whole so rare, and the language of exaggeration so common, that the simple reality seems tame; it is dull and uninteresting. and ordinary minds prefer and require to be stirred by noise and pretension. The writers of the sacred Scriptures might have taken this course, would certainly sometimes have fallen into it, had not the Spirit of God been their teacher. As it is, what simplicity, what unpretending announcement of the mightiest truths, what quietness in the manner, and what unadornment, nay, we had almost said, what rudeness and homeliness in the terms used!

The Bible again requires no more feeling than just that for which it lays the foundation, provides the fuel, and gives the reason. Here also it is different from all other books. Here is another internal evidence of its divine origin. We can find no false religion, in which there are not claims advanced, unsupported by the real dignity and worth of the system. But here, the simple proposal of the system establishes at once and forever the nature of the claim. It is supreme and infinite. The system is such in itself, as to make any thing less than such a claim incompatible; any thing more is impossible. The system could not require what it does, were it any thing less than what it is, were any of its parts deficient, were it not made up of the very truths, which it does contain.

But the moment we reject the grand cardinal

truths of the divinity of Christ, and the atonement by Him because He is divine, and by means of His being divine, we lose all power, all possibility of proving that the Bible is the Word of God. It is the Word of God, because these truths are taught in it, and God only could have struck them out, could have revealed them, could have provided the reality of which they are the manifestation. God only could have predestined, pre-arranged, created, those truths, conceived the plan of them, and fulfilled the reality; and God only could bear testimony in regard to them; man could not do it, but could only receive them, and believe them, as revealed from God. There they are; and if we deny them, we can not believe in the Bible as the Word of God. On the other hand, their being there compels us to believe; they could not have been there but by revelation from the Almighty, and the claims of the book containing them, and of the system in the book, would be baseless, false, contradictory, absurd, without them. The Word, in revealing Christ as a divine Saviour proves itself the Word of God, and Christ as a divine Saviour, a self-existent reality, is the life, the substance of that Word, the assurance of its truth to the soul, and the ground of its authority.

LIII.

COMPLEXITY, PARTICULARITY AND INDESTRUCTIBLE UNITY OF THE ARGUMENT—ITS POWER OF ANCHORAGE FOR THE SOUL THE SAME IN ALL AGES, BUT INCREASING THROUGH ALL—A NEVER ENDING NEW CREATING LIFE.

By the argument from the Old Testament to the New, promising mankind the Son of God, a Saviour;

By the argument and assurance also promising a Saviour from our sins, and the forgiveness of all sin, through faith in Him, and eternal redemption from that dying in our sins, otherwise inevitable to every unbelieving soul;

By the argument from the existence and character of Christ, as the Son both of David and of God, the DIVINE SAVIOUR;

By the argument from the concentration and fulfilment of prophecy in Him; also from the very delineation of His character, impossible for the human imagination to have wrought out, proving His *divine* existence, and from the answer of that existence to the prophecies, showing Him *beforehand* divine;

By the argument from His own expressed sanction and use of the Old Testament as the Word of God, infallible, and that can not be broken, and

His assertion of the inspiration of His apostles *equally* infallible;

By their appeals again, both to the Old Testament and to Christ;

By the argument from His prayer, *Sanctify them by Thy truth, Thy Word is truth;*

From the very necessity of the case, from the nature in detail of the materials in the whole mass of revelation, which, as they could not have been imagined by man, so could neither be rightly arranged nor presented, if left to the possibilities of man's limited reason and imperfect conception and utterance, but required as divine a wisdom in the handling as in the creating, and might be misrepresented and misconceived by the misplacing or defect of language even in a single word;

By the necessity therefore for a revelation, once for all, of absolute perfection, truth infinite, immutable, eternal, free from error, as perfect, as applicable, as direct from God, three hundred and sixty-five thousand years hence, as when first promulgated to constitute the sword of the Spirit, and for the determination of the destinies of eternity;

By the argument from the very penalties of unbelief, from the exaction of faith as an obligation outweighing all others;

By the argument from the very ideal of a divine

revelation, with an eternal penalty as the reason of it, and the certainty that any mixture of error impairs its indisputable authority, which, to admit a just eternal penalty, can not endure the least flaw in the indictment, nor any possibility of any serious mistake by any conscience enlightened by the Divine Spirit, which is a Spirit always acting by the truth, and never in the least respect sanctioning error;

From the necessity of such infallible perfection, imposed also by the scope and manner of God's providence, and by the microscopic minuteness and exactness of His works, in which we can never find error, nor admit its possibility;

By the necessity that that which is to be the key to the understanding of His providential administration through all time, and retributive through eternity, should command every secret ward and combination, with an exact predisposed and determined fitness;

By the necessity also of such an adaptation between the details of that revelation and the discoveries of science, in all ages, that there never shall be any possible ground for infidelity to stand upon, but temporary difficulties and obscurities shall result in greater light, as the nebulosities of the heavens, after furnishing a hopeful text for infidelity, are all resolved into whole and perfect worlds; from the impossibility of any contradiction between the Word and the Works of the Deity, the very affirmation of Jehovah being that of this difference between His Word and Works, that while heaven and earth shall pass away, His Word shall never pass away, nor in one jot or tittle fail, and that, while all flesh is grass, and all the glory of man as the flower of grass, the Word of the Lord LIVETH AND ABIDETH FOREVER, and is that by which the whole human race is to be judged;—

From all these pressures of necessity, and trains of demonstrative argument, the proof of an absolute fulness and literal perfection of inspiration is irresistible.

It is not to be evaded, and can not be nullified, nor rendered indistinct; and yet, to the unregenerate mind there is a veil over the face of all this truth, until the heart looks to Christ Himself, by faith, for salvation; for the veil is over the heart, nowhere else; and no man ever feels the power of this overwhelming majesty of proof, this transcendent all-penetrating presence of the light, and these thousand rainbows into which the very atmosphere and storms of human life and experience scatter it, except by the Spirit of God in the heart; the eyes of our understanding being enlightened that we may see the glory of the Redeemer, and know what is the hope of His calling, and what the riches of the glory of His inheritance in the saints.

We have said that the materials of a divine revelation must as necessarily be arranged and presented by the Author of them as created; the one necessity compels the other. Given, the raw materials of the universe, what being could understand them, or combine them under law, or manifest their harmonies, but He who created them? Their perfection in mutual relation and attraction, and their motions in obedience to one law, are as necessarily of God's arrangement, as their matter and form, of God's creation. A distinguished naturalist (was it not Agassiz?) has stated, as the results of a profound examination of the structure of plants, that the same law, the same harmony of proportion, regulates the distances between the leaves on a stem, as between the orbits and times of worlds in the solar system; and just so, for a perfect revelation, there is absolute necessity that the same wisdom and power that created its masses of light and appointed their revolutions, should govern every relation belonging to them; the law of language, the subtle analogies of words, the varieties of style, the choice of phrases, the minutest verbal niceties, being under the same law, as the mighty orbed ideas, the thoughts of God enclosed in human expression. Because the expression is human, it is not therefore the less superhuman and divine; because natural, not therefore the less supernatural; no more than the growth of the leaves, because it is the work of life, is therefore any less the arrangement of Jehovah, or less inevitably under His law and direct agency, than the orbits of the planets.

There are internal harmonies, and laws of adjustment in the Word of God, as subtle, as undiscovered, as wonderful, and minute, as any thing yet found out, or to be found out, in the composition and combinations of the universe. The divine Word is no more of man, because he speaks it, than the fruits of the earth are of the husbandman, because he sows the seeds of them, and from all that God has given him, chooses what to sow. But the sense and understanding of this testimony are only by the witness of the Spirit.

This then is the nature and secret of the independent authority and living power of the Word of God, and this is the talisman of omnipotence which those men wield, in whose hearts God has set His Word as a living fire, and has commissioned and commanded them to go forth and proclaim, THUS SAITH THE LORD. This is the commission, in a certain degree and sense, of the whole new-created Church of the Lord Jesus, but of His teaching and preaching ministers, in a special consecration and separation for that work; His ministers, whom He holds in His own right hand as stars, whom not the golden candlesticks support, but the Lord Jesus, and whom He keeps shining with His own light, living in His own life, given them, not through the church, nor through any historical or hierarchical succession, nor through any human instrumentality, but always directly from Himself, by His Spirit with His Word.

And indeed we can not be too grateful to God, that He has made our faith to stand not in the wisdom of men, but in the power of God, and that He allows no human mediator between Himself and us. We see the entire independence of our faith in regard to all human authority, and its entire and sole dependence upon God and His Spirit. We see that the evidences of Christianity are in the Word of God itself, and not in books containing merely the affidavits of uninspired men, transmitted down by fallible recorders. The body of such seeming evidence, composed merely of historical vouchers and commentaries, increases as the distance from the original transactions increases, learned men still adding to its accumulation in every age, though the fountain remains just where it was, and just the same.

But the Lord Jesus Christ declares plainly, "I receive not testimony from man"; and those who would believe must come to Him, and not to human historians. We are permitted to step across all these interminable libraries, all these dead carcasses of certificated ecclesiastical successions, and "Books of Origins," all these huge gulfs of human pride, philosophies, and affidavits, and to come right to the original, deep, living, eternal spring, where we drink, without waiting for an authorized dipper, or for an angel or a man of learning to trouble the waters. And the water of life is just as pure and potent to a man entirely ignorant of all that has taken place in churches and councils since the apostles' time, as to one who has waded through whole swamps and seas of evidence, and crossed gulfs and deserts of history, on the line where men testify that the high road to the fountain lies. Let us not be imposed upon by self-constituted mediators between us and the Word of God, as if the truth of God's testimony were nothing without the sanction and authority of men. In order to learn the truth, we must "LEARN CHRIST," and we have no real faith if it does not bring us to Him, or if it is merely a faith in history, and not in Him.

Does our faith stand in the opinion and judgment of men, or God? We must learn to believe, *because God says it*, not because history affirms it, or allows it. Some men talk of a faith not grounded in church history, as an unhistorical faith. But a faith in the

Word of God *can not be unhistorical*, but indeed is the only true historical faith; for the history that is in God's Word is the only *infallible* history. All other is mixed with lies. If we rely on man's testimony, because without it we can not rely on God's, and if we take our opinions at second hand, such a faith is but spiritual blindness and death. We must examine history by the Word of God, and not the Word of God by history. Human testimony and exposition, without this independent living faith, is like an awkward waiter with snuffers, who promises to make the candle burn brighter, but snuffs it out, leaving us nothing but a smoking wick. Not a few of the learned expositors calling themselves reconstructors of Israel's history and text, have been just such snuffers. We bring not the law and the testimony to be judged by these, but these and all things, to be judged by the law and the testimony.

LIV.

THE PROVERB OF "THE DEVIL TO PAY" ILLUSTRATED—BISHOP HOADLY ON THE KINGDOM OF CHRIST AND OF CONSCIENCE—CONJECTURAL CRITICISM AND CLINKERS OF THOUGHT—THE WAY TO DOUBTING CASTLE—THE FOG WITHIN AND BREAKERS WITHOUT—FRANKLIN'S EXPERIENCE AND BELIEF IN PRAYER.

The fabrication or supposition of legends, lost books, and assumed unknown authors, in order to displace the known books of Biblical history, as traditions, falsehoods and forgeries, in order to bring down the Scriptures into analogical harmony with the myths of all other nations, and therefore of no higher authority, is so like that of the tempter and destroyer of mankind, that it seems to realize in sober earnest the profound common proverb, taken out of Satan's ledger, "*The devil to pay.*" The consequences return upon the authors. False principles assumed as true, or true ones falsely stated, and the false statement carried out into working supremacy, are as rats carrying off phosphorous matches into their holes, where the gnawing of them sets the house on fire. Men's own souls are thus destroyed as by *delirium tremens*, and no man ever questioned the justice of such a retribution.

One of the most remarkable sermons ever preached in the English language was by Bishop Hoadly, March 31st, 1717, on the Nature of the kingdom of Christ, from John xviii. 36, "My kingdom is not of this world." The Lord Jesus the sole Lawgiver to His subjects, the sole Judge of their behavior, in matters of conscience and eternal salvation: no visible human authority, no interpreters on whom His subjects are absolutely to depend, no judges over the consciences or religion of His people. "The question with all men," said the bishop, "ought to be whether Christ did not know the nature of His own kingdom or church better than any since His time; whether we can suppose He left any such matters to be decided against Himself and His own express professions; and whether, if an angel from heaven should give us any account of His kingdom, contrary to what He Himself hath done, it can be of any weight or authority with Christians?"

"The only cure of eternal suspicions, doubts, and perplexities, is to go back to the New Testament itself, because there alone we shall find the original intention of such words, or the nature of the things designed to be signified by them, declared and fixed by our Lord, or His apostles from Him, *by some such marks as may, if we will attend to them, guide and guard us in our notions of those matters in which we are most of all concerned."* His kingdom is within, and His power and word a power that worketh within. The worth and destiny of the soul are decided by what is within, by the central principle and impulse of a conscience towards God.

Now it is no matter how rudely the machinery is made, if it obeys the divine impulse, if the central spring is there and the machinery answers to it. The wheels of a watch might be made of rough iron wire, and the hands of whittled wood, but if the mainspring were perfect, and the adjustment and motion of the parts accurate, that is all that you need for a trusty time-keeper. That makes a perfect watch. It is able to carry you through all countries, seas, and seasons, according to the power that worketh within. Able to take you on a voyage, and regulate your business, your appointments, your responsibilities, according to the power that worketh within.

A watch with a pewter case and wooden wheels would be better for you with that accurate, permanent, powerful action, than the most delicate, exquisite, costly machinery of gold and jewels, without the central guiding power. A turnip, if it kept time for you by a life and force within, would be better than the costliest chronometer ever constructed, without a good main-spring. According to the power *that worketh in you,* God is able to carry you through the battles and tempests of life, through temptation, difficulty, danger, through all worlds, up to His own throne in His likeness. But without that power working within, you might have the intellect of Newton, the genius of Shakspeare, the mathematics of Laplace, the mechanics of him of Syracuse, all the capacities and skilful tact of the most practical men of ability that ever lived, and you would have no permanent divine character; nothing but intellectual powers without a moral or spiritual regulator, and animating motive, holding you to God.

And it must hold you to God, while you are in the body, and under a veil or curtain in regard to the invisible world and God's government of it, by some external demonstration and guide, given you from God, to which the inward moral regulator shall accurately and intuitively answer. That external guide is, in the nature of the case, above man's power to construct or imagine. It is divine inspiration; it is God's work, God's Word, for man's guidance; and as a watch must run with reference to the universe, and the sun, moon, and stars set there for measurements of time, in hours, days, months, years, seasons, so the works of a man's heart and conscience, to be worth any thing for true practical purposes, must correspond with God's realities, God's principles, revealed in His Word. The conscience is useless without such correspondence; and equally useless if the revelation to which it must answer and correspond, be not a revelation of *absolute truth*. If the revelation be not perfect, neither can the inward watch be true. A mistake or falsehood in either case would render the whole worthless. *Out of season, out of reason;* especially, if eternal results are admitted; and if not, then the whole is of very little consequence.

There are such things in men's reasoning from conjectural criticism, and hypothesis without fact, as clinkers of thought. And how great is the absurdity of using them as if they were fresh coal! Some kinds of coal make them rapidly, and they cling to the reasoning processes so fast that they can not be broken off, or cleared away. The mind becomes like a house-furnace, and false opinions and prejudices are the clinkers.

Like an old Roman wall, the cement in which the stones were laid becomes stronger than the stone itself, and it is easier at length to break the stones than the prejudices. The prejudices become at length foundations and buttresses of the strongest buildings, and one generation is born, lives, worships and dies, in temples made out of the errors of the preceding. Hence the necessity, from the cradle to the grave, of being built up out of such stuff and with such cement as Paul describes, with such wonderful compound of love and logic, in his Epistles to the Ephesians and Colossians; "built upon the foundation of the apostles and prophets, Jesus Christ Himself being the chief corner-stone in whom all the building fitly framed together, GROWETH into a holy temple in the Lord, rooted and grounded in love, speaking the truth in love, and growing up in all things into Christ, our Head; from whom the whole body, fitly joined together, and compacted by that which every joint supplieth, according to the effectual working in the measure of every part, maketh increase of the body, unto the edifying of itself in love."

Now the moment we desert this divine plan and wisdom of temple-building for eternity, as a habitation of God through the Spirit, and betake ourselves to human virtue as our quarry, we build on quick-sands, for storms and destruction. There is such an architecture, that holds not by the propitiatory sacrifice of Christ, nor by the cement of His dying love, but by the virtues of sincerity in man, even amidst utter unbelief and error, and by a trust in the benevolence of God, without Christ as the foundation.

Over this stile lies the way to Doubting Castle kept by Giant Despair. The narrow way that the pilgrims had been treading was somewhat rough to their feet, and they were getting tired and dusty and foot-sore. The broad green meadow, beside the strait way, was soft and flowery and exceedingly inviting and tempting with its attractions. It seemed moreover to lie along-side the rough path where they had been travelling, and at any moment, if there was any danger or enemy occurrent, they could step back and be in safety again on the King's own highway. Might they not try it for a while? Was it not commanded them to prove all things, and then hold fast to that which is good? Well, at all events they would venture for a little. We all know the result; first doubtful, then dark and gloomy, then tempestuous and dreadful, became the way, till from terror and exhaustion they fell asleep, and waked only to behold Giant Despair standing over them, and in his face and words no mercy for them.

Now this Broad Church Theology smooths down and sows with flowers a wide meadow for men's thoughts and beliefs; and at length doubts themselves seem but the results of an earnest and disinterested pursuit after truth; and the pilgrims begin to think they are then giving the greatest proof of their sincerity, when they venture the experiment outside the straight and narrow path.

The effect of these speculations on the pilgrim is as the gathering of a fog upon the landscape, the dropping of a dark curtain before a scene of glory. You were travelling slowly up the mountain and at every turn in the zigzags of the road, admiring some new revelations of beauty. But the mists begin to rise around you before you are aware, and at length they steal every prospect from your sight, until above, around, below, a cloud of dripping mist envelops you, that if you staid in it would drench you to the bones. There are no more delectable mountains, there is no more heavenly horizon, nor sky, nor sun, nor shining light, but gloom, coldness, nightfall, darkness, despair. You saw Mont Blanc once; it was an unquestioned magnificent reality. Now you can not ascertain its place, nor a gleam of its regal glaciers nor its snowy dome. If you go down now again into the world you will have no remembrance of aught heavenwards, but clouds and endless depths of gloom; abysses, down which you are tempted to throw yourself as a plumb line for measurement.

If the fog were only on the landscape, another day, a day of sunshine, it may be removed. But when it enters into the soul, "if the light that is in thee be darkness, how great is *that* darkness!"

We know when we are *in a fog*, but when the fog is *within ourselves*, we are not aware of it; the moment we are, it is dissipated. A man in London may find himself in so thick a fog at noonday that all the street lamps have to be lighted, and bells rung in the streets to tell him where he is. The thicker the fog outside in such a case, the more certainly every body knows *what it is*. Yet at the very same time half the people in London may be enveloped *within* in so thick a darkness, that they put evil for good and good for evil and do not know it. So at sea, in the voyage to eternity.

And so with the fog of error and self-opinion in the soul. Some men's confidence is only the result of their having the understanding darkened, being alienated from the life of God through the ignorance that is in them because of the blindness of their heart. A fog is on their souls, yet they are driving on as if it were clear weather. If the fog were suddenly lifted, what a fearful revelation of breakers, on which they must inevitably strike, and be dashed to pieces, continuing that course. We have sailed in a fog on the Atlantic, when every minute or two the bell was sounded; an indication of danger indeed, but then also a comfort, because we knew our danger. But to have all precautions disregarded, and to be driving with all speed in a thick mist, was terrific. We drove one night with this presumption, our captain being tired of the foggy weather and determined to make haste, but in the morning we were entirely out of our reckoning, and the fog suddenly lifting for a few moments, disclosed a huge reef right before us, on which, five minutes later we should have struck.

In such a case, the letter killeth. It is the Spirit

that giveth light, and saveth life. It is the Spirit that teacheth the right interpretation and application of the letter. Dr. Franklin was always applying the incidents and escapes of common life in such a way that his observations may serve as exquisite illustrations of high principles in spiritual science.

"The model of a good sailing ship," says he, "has been exactly followed in a new one, which has proved on the contrary remarkably dull. I apprehend that this may partly be occasioned by the different opinions of seamen respecting the modes of loading, rigging and sailing of a ship; each has his method; and the same vessel laden by the method and orders of one captain shall sail worse than when by the orders of another.

"Unknown and unsuspected currents, different judgments in the officers commanding successive watches with the same wind, the watchmen sometimes answering mechanically and half asleep." Franklin was in this way near being wrecked. The light suddenly discovered seemed to Franklin as large as a constellated cart wheel, and they were running on the reef. In his letter to his wife giving an account of the escape, he says, "Were I a Roman Catholic, perhaps I should on this occasion vow to build a chapel to some saint, but as I am not, were I to vow at all, *it should be to build a lighthouse.*"

Apply all this to the voyage of life, and our escapes from shipwreck. *Over this stile.* The rich man would fain have sent Lazarus with the lantern, when it was too late. But John Bunyan, with the forces of the experience and truth of Christian and Hopeful, builds a warning by the wayside, *in this life.* Go not out of the King's highway. Walk in the light, as He is in the light, who lived and walked for our example, by the Word of His Father and our Father, His God and our God.

CONCLUSION.

"Sanctify THE LORD OF HOSTS Himself! Bind up THE TESTIMONY! Seal THE LAW among my disciples! For He established a TESTIMONY in Jacob, and appointed a LAW in Israel, which He commanded OUR FATHERS;"—before the first tabernacle and service in Shiloh; before the Era of the Judges and the Prophets; before David and Samuel and Solomon; before the Psalms and the Temple sanctuary and worship on Mount Zion; "that they should make them known to their children, that the generation to come might know them, and their children should arise and declare them to their children, to set their hope in God, and not forget His works, but keep His commandments; and not be as their fathers, a stubborn and rebellious generation, that kept not the Covenant of God, but refused to walk in His Law." ONE LAW OF LOVE; ONE COVENANT OF MERCY; ONE TESTIMONY OF NEW-CREATING GRACE IN CHRIST, FOREVER AND EVER.

It has pleased God to give us a Timepiece FOR ETERNITY because the impossibility is so great, for any created being, of measuring Time with any exactness except BY ETERNITY. For this reason God hath set ETERNITY IN MEN'S HEARTS; the conception of the central Divine Attribute is there, the measurement of all values by that, which in the nature of things is immeasurable; the search after that, which in the nature of things is unsearchable; the never-ceasing thirst of searching, and at the same time the impossibility of finding out. So all our days are limited, and yet eternal, by one sure gravitation of Worship, Faith and Love, infallible, towards God our Saviour; our Saviour because we have sinned; our God and Saviour, because He only, against whom we have sinned, can forgive; our Resurrection and our Life, because only in Him can we live forever; and in Him only by daily believing in Him with the confidence and love of little children; leaving forever all the anxieties of all our wants to be supplied by the loving kindness of our Heavenly Father.

It is not possible for the deepest profoundness and subtlety, or the highest majesty and glory of human reason, to conceive any thing more blissful than the Eternity of such a life of gratitude and love; any thing more divine, than the ETERNAL SELF-EXISTENCE of the Creative Fountain of such love and worship.

Our Timepiece for Eternity is the gift from God of such an infallible measurement of the moments and hours of our earthly existence; so filled with the Spirit of the Author and Giver of life, as to make every downward glimpse of His own life in us an upward thanksgiving reverberation in gratitude and love from ourselves to Him. In Him was life, and the life was the light of men; the true light which lighteth every man that cometh into the world, and returneth forever by faith and love, to the fountain from which it proceeded; the love of the only-begotten Son, who is in the bosom of the Father, and hath declared the invisible God unto us, in His own incarnate manifested being, as the Lamb of God, who taketh away the sin of the world. Oh the infinite blessedness and glory of having confessed by faith such a Saviour, in the midst of a world that comprehended Him not, because of the pride of reason and the ignorance of unbelieving sense!

> " GOOD WILL TO MAN !
> PEACE ON EARTH;
> GLORY TO GOD IN THE HIGHEST !
> FOR THINE IS THE KINGDOM,
> THE POWER AND THE GLORY,
> FOREVER, AMEN."

www.ingramcontent.com/pod-product-compliance
Lightning Source LLC
Chambersburg PA
CBHW051853300426
44117CB00006B/375